Lecture Notes in Computer Science 3130

Commenced Publication in 1973
Founding and Former Series Editors:
Gerhard Goos, Juris Hartmanis, and Jan van Leeuwen

Apostolos Syropoulos   Karl Berry
Yannis Haralambous   Baden Hughes
Steven Peter   John Plaice (Eds.)

TeX, XML, and Digital Typography

International Conference on TeX, XML, and Digital Typography
Held Jointly with the 25th Annual Meeting
of the TeX Users Group, TUG 2004
Xanthi, Greece, August 30 - September 3, 2004
Proceedings

 Springer

Volume Editors

Apostolos Syropoulos
Greek TeX Friends Group, 366, 28th October Str, 67100 Xanthi, Greece
E-mail: apostolo@ocean1.ee.duth.gr

Karl Berry
TeX Users Group, P.O. Box 2311, Portland, OR 97208-2311, USA
E-mail: karl@tug.org

Yannis Haralambous
ENST Bretagne, Département Informatique, CS 83818, 29238 Brest, France
E-mail: yannis.haralambous@enst-bretagne.fr

Baden Hughes
University of Melbourne
Department of Computer Science and Software Engineering
111 Barry Street, Carlton VIC 3053, Australia
E-mail: badenh@cs.mu.oz.au

Steven Peter
Beech Stave Press and TeX Users Group, 310 Hana Road, Edison, NJ 08817, USA
E-mail: speter@beechstave.com

John Plaice
University of New South Wales, School of Computer Science and Engineering
UNSW SYDNEY NSW 2052, Australia
E-mail: plaice@cse.unsw.edu.au

Library of Congress Control Number: 2004095630

CR Subject Classification (1998): I.7, H.5.4, G.4

ISSN 0302-9743
ISBN 3-540-22801-2 Springer Berlin Heidelberg New York

Springer is a part of Springer Science+Business Media

springeronline.com

© Springer-Verlag Berlin Heidelberg 2004
Printed in Germany

Typesetting: Camera-ready by author, data conversion by Olgun Computergrafik
Printed on acid-free paper   SPIN: 11306221   06/3142   5 4 3 2 1 0

Preface

This volume contains the papers that were accepted for presentation at the International Conference on TEX, XML, and Digital Typography, jointly held with the 25th Annual Meeting of the TEX Users Group in Xanthi, Greece in the summer of 2004. The term "Digital Typography" refers to the preparation of printed matter using only electronic computers and electronic printing devices, such as laser-jet printers. The document preparation process involves mainly the use of a digital typesetting system as well as data representation technologies. TEX and its offspring are beyond doubt the most successful current digital typesetters, while XML is the standard for text-based data representation for both business and scientific activities.

All papers appearing in this volume were fully refereed by the members of the program committee. The papers were carefully selected to reflect the research work that is being done in the field of digital typography using TEX and/or its offspring.

The problems for which comprehensive solutions have been proposed include proper multilingual document preparation and XML document processing and generation. The proposed solutions deal not simply with typesetting issues, but also related issues in document preparation, such as the manipulation of complex bibliographic databases, and automatic conversion of text expressed in one grammatical system to a more recent one (as for the Greek language, converting between monotonic Greek and polytonic Greek).

The conference is being graciously hosted by the Democritus University of Thrace in Xanthi and by the Greek TEX Friends. We wish to thank Basil K. Papadopoulos and Georgia Papadopoulou of the Democritus University for their generous help and support in the preparation of the conference. Also special thanks go to Stratos Doumanis, Georgios Maridakis, and Dimitrios Filippou for their invaluable help. Last but not least we thank the Manipulicity of Xanthi for their help and support.

Xanthi, Greece
July 2004

Apostolos Syropoulos
Karl Berry
Yannis Haralambous
Baden Hughes
Steven Peter
John Plaice

Official Sponsors:

«ΕΚΔΟΣΕΙΣ ΤΟΥ ΦΟΙΝΙΚΑ»

http://www.intersys.gr

Chikrii SoftLab GmbH has created these fine tools:

Table of Contents

Digital Typography in the New Millennium: Flexible Documents by a Flexible Engine

Christos K.K. Loverdos[1] and Apostolos Syropoulos[2]

[1] Department of Informatics and Telecommunications, University of Athens
TYPA Buildings, Panepistimiopolis
GR-157 84 Athens, Greece
loverdos@di.uoa.gr
http://www.di.uoa.gr/~loverdos
[2] Greek TEX Friends Group
366, 28th October Str.
GR-671 00 Xanthi, Greece
apostolo@obelix.ee.duth.gr
http://obelix.ee.duth.gr/~apostolo

Abstract. The TEX family of electronic typesetters contains the primary typesetting tools for the preparation of demanding documents, and have been in use for many years. However, our era is characterized, among others, by Unicode, XML and the introduction of interactive documents. In addition, the Open Source movement, which is breaking new ground in the areas of project support and development, enables masses of programmers to work simultaneously. As a direct consequence, it is reasonable to demand the incorporation of certain facilities to a highly modular implementation of a TEX-like system. Facilities such as the ability to extend the engine using common scripting languages (e.g., Perl, Python, Ruby, etc.) will help in reaching a greater level of overall architectural modularity. Obviously, in order to achieve such a goal, it is mandatory to attract a greater programming audience and leverage the Open Source programming community. We argue that the successful TEX-successor should be built around a microkernel/exokernel architecture. Thus, services such as client-side scripting, font selection and use, output routines and the design and implementation of formats can be programmed as extension modules. In order to leverage the huge amount of existing code, and keep document source compatibility, the existing programming interface is demonstrated to be just another service/module.

1 Introduction

The first steps towards computer typesetting took place in the 1950s, but it was not until Donald E. Knuth introduced TEX in 1978 [16] that true quality was brought to software-based typesetting. The history of TEX is well-known and the interested reader is referred to [16] for more details.

Today, the original TEX is a closed project in the sense that its creator has decided to freeze its development. As a direct consequence no other programs

A. Syropoulos et al. (Eds.): TUG 2004, LNCS 3130, pp. 1–16, 2004.

are allowed to be called TEX. In addition, the freely available source code of
the system was a major step on the road towards the formation of the Open
Source movement, which, in turn, borrowed ideas and practices from the Unix
world. Furthemore, the development of TEX and its companion system, META-
FONT, had made obvious the need for properly documented programs. This, in
turn, initiated Knuth's creation of the *literate programming* program development methodology. This methodology advances the idea that the program code
and documentation should be intermixed and developed simultaneously.

The source code of TEX and METAFONT being freely available has had enormous consequences. Anyone can not only inspect the source code, but also experiment freely with it. Combined with TEX's (primitive, we should note, but
quite effective for the time) ability to extend itself, this led to such success sto-
ries as LATEX and its enormous supporting codebase, in the form of packages.
As a direct consequence of the fact that the source code is frozen, stability was
brought forth. Note that this was exactly the intention Knuth had when developing his systems. A common referred-to core, unchanged in the passing of time
and almost free of bugs, offered a "secure" environment to produce with and
even experiment with.

However, in an everchanging world, especially in the fast-paced field of computer science, almost anything must eventually be surpassed. And it is the emerging needs of each era that dictate possible future directions. TEX has undoubtedly
served its purpose well. Its Turing-completeness has been a most powerful as-
set/weapon in the battles for and of evolution. Yet, the desired abstraction level,
needed to cope with increasing complexity, has not been reached. Unfortunately,
with TEX being bound to a fixed core, *it cannot be reached.*

Furthermore, the now widely accepted user-unfriendliness of TEX as a language poses another obstacle to TEX's evolution. It has created the myth of
those few, very special and quite extraordinary "creatures"[1] able to decrypt and
produce code fragments such as the following[2]:

```
\def\s@vig{{\E0@m=\E0@n
  \divide\E0@n by20 \relax
  \ifnum\E0@n>0\s@vig\fi
  \E0@k=\E0@n\relax
  \multiply\E0@k by-20\relax
  \advance\E0@m by \E0@k\relax
  \global\advance\E0@l by \@ne
  \expandafter\xdef\csname E0@d\@roman{\E0@l}\endcsname{%
      \ifnum\E0@m=0\noexpand\noexpand\E0zero
      \else\expandafter\noexpand
      \expandafter\csname E0\@roman{\E0@m}\endcsname\fi}
  \expandafter\@rightappend
    \csname E0@d\@roman{\E0@l}\endcsname
        \t@\epi@lmecDigits}}
```

Of course, to be fair, programmers in several languages (C and Perl among
others) are often accused of producing unundersstandable code and the well-
known *obfuscated code* contests just prove it. On the other hand, with the ad-

---

[1] The second author may be regarded as one of Gandalf's famuli, while the first author
is just a Hobbit, wishing to have been an Elf.

[2] Taken from the documentation of the epiolmec package by the second author.

vent of quite sophisticated assemblers, today one can even write well-structured assembly language, adhering even to "advanced" techniques/paradigms, such as object-oriented programming. Naturally, this should not lead to the conclusion that we should start writing in assembly (again)! In our opinion, software complexity should be tackled with an emphasis on abstraction that will eventually lead to increased productivity, as is shown in the following figure:

$$\text{Complexity} \xrightarrow{\text{requires}} \text{Abstraction} \xrightarrow{\text{increases}} \text{Productivity}$$

TeX's programming language is more or less an "assembly language" for electronic typesetting. It is true that higher level constructs can be made – macros and macro packages built on top of that. But the essence remains the same. Although it is true that TeX is essentially bug free and its macro expansion facility behaves the way it is specified (i.e., as defined in [9]), it still remains a fact that it takes a non-specialist quite some time to fully understand the macro expansion rules in spite of Knuth's initial intentions [12, page 6].

The fact that one should program in the language of his/her choice is just another reason for moving away from a low-level language. And it is true that we envision an environment where as many programmers as possible can – and the most important, wish to – contribute. In the era of the Open Source revolution, we would like to attract the Open Source community and not just a few dedicated low-level developers. Open Source should also mean, in our opinion, "open possibilities" to evolve the source. This is one of our major motivations for reengineering the most successful typesetting engine.

Richard Palais, the founding chairman of TUG, pointed out back in 1992 [12, page 7] that when developing TeX, Knuth

> ... had NSF grant support that not only provided him with the time and equipment he needed, but also supported a team of devoted and brilliant graduate students who did an enormous amount of work helping design and write the large quantity of ancillary software needed to make the TeX system work ...

and immediately after this, he poses the fundamental question:

> Where will the resources come from for what will have to be at least an equally massive effort? And will the provider of those resources be willing, at the end of the project, to put the fruits of all his effort in the Public Domain?

The answer seems obvious now. The way has been paved by the GNU/Linux/-BSD revolutionary development model, as has been explained crystal clearly in *The Cathedral and the Bazaar* [15].

This paper is an attempt to define a service-oriented architecture for a future typesetting engine, which will be capable of modular evolution. We take a layered approach of designing some core functionality and then define extensible services on top of the core. The engine is not restricted to a specific programming language either for its basic/bootstrapping implementation or, even more important, for its future enhancement. At the same time, we are bound to provide a 100% TeX-compatible environment, as the only means of supporting the vast quantity of existing TeX-based documents. We intend to achieve such a goal by leveraging the proposed architecture's own flexibility. Specifically, a TeX compatibility mode is to be supported and it should give complete "trip-test" compliance. Later on, we shall see that this compatibility is divided into two parts: source code compatibility and internal core compatibility. Both are provided by pluggable modules.

Structure of the Paper. In the following sections we briefly review the most important and influential approaches to extending or reengineering TeX, including TeX's inherent abilities to evolve. Then we discuss a few desired characteristics for any next generation typesetting engine. We advance by proposing an architecture to support these emerging needs. Finally, we conclude by discussing further and future work.

2   A Better TeX?

2.1   TeX the Program

TeX supports a Turing-complete programming language. Simply, this means that if it lacks a feature, it can be programmed. It contains only a few concepts and belongs to the LISP family of languages. In particular, it is a list-based macro-language with late binding [5, Sec. 3.3]:

> *Its data constructs are simpler than in Common Lisp: 'token list' is the only first order type. Glue, boxes, numbers, etc., are engine concepts; instances of them are described by token lists. Its lexical analysis is simpler than CL: One cannot program it. One can only configure it. Its control constructs are simpler than in CL: Only macros, no functions. And the macros are only simple ones, one can't compute in them.*

Further analysis of TeX's notions and inner workings such as *category codes*, TeX's *mouth* and *stomach* is beyond the scope of this paper and the interested reader is referred to the classic [9] or the excellent [3].

TeX the program is written in the WEB system of literate programming. Thus, its source code is self-documented. The programs tangle and weave are used to extract the Pascal code and the documentation, respectively, from the WEB code. The documentation is of course specified in the TeX notation. Although the TeX source is structured in a monolithic style, its architecture provides for some kind of future evolution.

First, TeX can be "extended" by the construction of large collections of macros that are simply called *formats*. Each format can be transformed to a quickly loadable binary form, which can be thought of as a primitive form of the module concept.

Also, by the prescient inclusion of the \special primitive command, TeX provides the means to express things beyond its built-in "comprehension". For example, TeX knows absolutely nothing about PostScript graphics, yet by using \special and with the appropriate driver program (e.g., dvips), PostScript graphics can be easily incorporated into documents. Color is handled in the same way. In all cases, all that TeX does is to expand the \special command arguments and transfer the command to its normal output, that is, the DVI file (a file format that contains only page description commands).

Last, but not least, there is the notion of *change file* [3, page 243]:

> *A change file is a list of changes to be made to the* WEB *file; a bit like a stream editor script. These changes can comprise both adaptations of the* WEB *file to the particular Pascal compiler that will be used and bug fixes to TeX. Thus the* TeX.web *file needs never to be edited.*

Thus, change files provide a form of incremental modification. This is similar to the patch mechanism of Unix.

Yet, no matter how foresighted these methods may be, twenty years after its conception TeX has started to show its age. Today's trends, and more importantly the programming community's continuing demand for even more flexible techniques and systems, call for new modes of expressiveness.

2.2   The LaTeX Format

LaTeX [10], which was released around 1985, is the most widely known TeX format. Nowadays, it seems that LaTeX is the de facto standard for the communication and publication of scientific documents (i.e., documents that contain a lot of mathematical notation). LaTeX "programs" have a Pascal-like structure and the basic functionality is augmented with the incorporation of independently developed collections of macro packages. In addition, classes are used to define major document characteristics and are in essence document types, such as *book*, *article*, etc. Thus, each LaTeX "program" is characterized by the document class to which it belongs, by the packages it utilizes, and any new macro commands it may provide.

The current version of LaTeX is called LaTeX 2_ε. Work is in progress to produce and widely distribute the next major version, LaTeX3 [11]. Among the several enhancements that the new system will bring forth, are:

- Overall robustness
- Extensibility, relating to the package interface
- Better specification and inclusion of graphical material
- Better layout specification and handling
- Inclusion of requirements of hypertext systems

The LaTeX3 core team expects that a major reimplementation of LaTeX is needed in order to support the above goals.

The ConTeXt [13] format, developed by Hans Hagen, is monolithic when compared to LaTeX. As a result, the lessons learned from its development are not of great interest to our study.

2.3 $\mathcal{N}_{\mathcal{T}}\mathcal{S}$: The New Typesetting System

The $\mathcal{N}_{\mathcal{T}}\mathcal{S}$ project [14] was established in 1992 as an attempt to extend TEX's typesetting capabilities and at the same time to propose a new underlying programmatic model. Its originators recognised that TEX lacked user-friendliness and as a consequence it attracted many fewer users than it could (or should). Moreover, TEX (both as a name and a program) was frozen by Knuth, so any enhancements should be implemented in a completely new system.

$\mathcal{N}_{\mathcal{T}}\mathcal{S}$ was the first attempt to recognize that TEX's monolithic structure and implementation in an obsolete language (i.e., the Pascal programming language) are characteristics that could only impede its evolution. The techniques used to implement TEX, particularly its "tight", static and memory conservative data structures have no (good) reason to exist today (or even when $\mathcal{N}_{\mathcal{T}}\mathcal{S}$ was conceived, in 1992), when we have had a paradigm shift to flexible programming techniques.

After considering and evaluating several programming paradigms [19] including functional, procedural and logic programming, the $\mathcal{N}_{\mathcal{T}}\mathcal{S}$ project team decided to proceed with a Java-based implementation. Java's object-oriented features and its network awareness were the main reasons for adopting Java, as $\mathcal{N}_{\mathcal{T}}\mathcal{S}$ was envisioned as a network-based program, able to download and combine elements from the network.

Today, there is a Java codebase, which has deconstructed the several functional pieces of TEX and reconstructed them in a more object-oriented way with cleaner interfaces, a property that the original TEX source clearly lacks. In spite of the promising nature of $\mathcal{N}_{\mathcal{T}}\mathcal{S}$, the directory listing at CTAN[3] shows that the project is inactive since 2001[4]. It seems that the main focus is now the development of ε-TEX, which is presented in the following section.

2.4 ε-TEX

ε-TEX [17] was released by the $\mathcal{N}_{\mathcal{T}}\mathcal{S}$ team as soon as it was recognized that $\mathcal{N}_{\mathcal{T}}\mathcal{S}$ itself was very ambitious and that a more immediate and more easily conceivable goal should be set. So, it was decided that the first step towards a new typesetting system was to start with a reimplemented but 100% TEX compatible program.

ε-TEX was released in 1996, after three years of development and testing. It adds about thirty new primitives to the standard TEX core, including handling of bidirectional text (right-to-left typesetting). It can operate in three distinct modes:

1. "compatibility" mode, where it behaves exactly like standard TEX.
2. "extended" mode, where its new primitives are enabled. Full compatibility with TEX is not actually sought and the primary concern is to make typesetting easier through its new primitives.
3. "enhanced" mode, where bidirectional text is also supported. This mode is taken to be a radical departure from standard TEX.

---

[3] http://www.ctan.org/tex-archive/systems/nts/
[4] We have last accessed the above URL in March 2004.

Today, ε-TEX is part of all widely used TEX distributions and has proven to be very stable. Indeed, in 2003 the LATEX team requested that future distributions use ε-TEX by default for LATEX commands, which has since been implemented in TEX Live and other distributions.

2.5 Ω

Ω [16], which was first released in 1996, is primarily the work of two people: Yannis Haralambous and John Plaice. It extends TEX in order to support the typesetting of multilingual documents. Ω provides new primitives and new facilities for this reason. Ω's default character encoding is the Unicode UCS-2 encoding, while it can easily process files in almost any imaginable character encoding. In addition to that, Ω supports the parameterization of paragraph and page direction, thus allowing the typesetting of text in almost any imaginable writing method[5].

Much of its power comes from its new notion of ΩTPs (Ω Translation Processes). In general, an ΩTP is normally used to transform a document from a particular character encoding to another. Obviously, an ΩTP can be used to transform text from one character set to another. An ΩTP is actually a finite state automaton and, thus, it can easily handle cases where the typesetting of particular characters are context dependent. For example, in traditional Greek typography, there are two forms of the small letter theta, which are supported by Unicode [namely ϑ (03D1) and θ (03B8)]. The first form is used at the beginning of a word, while the second in the middle of a word. The following code borrowed from [16] implements exactly this feature:

```
input: 2; output: 2;
aliases:
LETTER  = (@"03AC-@"03D1 | @"03D5 | @"03D6 |
           @"03F0-@"03F3 | @"1F00-@"1FFF) ;
expressions:
^({LETTER})@"03B8({LETTER} | @"0027)
  => \1 @"3D1 \3;
. => \1;
```

For performance reasons, ΩTPs are compiled into ΩCPs (Ω Compiled Processes).

External ΩTPs are programs in any programming language that can handle problems that cannot be handled by ordinary ΩTPs. For example, one can prepare a Perl script that can insert spaces in a Thai language document. Technically, external ΩTPs are programs that read from the standard input and write to the standard output. Thus, Ω is forking a new process to allow the use of an external ΩTP. In [16] there are a number of examples (some of them were borrowed from [7]).

We should note that the field of multilingual typesetting is an active research field, which is the main reason why Ω is still an experimental system. We should also note that ε-Ω [4], by Giuseppe Bilotta, is an extension of Ω that tries to incorporate the best features of ε-TEX and Ω in a new typesetting engine.

---

[5] Currently the boustrophedon writing method is the only one not supported.

2.6   pdfTeX

pdfTeX [18] is yet another TeX extension that can directly produce a file in Adobe's PDF format. Recently, pdf-ε-TeX was introduced, merging the capabilities of both pdfTeX and ε-TeX.

3   Towards a Universal Typesetting Engine

From the discussion above, it is obvious that there is a trend to create new typesetting engines that provide the best features of different existing typesetting engines. Therefore, a Universal Typesetting Engine should incorporate all the novelties that the various TeX-like derivatives have presented so far. In addition, such a system should be designed by taking into serious consideration all aspects of modern software development and maintenance. However, our departure should not be too radical, in order to be able to use the existing codebase. Let us now examine all these issues in turn.

3.1   Discussion of Features

Data Structures. TeX's inherent limitations are due to the fact that it was developed in a time when computer resources were quite scarce. In addition, TeX was developed using the now outdated structured programming program development methodology.

Nowadays, hardware imposes virtually no limits in design and development of software. Also, new programming paradigms (e.g., aspect-oriented programming [8], generative programming [2], etc.) and techniques (e.g., extreme programming [1]) have emerged, which have substantially changed the way software is designed and developed.

These remarks suggest that a new typesetting engine should be free of "artificial" limitations. Naturally, this is not enough as we have to leave behind the outdated programming techniques and make use of modern techniques to ensure the future of the Universal Typesetting Engine. Certainly, $\mathcal{NTS}$ was a step in the right direction, but in the light of current developments in the area of software engineering it is now a rather outdated piece of software.

New Primitive Commands. Modern document manipulation demands new capabilities that could not have been foreseen at the time TeX was created. A modern typesetting engine should provide a number of new primitive commands to meet the new challenges imposed by modern document preparation. Although the new primitives introduced by ε-TeX and Ω solve certain problems (e.g., bidirectional or, more generally, multidirectional typesetting), they are still unable to tackle other issues, such as the inclusion of audio and/or animation.

Input Formats. For reasons of compatibility, the current input format must be supported. At the same time the proliferation of XML and its applications makes it more than mandatory to provide support for XML content. Currently,

XMLTEX is a TEX format that can be used to typeset validated XML files[6]. In addition, XLATEX [6] is an effort to reconcile the TEX world with the XML world. In particular, XLATEX is an XML Document Type Definition (DTD) designed to provide an XMLized syntax for LATEX. However, we should learn from the mistakes of the past and make the system quite adaptable. This means that as new document formats emerge, the system should be easily reconfigurable to "comprehend" these new formats.

Output Formats. The pdfLATEX variant has become quite widespread, due to its ability to directly produce output in a very popular document format (namely Adobe's Portable Document Format). Commercial versions of TEX are capable of directly generating PostScript files without the need of any driver programs. However, as in the case of the input formats, it is quite possible that new document formats will appear. Thus, we need to make sure that these document formats will find their way into TEX sooner or later.

In addition, XML initiatives such as MathML and SVG (Scalable Vector Graphics) are increasingly common in electronic publishing of scientific documents (i.e., quite demanding documents from a typographical point of view). Thus, it is absolutely necessary to be able to choose the output format(s) from a reasonable list of options. For example, when one makes a drawing using LATEX's `picture` environment, it would be quite useful to have SVG output in addition to the "standard" output. Currently, Ω can produce XML content, but it cannot generate PDF files.

Innovative Ideas. The assorted typesetting engines that follow TEX's spirit are not mere extensions of TEX. They have introduced a number of useful features and/or capabilities. For example, Ω's ΩTPs and its ability to handle Unicode input by default should certainly make their way into a new typesetting engine. In addition, ε-TEX's new conditional primitives are quite useful in macro programming.

Typesetting Algorithms. The paragraph breaking and hyphenation algorithms in TEX make the difference when it comes to typographic quality. Robust and adaptable as they are, these algorithms may still not produce satisfactory results for all possible cases. Thus, it is obvious that we need a mechanism that will adapt the algorithms so they can successfully handle such difficult cases.

Fonts. Typesetting means to put type (i.e., font glyphs) on paper. Currently, only METAFONT fonts and PostScript Type 1 fonts can be used with all different TEX derivatives. Although Ω is Unicode aware, still it cannot handle TrueType fonts in a satisfactory degree (one has to resort to programs like `ttf2tfm` in order to make use of these fonts). In addition, for new font formats such as

---

[6] Validation should be handled by an external utility. After all, there are a number of excellent tools that can accomplish this task and thus it is too demanding to ask for the incorporation of this feature in a typesetting engine.

OpenType and SVG fonts there is only experimental support, or none at all. A new typesetting engine should provide font support in the form of plug-ins so that support for new font formats could be easily provided.

Scripting. Scripting is widely accepted as a means of producing a larger software product from smaller components by "gluing" them together. It plays a significant role in producing flexible and open systems. Its realization is made through the so-called "scripting languages", which usually are different from the language used to implement the individual software components.

One could advance the idea that scripting in TeX is possible by using TeX the language itself. This is true to some extent, since TeX works in a form of "interpretive mode" where expressions can be created and evaluated dynamically at runtime – a feature providing the desired flexibility of scripting languages. But TeX itself is a closed system, in that almost everything needs to be programmed within TeX itself. This clearly does not lead to the desired openness.

A next generation typesetting engine should be made of components that can be "glued" together using any popular scripting language. To be able to program in one's language of choice is a highly wanted feature. In fact, we believe it is the only way to attract as many contributors as possible.

Development Method. Those software engineering techniques which have proven successful in the development of real-world applications should form the core of the program methodology which will be eventually used for the design and implementation of a next generation typesetting engine. Obviously, generic programming and extreme programming as well as aspect-oriented programming should be closely examined in order to devise a suitable development method.

All the features mentioned above as well as the desired ones are summarized in Table 1.

Table 1. Summary of features of TeX and its extensions.

	TeX	$\mathcal{NTS}$	ε-TeX	Ω	LaTeX(3)	**Desired**
implementation language	traditional	Java	traditional	traditional	traditional	perhaps scripting
architecture	monolithic	modular?	monolithic	monolithic	monolithic	modular
TeX compatibility	100%	yes	100%	100%	100%	via module
input transformations				ΩTPs		pluggable
Unicode	(Babel)	(Java)	(Babel)	true		true
XML				yes	via package	yes
typesetting algorithms	TeX	TeX-like	TeX-like	TeX-like	TeX-like	pluggable
scripting language	TeX	$\mathcal{NTS}$ (?)	ε-TeX	Ω	TeX	any
output drivers	dvi(ps,pdf)	dvi(?)	dvi(ps,pdf)	dvi(ps,pdf)	dvi(ps,pdf)	any
TRIP-compatible	yes	almost	ε-TRIP	yes	yes	yes (via module)
library mode	no	no	no	no	no	yes
daemon (server) mode	no	no	no	no	no	yes
programming community	< LaTeX	1 person?	< TeX	very small	big	> LaTeX

3.2   Architectural Abstractions

Roughly speaking, the *Universal Typesetting Engine* we are proposing in this paper, is a project to design and, later, to implement a new system that will support all the "good features" incorporated in various TEX derivatives plus some novel ideas, which have not found their way in any existing TEX derivative.

Obviously, it is not enough to just propose the general features the new system should have – we need to lay down the concrete design principles that will govern the development of the system. A reasonable way to accomplish this task is to identify the various concepts that are involved. These concepts will make up the upper abstraction layer. By following a top-down analysis, eventually, we will be in position to have a complete picture of what is needed in order to proceed with the design of the system.

The next step in the design process is to choose a particular system architecture. TEX and its derivatives are definitely monolithic systems. Other commonly used system architectures include the microkernel and exokernel architectures, both well-known from operating system research.

Microkernel Architecture. A microkernel-based design has a number of advantages. First, it is potentially more reliable than a conventional monolithic architecture, as it allows for moving the major part of system functionality to other components, which make use of the microkernel. Second, a microkernel implements a flexible set of primitives, providing high level of abstraction, while imposing little or no limitations on system architecture. Therefore, building a system on top of an existing microkernel is significantly easier than developing it from scratch.

Exokernel Architecture. Exokernels follow a radically different approach. As with microkernels, they take as much out of the kernel as possible, but rather than placing that code into external programs (mostly user-space servers) as microkernels do, they place it into shared libraries that can be directly linked into application code. Exokernels are extremely small, since they arbitrarily limit their functionality to the protection and multiplexing of resources.

Both approaches have their pros and cons. We believe that a mixed approach is the best solution. For example, we can have libraries capable of handling the various font formats (e.g., Type 1, TrueType, OpenType, etc.) that will be utilized by external programs that implement various aspects of the typesetting process (e.g., generation of PostScript or PDF files). Let us now elaborate on the architecture we are proposing. The underlying components are given in Figure 1.

The *Typesetting Kernel* (TK) is one of the two core components at the first layer. It can be viewed as a "stripped-down" version of TEX, meaning that its role as a piece of software is the orchestration of several typesetting activities. A number of basic algorithms are included in this kernel both as abstract notions – necessary for a general-purpose typesetting engine – and concrete implementations. So, TK incorporates the notions of paragraph and page breaking, mathematical typesetting and is Unicode-aware. It must be emphasized that TK "knows" the concept of paragraph breaking and the role it plays in typeset-

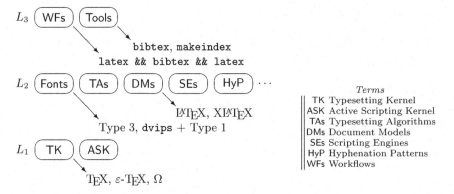

Fig. 1. The proposed microkernel-based layered architecture. The arrows show rough correspondence between the several architectural abstractions and their counterparts in existing monolithic typesetting engines.

ting but it is not bound to a specific paragraph breaking algorithm. The same principle applies to all needed algorithms.

The *Active Scripting Kernel* (ASK) is the second of the core components and the one that allows scripting at various levels, using a programming (scripting) language of one's choice. It is in essence a standardized way of communicating between several languages (TeX, Perl, Python), achieved by providing a consistent Application Programming Interface (API). The most interesting property of ASK is its *activeness*. This simply means that any extension programmed in some language is visible to any other available languages, as long as they adhere to the standard Active Scripting Kernel API. For example, an external module/service written in Perl that provides a new page breaking algorithm is not only visible but also available for immediate use from Python, C, etc.

Above TK and ASK, at the second layer, we find a collection of typesetting abstractions.

Fonts are at the heart of any typesetting engine. It is evident that font architectures change with the passing of time, and the only way to allow for flexibility in this part is to be open. Although there many different font formats, all are used to define glyphs and their properties. So instead of directly supporting all possible font formats, we propose the use of an abstract font format (much like all font editors have their own internal font format). With the use of external libraries that provide access to popular font formats (e.g., a Free Type library, a Type 1 font library, etc.), it should be straightforward to support any existing or future font format.

The various *Typesetting Algorithms* (TAs) – algorithms that implement a particular typographic feature – should be coded using the Active Scripting Kernel API. In a system providing the high degree of flexibility we are proposing, it will be possible to exhibit, *in the same document*, the result of applying several paragraph and page breaking algorithms. By simply changing a few runtime parameters it will be possible to produce different typographic "flavors" of the same document.

A *Scripting Engine* (SE) is the realization of the ASK APIs for a particular scripting language. For reasons of uniformity, the TEX programming language will be provided as a Scripting Engine, along with engines for Perl, Ruby and Python. This will make all the existing TEX codebase available for immediate use and it will provide for cooperation between existing LATEX packages and future enhancements in other languages. Thus, a level of 100% TEX compatibility will be achieved, merely as a "side-effect" of the provided flexibility.

The idea of a *Document Model* (DM) concerns two specific points: The document *external* representation, as it is "edited" for example in an editor, or "saved" on a hard disk, and its *internal* representation, used by the typesetting engine itself. It is clear that under this distinction, current LATEX documents follow the (fictional) "LATEX Document Model", XLATEX documents follow the "XLATEX document model" and an XML document with its corresponding DTD follows an analogous "XML+DTD Document Model".

We strongly believe that how a document is written should be separated from its processing. For the last part, an *internal* representation like the *Abstract Syntax Trees* (ASTs) used in compiler technology is highly beneficial. One way to think of DM is as the typographic equivalent of the Document Object Model (DOM). That is, it will be a platform-neutral and language-neutral representation allowing scripts to dynamically access and update the content, structure and style of documents.

Several *Document Processors* (DPs) may be applied to a specific document before actual typesetting takes place. DPs are the analog of ΩTPs. By leveraging the scripting power of ASK, the representation expressiveness of DPs is increased – as opposed to algorithmic expressiveness (Turing-completeness), which is evident, e.g., in Ω, but is not the sole issue.

The *Workflows* (WF) and *Tools* are at the highest architectural layer. Currently, there are a number of tools that may not produce a final typeset result, but are important for the proper preparation of a document. For example, such tools include bibliography, index and glossary generation tools. In the proposed architecture, all these programs will take advantage of other architectural abstractions – such as the Document Model or the Scripting Engines – in order to be more closely integrated in the typesetting engine as a whole.

Of particular importance is the introduction of the *Workflows* notion. A workflow is closely related to the operation or, to be more precise, *co*operation of several tools and the typesetting engine in the course of producing a typeset document. In effect, a workflow specifies the series of execution (probably conditional) steps and the respective inputs/outputs during the "preparation" of a document. By introducing a workflow specification for each tool, we relieve the user from manually specifying all the necessary actions in order to get a "final" `.pdf` (or whatever output format has been requested). Instead, the user will declaratively specify that the services of a tool are needed and the engine will load the respective workflows, compose them and execute them.

We shall give a workflow example concerning a BIBTEX-like tool. What we do here is to transform our experience of using `bibtex` into declarations specifying its behaviour in cooperation with `latex`:

```
WORKFLOW DEFINITION bibtex

SERVICE bibtex NEEDS latex
SERVICE bibtex INTRODUCES latex
```

In effect, this translates a hypothetical `Makefile`:

```
all:
    latex mydoc
    bibtex mydoc
    latex mydoc
```

for the preparation of the fictitious `mydoc.tex` document into a declarative specification that is given only *once* as part of the `bibtex` tool!

3.3   On Design and Evolution

Recent advances in software engineering advocate the use of multidimensional separation of concerns as a guiding design principle. Different concerns should be handled at different parts of code and ideally should be separated. For example, the representation of a document and its processing are two separate concerns and should be treated as such. Their interaction is better specified out of their individual specifications. Thus, we have introduced the Document Models notion to cope with the existing TEX/LATEX base as well as any future document representation.

Several architectural abstractions of Figure 1 are candidates to be specified as "services" at different granularities. For example, any *Tool* of the third layer can be thought of as a service that is registered with a naming authority and discovered dynamically, for immediate use on demand. A TrueType Font Service, regarding the second layer *Font* abstraction, is another example, this time more of a fine-grained nature, in the sense that a *Tool* (coarse-grained service) utilizes a *Font* (fine-grained service).

The proposed architecture makes special provisions for evolution by keeping rigid design decisions to a minimum. Built-in Unicode awareness is such a notable rigid design decision, but we feel that its incorporation is mandatory. Besides that, the ideas of pluggable algorithms and scripting are ubiquitous and help maintain the desired high degree of flexibility.

At the programming level, any style of design and development that promotes evolution can be applied. In the previous section we have actually demonstrated that the proposed architecture can even handle unanticipated evolution at the workflow level: the `bibtex` tool workflow specification causes the execution of an existing tool (`latex`) but we have neither altered any workflow for `latex` nor does `latex` need to know that "something new" is using it. In effect, we have *introduced* (the use of the keyword INTRODUCE was deliberate) a new *aspect* [8].

4   Conclusions and Future Work

In this paper we have reviewed the most widespread modern approaches to extending TEX, THE typesetting engine. After analyzing weaknesses of the approaches and the existing support for several features, we have presented our views on the architecture of an open and flexible typesetting engine.

We have laid down the basic architectural abstractions and discussed their need and purpose. Of course, the work is still at the beginning stages and we are now working on refining the ideas and evaluating design and implementation approaches.

The introduction of the Active Scripting Kernel is of prime importance and there is ongoing work to completely specify a) the form of a standard procedural API and b) support for other programming styles, including object-oriented and functional programming. This way, an *object* may for example take advantage of an algorithm that is better described in a *functional* form. There are parallel plans for transforming TEX into a Scripting Engine and at the same time providing Engines powered by Perl and Python.

We are also investigating the application of the workflow approach at several parts in the architecture other than the interaction among tools. This, in turn, may raise the need for the incorporation of a *Workflow Kernel* at the core layer, along with the Typesetting Kernel and the Active Scripting Kernel.

References

1. chromatic. *Extreme Programming Pocket Guide*. O'Reilly & Associates, Sebastopol, CA, USA, 2003.
2. Krzysztof Czarnecki and Ulrich Eisenecker. *Generative Programming: Methods, Tools, and Applications*. Addison–Wesley Publ. Co., Reading, MA, USA, 2002.
3. Victor Eijkhout. TEX by Topic. http://www.cs.utk.edu/~eijkhout/tbt
4. ε-Ω Project home page. http://www.ctan.org/tex-archive/systems/eomega/
5. $\mathcal{N_TS}$ FAQ. http://www.ctan.org/tex-archive/info/NTS-FAQ
6. Yannis Haralambous and John Plaice. Omega, OpenType and the XML World. *The 24th Annual Meeting and Conference of the TeX Users Group, TUG 2003.*
7. Yannis Haralambous and John Plaice. Traitement automatique des langues orientales et composition sous Omega. *Cahiers GUTenberg*, pages 139–166, 2001.
8. Gregor Kiczales, John Lamping, Anurag Mendhekar, Chris Maeda, Cristina Lopes, Jean-Marc Loingtier, and John Irwin. Aspect-Oriented Programming. In M. Aksit and S. Matsuoka, editors, *ECOOP '97 – Object-Oriented Programming: 11th European Conference, Jyväskylä, Finland, June 1997. Proceedings*, number 1241 in Lecture Notes in Computer Science, pages 220–242. Springer-Verlag, Berlin, 1997.
9. Donald Erwin Knuth. *The TEXbook*. Addison-Wesley, 1984.
10. Leslie Lamport. *LATEX: A Document Preparation System*. Addison–Wesley Publ. Co., Reading, MA, USA, 2nd edition, 1994.
11. LATEX3 Project home page. http://www.latex-project.org/latex3.html.
12. Richard Palais. Position Paper on the future of TEX. http://www.loria.fr/services/tex/moteurs/nts-9207.dvi, reached from http://tex.loria.fr/english/moteurs.html, October 1992.

13. PRAGMA Advanced Document Engineering. ConTEXt home page.
    http://www.pragma-ade.com/
14. $\mathcal{N_TS}$ Project home page. http://www.dante.de/projects/nts/
15. Eric E. Raymond. The Cathedral and the Bazaar.
    http://www.catb.org/~esr/writings/cathedral-bazaar/
16. Apostolos Syropoulos, Antonis Tsolomitis, and Nick Sofroniou. *Digital Typography Using LATEX*. Springer-Verlag, New York, NY, USA, 2003.
17. $\mathcal{N_TS}$ Team and Peter Breitenlohner. The ε-TEX manual, Version 2. MAPS, (20):248–263, 1998.
18. Hàn Thế Thành, Sebastian Rahtz, and Hans Hagen. The pdfTEX users manual. MAPS, (22):94–114, 1999.
19. Jiri Zlatuska. $\mathcal{N_TS}$: Programming Languages and Paradigms. EuroTEX 1999, http://www.uni-giessen.de/partosch/eurotex99/zlatuska.pdf

Moving Ω to an Object-Oriented Platform

John Plaice[1], Yannis Haralambous[2], Paul Swoboda[1], and Gábor Bella[2]

[1] School of Computer Science and Engineering
The University of New South Wales
UNSW SYDNEY NSW 2052, Australia
{plaice,pswoboda}@cse.unsw.edu.au
[2] Département Informatique
École Nationale Supérieure des Télécommunications de Bretagne
CS 83818, 29238 Brest Cédex, France
{yannis.haralambous,gabor.bella}@enst-bretagne.fr

Abstract. The code for the Ω Typesetting System has been substantially reorganised. All fixed-size arrays implemented in Pascal Web have been replaced with interfaces to extensible C++ classes. The code for interaction with fonts and Ω Translation Processes (ΩTP's) has been completely rewritten and placed in C++ libraries, whose methods are called by the (now) context-dependent typesetting engine. The Pascal Web part of Ω no longer uses change files. The overall Ω architecture is now much cleaner than that of previous versions.

Using C++ has allowed the development of object-oriented interfaces without sacrificing efficiency. By subclassing or wrapping existing stream classes, character set conversion and ΩTP filter application have been simultaneously generalised and simplified. Subclassing techniques are currently being used for handling fonts encoded in different formats, with a specific focus on OpenType.

1 Introduction

In this article, we present the interim solution for the stabilisation of the existing Ω code base, with a view towards preparing for the design and implementation of a new system. We focus on the overall structure of the code as well as on specific issues pertaining to characters, fonts, ΩTP's and hyphenation.

Since the first paper on Ω was presented at the 1993 Aston TUG Conference, numerous experiments with Ω have been undertaken in the realm of multilingual typesetting and document processing. This overall work has given important insights into what a future document processing system, including high quality typesetting, should look like. We refer the reader to the 2003 TUG presentation [7], as well as to the position papers presented to the Kyoto Glyph and Typesetting Workshop [3, 6, 8]. Clearly, building an extensive new system will require substantial effort and time, both at the design and the implementation levels, and so it is a worthwhile task to build a production version of Ω that will be used while further research is undertaken.

A. Syropoulos et al. (Eds.): TUG 2004, LNCS 3130, pp. 17–26, 2004.

The standard `web2c` infrastructure, which assumes that a binary is created from a single Pascal Web file and a single Pascal Web change file, is simply not well suited for the development of large scale software, of any genre. For this reason, we have eliminated the change files, and broken up the Pascal Web file into chapter-sized files. All fixed-size arrays have been reimplemented in C++ using the Standard Template Library. Characters are now 32 bits, using the `wchar_t` data type, and character set conversion is done automatically using the routines available in the `iconv` library. The entire Pascal Web code for fonts and ΩTP's, including that of Donald Knuth, has been completely rewritten in C++ and placed in libraries. Clean interfaces have been devised for the use of this code from the remaining Pascal code.

2   Problems with Pascal Web

When we examine the difficulties in creating Ω as a derivation of `tex.web`, we should understand that there is no single source for these difficulties.

Pascal was designed so that a single-pass compiler could transform a monolithic program into a running executable. Therefore, all data types must be declared before global variables; in turn, all variables must be declared before subroutines, and the main body of code must follow all declarations. This choice sacrificed ease of programming for ease of compiler development; the resulting constraints can be felt by anyone who has tried to maintain the TEX engine.

Pascal Web attempts to alleviate this draconian language vision by allowing the arbitrary use within code blocks – called *modules* – of pointers to other modules, with a call-by-name semantics. The result is a programming environment in which the arbitrary use of GOTOs throughout the code is encouraged, more than ten years after Dijkstra's famous paper. Knuth had responded correctly to Dijkstra's paper, stating that the reasonable use of GOTOs simplifies code. However, the arbitrary use of GOTOs across a program, implicit in the Pascal Web methodology, restricts code scalability. Knuth himself once stated that one of the reasons for stopping work on TEX was his fear of breaking it.

For a skilled, attentive programmer such as Knuth, developing a piece of code that is not going to evolve, it is possible to write working code in Pascal Web, *up to a certain level of complexity*. However, for a program that is to evolve significantly, this approach is simply not tenable, because the monolithic Pascal vision is inherited in Pascal Web's change file mechanism. Modifications to TEX are supposed to be undertaken solely using change files; the problem with this approach is that the vision of the code maintainer is that they are modifying functions, procedures, and so on. However, the *real* structure of a Pascal Web program is the interaction between the Pascal Web *modules*, not the functions and procedures that they define. Hence maintaining a Pascal Web program is a very slow process. Back in 1993, when the first Ω work was being undertaken, "slow" did not just mean slow in design and programming, but also in compilation: the slightest modification required a 48-minute recompilation.

The size limitations created by `tex.web`'s compile-time fixed-size arrays are obvious and well known. This issue was addressed publicly by Ken Thompson in the early 1980s, and both the existing Ω and the `web2c` distribution have substantially increased the sizes. However, these arrays raise other problems. The `eqtb`, `str_pool`, `font_info` and `mem` arrays all have documented programming interfaces. However, whenever these interfaces are insufficient, the TEX code simply makes direct accesses into the arrays. Hence any attempt to significantly modify these basic data structures requires the modification of the *entire* TEX engine, and not simply the implementations of the structural interfaces.

In addition, the single input `buffer` for all active files of `tex.web` turns out to be truly problematic for implementing ΩTP's. Since an ΩTP can read in an arbitrary amount of text before processing it, a new input buffer had to be introduced to do this collection. The resulting code is anything but elegant, and could certainly be made more efficient.

Finally, problems arise from the `web2c` implementation of Pascal Web. Many of the routines written in C to support the `web2c` infrastructure make the implicit assumption that all characters are 8 bits, making it difficult to generalise to Unicode (currently 21 bits), even though C itself has a datatype called `wchar_t`.

3   Suitability of C++

The advantages of the use of C++ as an implementation language for stream-oriented typesetting, over the Pascal Web architecture, are manifold. The chief reason for this is that the rich set of tools and methodologies that have evolved in the twenty-five years since the introduction of TEX includes developments not only in programming languages and environments, but in operating systems, file structure, multiprocessing, and in the introduction of whole new paradigms, including object-oriented software and generic programming.

C++ is the *de facto* standard for object-oriented systems development, with its capability to provide low-level C-style access to data structures and system resources (and, in the case of Unix-like systems, direct access to the kernel system call API), for the sake of efficiency.

In addition, the C++ Standard Template Library (STL) offers built-in support for arbitrary generic data structures and algorithms, including extensible, random-access arrays. It would be foolish to ignore such power when it is so readily available.

Since C++ is fully compatible with C, one can still take advantage of many existing libraries associated with TEX, such as Karl Berry's `kpathsea` file searching library, and the `iconv` library character-set conversion between Unicode and any other imaginably-used character set.

The abilities to use well-known design patterns for generic algorithm support (plug-in paragraphers, generic stream manipulation), as well as generic representation of typesetting data itself, add a wealth of possibilities to future, open typesetting implementations.

4   Organisation of the Ω Code Base

Obviously, we are moving on. Our objective is to include the existing Ω functionality, to stretch it where appropriate, leaving clean interfaces so that, if others
wish to modify the code base, they can do so. Our current objective is not to
rewrite TEX, but its underlying infrastructure.

4.1   Reorganising the Pascal Web Code

The `tex.web` file has been split into 55 files called `01.web` to `55.web`. The `tex.ch`
file has been converted into 55 files, `01.ch` to `55.ch`. Data structure by data
structure – specifically the large fixed-size arrays – we have combed the code,
throwing out the definitions of the data structures and replacing their uses with
Pascal procedure calls which, once passed through the `web2c` processor, become
C++ method calls. In the process, most of the code in the change files ends up
either being unnecessary, or directly integrated in the corresponding `.web` files.

4.2   The External Interface with Ω

We envisage that Ω will be used in a number of different situations, and not
simply as a batch standalone program. To facilitate this migration, we have
encapsulated the interface to the external world into a single class. This interface
handles the interpretation of the command line, as well as the setup for the file
searching routines, such as are available in the `kpathsea` library. Changing this
class will allow the development of an Ω typesetting server, which could be used
by many different desktop applications.

4.3   Characters, Strings and Files

The other interface to the outside world is through the data passed to Ω itself.
This data is in the form of text files, whose characters are encoded in a multitude
of different character encodings.

For characters, TEX has two types, `ASCII_code` and `text_char`, the respective internal and external representations of 8-bit characters. The new Ω uses the
standard C/C++ data type, `wchar_t`. On most implementations, including GNU
C++, `wchar_t` is a 32-bit signed integer, where the values 0x0 to 0x7fffffff
are used to encode characters, and the value 0xffffffff (-1) is used to encode
`EOF`. Pascal Web strings are converted by the `tangle` program into `str_number`,
where values 0 to 255 are reserved for the 256 8-bit characters. We have modified `tangle` so that the strings are numbered -256 downwards, rather than 256
upwards. Hence, `str_number` and `wchar_t` are both 32-bit signed integers.

When dealing with files, there are two separate issues, the file names, and the
file content. Internally, all characters are 4-byte integers, but on most systems, file
names are stored using 8-bit encodings, specified according to the user's locale.
Hence, character-set conversion is now built into the file-opening mechanisms,
be they for reading or writing.

The actual content of the files may come from anywhere in the world and a single file system may include files encoded with many different encoding schemes. We provide the means for opening a file with a specified encoding, as well as opening a file with automatic character encoding detection, using a one-line header at the beginning of the file. The actual character set conversion is done using the `iconv` library. As a result of these choices, the vast majority of the Ω code can simply assume that characters are 4-byte Unicode characters.

In addition to the data files, the following information must be passed through a character encoding converter: command line input, file names, terminal input, terminal output, log file output, generated intermediate files, and `\special` output to the `.dvi` file.

4.4   The Fixed-Size Arrays

The core of the the new Ω implementation is the replacement of the large fixed-size arrays, which are quickly summarized in the table below:

`str_pool`	string pool
`buffer`	input buffer
`eqtb`, etc.	table of equivalents
`font_info`, etc.	font tables
`mem`	dynamically allocated nodes
`trie`, etc.	hyphenation tables

For the cumulative data arrays, such as the string pool, we have created a new class, `Collection`, subclass of `vector`, that can be dump'ed to and undump'ed from the format file.

Currently no work has been done with the dynamically allocated nodes and the hyphenation tables. Replacing the `mem` array with any significantly different structure would effectively mean rewriting all of TEX, which is not our current goal.

4.5   The String Pool

The TEX implementation used two arrays: `str_pool` contained all of the strings, concatenated, while `str_start` held indices into `str_pool` indicating the beginning of each string. This has all been replaced with a `Collection<wstring*>`, where `wstring` is the STL string for 4-byte characters. As a result, we can directly take advantage of the hashing facilities provided in the STL. Note that the `omega.pool` file generated by `tangle` has been transformed into a C++ file.

4.6   The Input Buffer

The TEX implementation used a single array `buffer`, holding all the active lines, concatenated. This has now been broken up into a `Collection` of string streams. This setup simplifies the programming of ΩTPs, which must add to the input buffer while a line is being read.

4.7   The Table of Equivalents

The table of equivalents holds the values for the registers, the definitions for macros, and the values for other forms of globally accessible data. The TEX implementation used three arrays: `eqtb` held all of the potential equivalent entries, `hash` mapped string numbers to equivalent entries, and `hash_used` was an auxiliary Boolean table supporting the hashing.

The table has now been broken into several tables `map<unsigned,Entry*>` (for characters or register numbers) or `map<wstring,Entry*>` (for macro definitions), where `Entry` is some kind of value. Support is provided for characters up to `0x7fffffff`, and the STL hashing capabilities are used. This infrastructure has been built using the `intense` library [9], thereby allowing each `Entry` to be *versioned.* allowing different definitions of a macro for different contexts.

4.8   Fonts and ΩTPs

In terms of numbers of lines written, most of the new code in Ω is for handling fonts and ΩTPs. However, because we are using standard OO technology, it is also the most straightforward.

The original TEX and Ω code for fonts was concerned mostly with bit packing of fields in the `.tfm` and `.ofm` files, and unpacking this information inside the typesetting engine whenever necessary. This approach was appropriate when space was at a premium, but it created very convoluted code. By completely separating the font representations in memory and on disk, we have been able to provide a very simple OO interface in the character-level typesetter of the Ω engine, greatly simplifying the code for ligatures and kerning inside the typesetter, as well as for the font conversion utilities.

Similarly, for the ΩTPs, filters can be implemented as function objects over streams using iterators, tremendously simplifying the code base.

5   Supporting OpenType

Since we are using a programming language supporting type hierarchies, it is possible to support many different kinds of font formats. In this section, we consider different options for supporting OpenType, the current de facto standard.

The OpenType font format has been officially available since 1997. Unlike its predecessors, TrueType and PostScript Type 1 and 2, it facilitates handling of LGC (Latin-Greek-Cyrillic) scripts and also provides essential features for proper typesetting of non-LGC ones. Competing formats with similar capabilities (Apple GX/AAT and Graphite) do exist, but the marketing forces are not as strong.

At the EuroTEX conference in the summer of 2003, we presented our first steps towards an OpenType-enabled Ω system. At the time, OpenType and Ω were just flirting, but since last year their relationship has become more and more serious. In other words, what began simply as the adaptation of Ω to OpenType fonts has now become a larger-scale project: the authors are planning to restructure Ω's font system and make OpenType a base font format. As it will be shown, full OpenType compatibility requires serious changes inside both Ω and `odvips`. The other goal of the project is to simplify the whole font interface, eliminating the need for separate metric files, virtual fonts and the like (while the old system will of course continue to be supported).

Such a project, however, will certainly need some time to finish. Fortunately, the work done until now already provides users with the possibility to typeset using OpenType fonts, even if only a limited number of features are supported. It will be shown below that further development is not possible without major restructuring of the Ω system. Nevertheless, the present intermediate solution is in fact one of the three that we will retain.

Before getting to the discussion of possible solutions, let us briefly present the most important aspects of OpenType and their implications for Ω development.

5.1   OpenType vs. Omega

The key features of the OpenType format are summarised in the list below. As each one of these features raises a particular compatibility issue with Ω, they will all be elaborated below.

1. Font and glyph metric information;
2. Type 2 or TrueType glyph outlines (and hints or instructions);
3. Advanced typographic features (mainly GSUB and GPOS);
4. Clear distinction between character and glyph encodings;
5. Pre-typesetting requirements;
6. Extensible tabular file format.

Font and Glyph Metrics. OpenType provides extensive metric information dispersed among various tables (`post`, `kern`, `hmtx`, `hdmx`, `OS/2`, `VORG`, etc.), both for horizontal and vertical typesetting. Although in most cases Ω's and Open-Type's metrics are interconvertible a few but important exceptions do exist (e.g., height/depth) where conversion is not straightforward. See [1, 4].

Glyph Outlines, Hints and Instructions. Since the OpenType format it-self is generally not understood by PostScript printers, a conversion to more common formats like Type 1 or Type 42 is necessary. As explained in [1], to speed up this conversion process, we create Type 1 charstring collections using our own PFC tables which are used by `odvips` to create small, subsetted Type 1 fonts (a.k.a. *minifonts*) on the fly. This solution, on the other hand, does not preserve hints nor instructions, at least not in the present implementation. We are therefore planning to also provide Type 42 support for TrueType-flavoured OpenType. This solution would allow us to preserve instructions, at the expense of subsetting and compatibility.

Advanced Typographic Features. These are perhaps the most important aspect of OpenType. Its GSUB (glyph substitution) and GPOS (glyph positioning) tables are essential for typesetting lots of non-LGC scripts. In Ω, the equivalent of GSUB features are the ΩTP's: they can do everything GSUB features can, including contextual operations. Glyph positioning is a different issue: since the ΩTPs are designed for text rearrangement (substitutions, reordering etc.), they are not suitable for doing glyph placement as easily. Context-dependent typesetting *microengines* for character-level typesetting have been proposed for Ω to provide modular, script- and language-specific positioning methods, along the lines of ΩTP files; however, they have yet to be implemented. The positioning features in OpenType GPOS tables are in fact the specifications for microengines.

Character and Glyph Encodings. The above discussion of advanced typographic features brings us to a related issue: the fundamental difference between Ω's and OpenType's way of describing them. Although both Ω and OpenType are fully Unicode compatible, OpenType's GSUB and GPOS features are based on strings made of glyph ID's and not of Unicode characters. As for Ω and some of its ΩTP's, tasks such as contextual analysis or hyphenation are performed on character sequences and the passage from characters to "real" glyph ID's happens only when `odvips` replaces virtual fonts by real ones. To convert a glyph-based OpenType feature into a character-based ΩTP would require Ω to offer means of specifying new "characters" (the glyph ID's) that do not correspond to any Unicode position. The conversion itself would not be difficult since Ω's possible character space is much larger than Unicode's. This, however, would lead us to glyph ID-based, hence font-specific, ΩTP's and hyphenation, which is not a lovely prospect, to say the least. To solve this problem, it will certainly be necessary to keep both character and glyph information of the input text in parallel during the whole typesetting and layout process. This dual representation of text is also crucial for the searchability and modifiability of the output (PDF, PS, SVG or any other) document.

Pre-typesetting Requirements. OpenType relies on input text reordering methods for its contextual lookups to work correctly. If Ω is to use the same lookups, these reordering methods must also be implemented, either by ΩTP's or by an external library.

Extensibility. Finally, the OpenType format has the important feature of being extensible: due to its tabular structure, new tables can be added into the font file, containing, for example, data needed by Ω with no OpenType-equivalents (like metrics or PFC charstrings, see below). However, it is necessary that the given font's license allow additions.

5.2   Solutions

From the above discussion it should now be clear that complete and robust OpenType support is not a simple patch to Ω and `odvips`. Three solutions are proposed below, in order of increasing difficulty and of our working plan.

1. Convert OpenType fonts into existing Ω font metrics and ΩTP's;
2. Provide built-in support within Ω for a fixed but extensive set of OpenType features and read data directly from the OpenType font file;
3. Finally, provide extensible means for using the full power of OpenType fonts.

The Current Solution. This, described in detail in the EuroTEX article [1], corresponds to the first solution. Here we give a short summary.

The initial solution was based on the approach that OpenType fonts should be converted to Ω's own formats, i.e., `.ofm` (metrics), `.ovf` (virtual fonts) and ΩTP. Anish Mehta wrote several Python scripts to generate these files, of which the most interesting is perhaps the one that converts the whole OpenType GSUB table into ΩTP's. Type 2 and TrueType outlines themselves are converted into the Type 1-based PFC format and are subsetted on the fly by a modified `odvips`.

In summary, the present solution is a *working one*. Admittedly far from being complete (GPOS support is missing, among others), it is intended to provide Ω users with the possibility to typeset using OpenType fonts, including even some of its advanced features, while further development is being done.

Future Solutions. The second and third solutions mentioned above require that the Ω engine be capable of directly reading OpenType fonts, which can be done using a public library such as `freetype` or Kenichi Handa's `libotf`. This would also eliminate the need to create `.ofm` and `.ovf` files.

Providing built-in support for a fixed set of features corresponds to the aforementioned microtypesetting engines. For a given set of features, a new engine can be written. This approach can be taken using standard OO techniques.

A more general approach requires the ability to reach into an OpenType font, reading tables that were not known when the Ω engine was written. For this to work requires some kind of programming language to be able to manipulate these new tables. A simple such language is Handa's Font Layout Tables [2].

It should be clear that these solutions are not mutually exclusive and that backwards compatibility with the classic font system will be maintained.

6   Conclusions

At the time we are writing, this work is not completely finished. Nevertheless, it is well advanced: the infrastructure is substantially cleaned up, and is extensible, with clear API's. Detailed documentation will be forthcoming on the Ω website.

If we view things in the longer term, we are clearly moving forward with two related goals, the stabilisation of existing Ω infrastructure, and abandonment of the TEX infrastructure for the design and implementation of a next-generation open typesetting suite.

Such a suite should be a generic framework with an efficient C++ core, that is universally extensible through a number of well-known scripting interfaces, for example, Perl, Python, and Guile. Implementation of libraries similar to the popular LATEX suite could then be done directly in C++, on top of the core API, or as a linked-in C++ stream filter.

References

1. Gábor Bella and Anish Mehta. Adapting Ω to OpenType Fonts. *TUGboat*, 2004. In press.
2. Kenichi Handa, Mikiko Nishikimi, Naoto Takahashi and Satoru Tomura. FLT: Font Layout Table. Kyōto University 21st Century COE Program, 2003.
   http://coe21.zinbun.kyoto-u.ac.jp/papers/ws-type-2003/052-handa.pdf
3. Tereza Haralambous and Yannis Haralambous. Characters, Glyphs and Beyond. Kyōto University 21st Century COE Program, 2003.
   http://coe21.zinbun.kyoto-u.ac.jp/papers/ws-type-2003/017-tereza.pdf
4. Yannis Haralambous and John Plaice. Omega and OpenType Fonts. Kyōto University 21st Century COE Program, 2003.
   http://coe21.zinbun.kyoto-u.ac.jp/papers/ws-type-2003/067-yannis.pdf
5. The OpenType Specification v1.4.
   http://www.microsoft.com/typography/otspec/default.htm
6. John Plaice and Chris Rowley. Characters are not simply names, nor documents trees. Kyōto University 21st Century COE Program, 2003.
   http://coe21.zinbun.kyoto-u.ac.jp/papers/ws-type-2003/009-plaice.pdf
7. John Plaice, Paul Swoboda, Yannis Haralambous and Chris Rowley. A multidimensional approach to typesetting. *TUGboat*, 2003. In press.
8. Chris Rowley and John Plaice. New directions in document formatting: What is text? Kyōto University 21st Century COE Program, 2003.
   http://coe21.zinbun.kyoto-u.ac.jp/papers/ws-type-2003/001-rowley.pdf
9. Paul Swoboda and John Plaice. A new approach to distributed context-aware computing. In A. Ferscha, H. Hoertner and G. Kotsis, eds., *Advances in Pervasive Computing*. Austrian Computer Society, 2004. ISBN 3-85403-176-9.

Basque: A Case Study
in Generalizing LaTeX Language Support

Jagoba Arias Pérez[1], Jesús Lázaro[2], and Juan M. Aguirregabiria[3]

[1] Alameda Urquijo s/n
Bilbao, 48013
Spain
http://det.bi.ehu.es/~apert
jtparpej@bi.ehu.es
[2] Alameda Urquijo s/n
Bilbao, 48013
Spain
http://det.bi.ehu.es/~apert
jtplaarj@bi.ehu.es
[3] Bº Sarriena s/n
Leioa, 48940
Spain
http://tp.lc.ehu.es/jma.html
wtpagagj@lg.ehu.es

Abstract. The multilingual support of LaTeX presents many weak points, especially when a language does not present the same overall syntactic scheme as English. Basque is one of the official languages in the Basque Country, being spoken by almost 650,000 speakers (it is also spoken in Navarre and the south of France). The origins of the Basque language are unknown. It is not related to any neighboring language, nor to other Indo-European languages (such as Latin or German). Thus, dates, references and numbering do not follow the typical English pattern. For example, the numbering of figure prefixes does not correspond to the `\figurename\thefigure` structure, but is exactly the other way round. To make matters worse, the presence of declension can turn this usually simple task into a nightmare. This article proposes an alternative structure for the basic classes, in order to support multilingual documents in a natural way, even in those cases where the languages do not follow the typical English-like overall structure.

1 Introduction

The origins of LaTeX are tied closely to the English language. Since those days, however, it has spread to many different languages and different alphabets. The extent of the differences among these languages is not only related to lexical issues, but to the structure of the languages themselves.

The main problem arises when the syntactic structure of the language does not follow the English patterns. In these cases the adoption of a new multilingual approach is required in order to produce documents for these languages.

A. Syropoulos et al. (Eds.): TUG 2004, LNCS 3130, pp. 27–33, 2004.

Although LATEX is a highly parameterizable environment, it lacks resources to alter the order of the parameters themselves. This is due to the fact that both Germanic languages (such as English and German) and Romance languages (such as French, Italian, Spanish) – and therefore the most widely spread European research languages that use the Latin alphabet – share a similar word order for numeric references. To make matters worse, the presence of declension in structure such as dates and numbers leads to a complicated generalization of procedures.

This paper describes an alternative structure for the basic classes, in order to support multilingual documents in a natural way, even in those cases where the languages do not follow the typical English-like overall structure. Specifically, the paper focuses on Basque, one of the official languages in the Basque Country, being spoken by over half a million speakers (it is also spoken in Navarre and the south of France).

The rest of the paper is organized as follows: section 2 describes the specific details of the Basque language, in section 3 a brief description of prior work is presented, section 4 describes the different approaches that can be followed to solve the problem, section 5 shows the advantages and drawbacks of the different solutions and finally, in section 6 some brief conclusions are presented.

2   Specific Details of the Basque Language

The origins of the Basque language are unknown. It is not related to any neighboring language, nor to other Indo-European languages (such as Latin or German). This is one of the reasons why word order and numbering schemes are different from those in English.

Dates and numbers. Basque uses declension instead of prepositions as many other languages. The main difference from other languages that use declension, such as German, is that in Basque numbers are also fully declined, even in common structures such as dates. These declensions depend not only on the case, number and gender, but on the last sound of the word. Another peculiarity of Basque is the use of a base 20 numerical system instead of the traditional decimal one.

This forces us to take into account not just the last figure of the number but the last two figures, in order to determine the correct declension for the number [3]. In the following example, two dates are represented using ISO 8601 and its translation into Basque.

2004-01-11 : 2004ko urtarrilaren 11n
2005-01-21 : 2005eko urtarrilaren 21ean

Note that although both days end in the same figure, the declension is slightly different. The same happens to the year. The extra phonemes have been added to avoid words that are difficult to pronounce. This makes automatic date generation difficult, because it must take into account all the possible cases (as

Table 1. Endings.

Number	Ending (year)	Ending (day)
00	ko	-
01	eko	ean
02	ko	an
03	ko	an
04	ko	an
05	eko	ean
06	ko	an
07	ko	an
08	ko	an
09	ko	an
10	eko	ean
11	ko	n
12	ko	an
13	ko	an
14	ko	an
15	eko	ean
16	ko	an
17	ko	an
18	ko	an
19	ko	an
20	ko	an

base 20 is used, there may be as many as 20 different possibilities). The different number endings are shown in table 1. Note that there are only twenty possible terminations, and two declension classes are necessary.

Word order. When numbering a certain chapter, section, etc., in English-like languages the order is always the following: first, the item class (e.g. "figure") is named and, afterwards, the number is written. For example, we have "Figure 1.1" or "Table 2.3". However, this is not the case in Basque. In this language, we must reverse this order: "1.1 Irudia" or "2.3 Taula". The same applies for chapters, sections and other kind of text partitioning structures.

3   Related Work

Multilingual support for LaTeX is traditionally performed using the Babel package [2]. In this package, the overall structure of documents, such as books, articles, etc., is fitted to different languages by using different variables for the different strings in each language.

For example, we can take the way figure captions are numbered in these types of documents: a variable called \figurename contains the string corresponding to the word "figure" in the first part of the caption, while another variable, \thefigure contains the number assigned to that caption. When a new figure is inserted in the document, the string preceding the caption is always formed by using a concatenation of both variables. However, this process is not performed by Babel, which would allow a general description of the language, but in the different files that describe the document format: `book.cls`, `article.cls`, etc. Thus, some of the work that should be performed by the module in charge of the multilingual support is made by the formatting part of the typesetting software.

The file `basque.ldf` [1] currently provides support for Basque in Babel. In this file, the most commonly used words have been translated. However, this does not solve the problem of the different order of strings. In [1], a possible solution is proposed using a new package for the document definition: instead of using the multilingual capabilities of Babel to solve the problem, a new document formatting file is defined, where the specific corrections for the language are performed. The limitation for multilingual document generation is obvious in this scheme: the format must be redefined whenever the language of the document is changed. Besides, a new definition for every single class of document must be performed for this particular language – as we are not philologists, we do not know if the same happens in other languages.

4   Approaches to the Solution

The solution to the problem described in this paper must deal with the following issues:

- It must respect all the translations of the different strings generated automatically.
- It must respect not only the translation, but the order of words as well.
- The last problem to solve is the use of the `\selectlanguage` directive, which would allow us to change the hyphenation patterns and the automatic text generation structures dynamically in the same document. This directive is particularly useful for documents which contain the same text in different languages (e.g. user's guides, where the manual has been translated).

The main possible avenues to the solution are the following:

- **Use of specific classes for the language:** This solution implies the redefinition of every document format, in order to embed the corresponding word order alteration for automatic string generation. The main drawback of this alternative is the need for rewriting and adapting all the existing document formats.
- **Use of a specific package for the language:** A second possibility could include the definition of a new package for those languages that require a word order alteration. This package should redefine the `\fnum@figure` and the `\fnun@table` variables (among others, which define the chapter or section name) in order to adapt them to the needs of the languages used. A macro should be used to switch between the two nodes.
- **Inclusion of order parameters in the document class definition files:** This option requires that a new input parameter is defined in the document

class to define the order of the words. Basically, it is the same solution as the first one, but merging all the different files for a document class into a single (larger and more complex) file.

- **Redefinition of existing multilingual support files:** This solution implies the addition of several lines to every language support file, where the definition of the automatic strings such as the figure captions or the table captions is performed. For example, for the case of table and figure captions, the definitions for the Basque language would be the following:

```
\def\fnum@figure{\thefigure~\figurename}
\def\fnum@table{\thetable~\tablename}
```

These definitions should go into the `basque.ldf` file, immediately after the definition of the terms for caption or table names. Thus, whenever a \selectlanguage directive is introduced in the document, the Babel package will read the definitions for the new language, which will include the definitions for every string.

5   Comparison of Solutions

We use the following criteria to compare the different solutions:

- **Extent of modification to existing files:** This criterion measures how many existing files will be altered to fix the problem and how complicated this alteration is.
- **Addition of new files:** This criterion measures how many new files are to be added to the LATEX distribution for each solution.
- **The \selectlanguage issue:** This criterion measures how well the solution deals with possibly changing the language of the document dynamically.
- **How easily new automatically-generated strings are included:** In the future, translation of new strings may be required. Therefore, the proposed solution must provide an easy way to include these new strings.

5.1   Extent of Modification

Here is how the solutions fare with respect to the first criterion:

- **Use of specific classes for the language:** This option does not require that any file be modified, because new definitions are described in new files.
- **Use of specific package for the language:** This approach requires no modifications of existing files, since all modifications are included in a new package.
- **Inclusion of order parameters in the document class definition files:** This alternative entails the redefinition of every document class. These should admit a language parameter to determine the correct word order.
- **Redefinition of existing multilingual support files:** This choice implies that every file containing the translation and definition of the automatically-generated strings provides order information for them, and therefore, all the files in Babel should be changed.

5.2 Addition of New Files

Here's how the solutions fare with respect to adding new files:

- **Use of specific classes for the language:** This option requires all document classes to be rewritten for every language that does not follow the English-like structure.
- **Use of specific package for the language:** This approach requires one new file for every language that has not been described successfully in the Babel approach.
- **Inclusion of order parameters in the document class definition files:** This alternative entails no new files, as it is based on the modification of the existing files.
- **Redefinition of existing multilingual support files:** This choice does not need new files, as it is based on the modification of the existing files.

5.3 The \selectlanguage Issue

Depending on how generalization of the multilingual support is implemented, the different solutions may (or not) solve the \selectlanguage problem:

- **Use of specific classes for the language:** This option does not really use Babel and its macros. As part of the translation of automatic strings is performed by the file defining the format of the document class, support for the \selectlanguage directive should be implemented in each document class for every language (not only for those incorrectly supported by the Babel system, but for all of them).
- **Use of specific package for the language:** This approach requires one new file for every language. Hence, a macro would be required in each package to leave things as they were *before* the package was initiated.
- **Inclusion of order parameters in the document class definition files:** This alternative cannot solve the problem, because the order specification is only made at the beginning of the document. A macro could be added to alter its value dynamically throughout the document, but it would be an artificial patch that would not fit naturally in the Babel structure.
- **Redefinition of existing multilingual support files:** This choice does solve the problem, because when a new \selectlanguage command is issued, the definitions for the new language are reloaded. It requires no new macro definitions to suit the Babel scheme for multilingual documents.

5.4 Inclusion of New Strings

Here's how the solutions fare with respect to the possibility of including further modifications for strings that could be necessary in the future:

- **Use of specific classes for the language:** As some of the linguistic characteristics of the document are included in the document class, this option does not provide a straightforward method for including changes for problems that may arise.

- **Use of specific package for the language:** The use of a package gives flexibility to the scheme, allowing the insertion of new macros to adapt to the peculiarities of the language. However, the range of possibilities is so wide that a very well-defined structure must be laid down in order to keep a modicum of coherence for creating a document in a different language.
- **Inclusion of order parameters in the document class definition files:** This scheme requires updating several files whenever a new string or scheme must be added.
- **Redefinition of existing multilingual support files:** As this choice uses a single file for every language, it makes updating the elements for Babel very easy.

6 Conclusions

This paper discusses some alternatives to solve the ordering problems that may arise in multilingual documents.

Table 2. Solution comparison.

Solution	Mod.	Cr.	Multi.	Updates
Specific class	X	✓	Dif.	Dif.
Specific pack.	X	✓	Dif.	Dif.
Parameters	✓	X	Dif.	Dif.
Redefinition	✓	X	✓	✓

The characteristics of the different proposed solutions are summarized in table 2. Among the solutions, the most suitable would be the redefinition of all the existing Babel files. The reason is simple: it requires the addition of two lines to approximately 45 files, and allows the update of the system in the future, as it maintains *all* the translating issues within their natural context (Babel).

References

1. Juan M. Aguirregabiria. Basque language definition file. http://tp.lc.ehu.es/jma.html, 2001.
2. Johannes Braams. Babel, a multilingual package for use with LaTeX's standard document classes. CTAN://macros/latex/required/babel/, 2001.
3. Euskaltzaindia. Data nola adierazi. http://www.euskaltzaindia.net/arauak/dok/ProNor0037.htm, 1995.

μονο2πολυ: Java-Based Conversion of Monotonic to Polytonic Greek

Johannis Likos

ICT Consulting
Rusthollarintie 13 E 35
Helsinki 00910
Finland
likosjo@yahoo.com

Abstract. This paper presents a successfully tested method for the automatic conversion of monotonic modern Greek texts into polytonic texts, applicable on any platform. The method consists of combining various freely available technologies, which have much better results than current commercially available solutions. The aim of this presentation is to introduce a way of applying this method, in order to convert thousands of digitally available single-accented modern Greek pages into attractive artworks with multi-accented contents, which can be easily transferred either to the Web or a TEX-friendly printer. We will discuss the preparatory and postprocessing efforts, as well as the editing of syntax rulesets, which determine the quality of the results. These rulesets are embedded in extendable tables, functioning as flat databases.

1   Introduction

During the past centuries, Greek and Hellenic scholars have introduced and refined polytonism (multiple accenting) in the written word for the precise pronounciation of ancient Greek. Since spoken modern Greek is comparatively less complicated, the Greek government has officially replaced polytonism by monotonism (single accenting) for purposes of simplification, especially in the educational system. Also, Greek authors commonly use monotonism, since it is so much simpler to produce.

Classical, polytonic, Greek has three accents (acute, grave, and circumflex) and two *breathings* (rough and smooth – equivalent to an initial 'h' and lack thereof). Accents are lexically marked, but can change based on other factors, such as *clitics* (small, unstressed words that lean on another word to form a *prosodic word* – a single word for accent placement). In addition, two other symbols were used: diaeresis (to indicate two vowels that are not a diphthong) and iota subscript (a small iota that was once part of a diphthong but subsequently became silent).

Monotonic Greek retains only the acute accent, which was usually, though not always, the same as the classical acute. To make a graphic break with the

A. Syropoulos et al. (Eds.): TUG 2004, LNCS 3130, pp. 34–54, 2004.

past, the new acute accent was written as a new *tonos* glyph, a dot or a nearly vertical wedge, although this was officially replaced by a regular acute in 1986.

So, why bother with the complexities of polytonism? The benefits are increased manuscript readability and, even more important, reducing ambiguity. Despite the simplification efforts and mandates, the trend nowadays is *back to the roots*, namely to polytonism. More and more publishers appreciate, in addition to the content, the public impression of the quality of the printed work.

This paper discusses an innovative and flexible solution to polytonism with an open architecture, enabling the automatic multiple accenting of existing monotonic Greek digital documents.

2   Terminology

In this article, we will use the terms *polytonism* and *multiple accenting* interchangeably to mean the extensive usage of *spiritus lenis, spiritus asper, iota subscript, acute, gravis* and *circumflex*. Similarly, we use the terms *monotonism* and *single accenting* to mean the usage of simplified accenting rules in Modern Greek documents.

3   Historic Linguistic Development

During the last four decades the printed Greek word has undergone both minor and radical changes. Elementary school text during the late 1960s and early 1970s made Purified Greek (καθαρεύουσα), by strict government law of the time. The mid-1970s saw a chaotic transition period from Purified Greek to Modern Greek (δημοτική) with simplified grammar, where some publications were printed with multiple accenting, some with single accenting and even some without any accenting at all!

Even after the government officially settled on monotonism in the early 1980s, Greek publishers were not able to switch immediately to the monotonic system. During the last decade, many computerized solutions have been invented for assistance in typing monotonic Greek. Today, there is a trend toward a mixture of simplified grammar with multiple accenting, decorated with Ancient Greek phrases. See Table 3.

4   Polytonic Tools

There are two programs for Microsoft Word users, namely *ΤΟΝΙΣΜΟΣ* by DATA-SOFT and *ΑΥΤΟΜΑΤΟΣ ΠΟΛΥΤΟΝΙΣΤΗΣ* (academic and professional version) by MATZENTA. A third is the experimental μονο**2**πολυ, an open source project, which is the subject of this discussion.

These solutions are independent. The major difference between the commercial and open source programs is the control of the intelligence, such as logic, rule sets and integrated databases. In the case of the commercial solutions, users

Table 1. Selected examples of Greek publications from the last four decades.

Date Publisher	Author	Subject/Title	Language	Remarks	Example
1968 ΕΚΔΟΣΕΙΣ A. ΚΑΡΑΒΙΑ	S. TIMOSHENKO	Ἀντοχὴ τῶν ῾Υλικῶν	purified	polytonic translation including gravis	
1971 O.E.Δ.B.	D.H. YOUNG M. ΚΑΤΣΙΚΑΣ	ΓΕΩΓΡΑΦΙΑ ΣΤ' ΔΗΜΟΤΙΚΟΥ	purified	no dative at all and iota subscript seldom used	νὰ ἐπιδιωχθῇ
1978 ΙΔΡΥΜΑ ΕΥΓΕΝΙΔΟΥ	I. ΧΑΣΤΑΣ	βιβλ. Τεχν. κ. Ἐπαγγ. Λυκείου	modern	polytonic without gravis	
1980 self-published	P. ΓΡΑΙΚΟΥΣΗΣ	ΣΤΟΙΧΕΙΑ ΜΗΧΑΝΩΝ	modern	acute used instead of gravis in polytonic text, some feminine singular genitive in purified version	τῆς κλίσεως
1982 self-published	Ε.Σ.Μ.Α.	ΠΡΑΚΤΙΚΑ ΕΘΝ. ΑΕΡΟΠΟΡΙΚΟΥ ΣΥΝΕΔΡΙΟΥ	modern	monotonic typewriter text style	
1989 INTERBOOKS	ΓΡ. ΣΦΑΚΙΑΝΟΣ	ΕΜΠΟΡΙΚΗ ΑΛΛΗΛΟΓΡΑΦΙΑ	modern	monotonic with neutral accent and acute	εκτός από τόν
1998 ΠΑΡΑΤΗΡΗΤΗΣ	A. ΣΥΡΟΠΟΥΛΟΣ	LᴬTᴇX	modern	acute only accent type in monotonic text	τό τόπι
2003 A. ΦΩΤΙΕΡΗΣ	several authors	ἡ λέξη	modern	polytonic without gravis	καί ἀπ' τό

depend on the software houses; in the open source case, users depend on their own abilities. See Table 2.

There is no absolutely perfect tool for polytonism, so the ultimate choice is of course up to users themselves.

Table 2. Comparison of polytonic tools.

	ΤΟΝΙΣΜΟΣ	ΑΥΤΟΜΑΤΟΣ ΠΟΛΥΤΟΝΙΣΤΗΣ	μονο2πολυ
Greek language support			
Ancient	yes	yes	later
Hellenistic	yes	yes	later
Byzantine	no	no	later
Church/Biblical/NT	yes	yes	later
Purified	yes	yes	later
Modern	yes	yes	yes
Mixed (Ancient and Modern)	selectable	selectable	fixed
Editing assistance	no	yes	no
Database	fixed (binary)	fixed (binary), editable exception list interactively	editable (XML)
Manual corrections		yes	post-processed
Automatic hyphenation	unknown	ID	external task
Protection	hardlock		no
File formats			
Input	Word (Win, Mac)	Word (Win, Mac), other Greek formats	ISO 8859-7 encoded, ASCII on any platform
Output	Word (Win, Mac)	Word (Win, Mac), other Greek formats	ASCII (ISO 10646-1 encoded), HTML (ISO 10646-1 encoded)
Unicode support	yes	yes	yes
TeX-specific filters	TeXto737.lex, 737toTeX.lex	no	Writer2LaTeX
Requirements	Microsoft Word	Microsoft Word	JDK 1.4
Platforms			
Microsoft Windows	95, 98, ME, NT, 2000, XP	95, 98, ME, NT, 2000, XP	95, 98, ME, NT, 2000, XP
Apple Macintosh	no	no	Mac OS 9, Mac OS X
Linux	no	no	Mandrake, Red Hat, SuSE
Unix	no	no	AIX, HP-UX, Sinix, Solaris
Availability	immediately	immediately	under development
Distribution	purchased license	purchased license	open source

5 Open Source Concept

μονο2πολυ implements a modular mechanism for multiple accenting of single-accented Greek documents. See Figure 1.

5.1 Architecture

The μονο2πολυ architecture consists of (Figure 2):

- methods: DocReader, DocWriter,
  DBParser, Converter
- configuration file: *.cfg

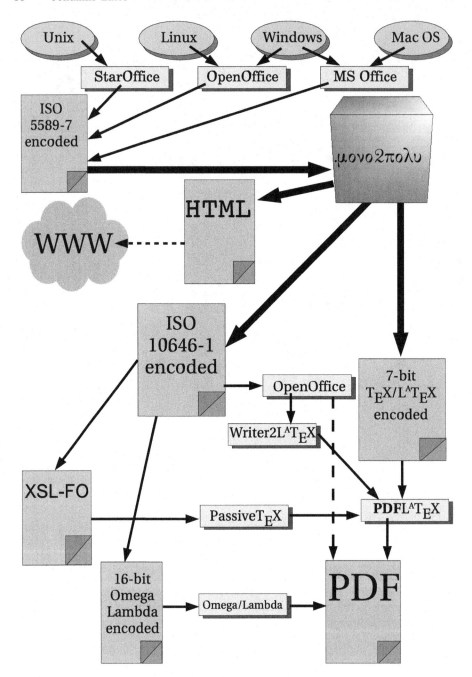

Fig. 1. Overview of the overall multiple accenting concept, which involves many external tools.

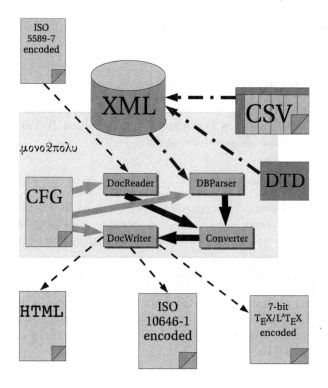

Fig. 2. Overview of internal architecture, with external interfaces to existing standards.

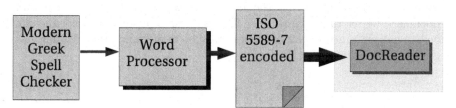

Fig. 3. External creation of monotonic Greek with any word processor (e.g., OpenOffice) using a separate spellchecker (e.g., elspell).

- flat database: `*.xml`
- document type definition: `*.dtd`
- optional spreadsheet: `*.csv`, `*.xls`

5.2   Configuration

The plain text configuration file defines (gray arrows in Figure 2) the necessary filenames and pathnames. The μονο2πολυ components read this during initialization to determine where to find the input files and where to write the output files (by default, the current working directory).

5.3 Database Connectivity

The dotted arrows in the architecture figure (Figure 2) show the connection between a CSV spreadsheet, a Document Type Definition (DTD), the actual XML flat database, and the database parser.

5.4 Input Prerequisites

During the conversion process, invisible special control codes for formatting features (superscript, bold, etc.) make it difficult to coherently step through paragraphs, sentences and words. Therefore, plain text files serve best for polytonism input.

The DocReader component of $\mu o\nu o2\pi o\lambda\upsilon$ expects the source document to be in the ISO 8859-7 encoding, and to be written according to the Modern Greek grammar, especially regarding the monotonic accenting rules.

Assistance for monotonic accenting while typing Modern Greek documents is provided by Microsoft's commercially bundled spellchecker, or any downloadable Open Source spellchecker.

5.5 Converter

The bold arrows in the architecture figure (Figure 2) show the data exchange between the internal components, the document reader, the database parser and the document writer to the converter. The conversion process does not include grammar analysis, since $\mu o\nu o2\pi o\lambda\upsilon$ expects that monotonic proof reading has been done previously, with other tools.

6 External Interfaces

The output from $\mu o\nu o2\pi o\lambda\upsilon$ (DocWriter method) is in the ISO 10646-1 encoding, in various formats, which are then post-processed. The dashed arrows in Figure 2 show the relationship between the external files.

6.1 Web Usage

For background, these web pages discuss polytonic Greek text and Unicode[1] (UTF) fonts:

---

[1] Concerning missing Greek characters and other linguistic limitations in Unicode, see *Guidelines and Suggested Amendments to the Greek Unicode Tables* by Yannis Haralambous at the 21st International Unicode Conference on May 2002 in Dublin, Ireland (`http://omega.enstb.org/yannis/pdf/amendments2.pdf`).

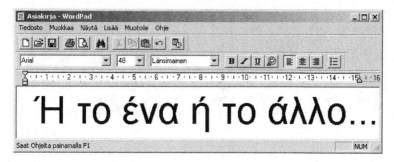

Fig. 4. Example of original monotonic input.

- http://www.ellopos.net/elpenor/lessons/lesson2.asp
- http://www.stoa.org/unicode/
- http://www.mythfolklore.net/aesopica/aphthonius/1.htm

Using the direct HTML polytonic output from μονο2πολυ requires that the layout of the web page be done in advance, since manually editing the numeric Unicode codes in the *.html file is impractical (see figure 5). Dynamic web pages created through CGI scripts, PHP, etc. have not yet been tested.

```
<font
FACE="Arial Unicode MS"
SIZE="36">
&#7978;&#32;
&#964;&#8056;&#32;
&#7957;&#957;&#945;&#32;
&#7970;&#32;
&#964;&#8056;&#32;
&#7940;&#955;&#955;&#959;;
&#46;&#46;&#46;
</font>
```

Fig. 5. Example of polytonic HTML output.

6.2   OpenOffice Usage

The ISO 10646-1 encoded polytonic output (Figure 6) from μονο2πολυ could be inserted into the OpenOffice Writer software, since the newest version can directly output polytonic Greek .pdf files. Unfortunately, the quality of the result leaves much to be desired. Better results can be produced by converting from Writer to LATEX and doing further processing in the LATEX environment.

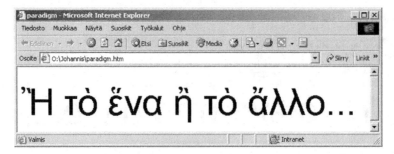

Fig. 6. Example of polytonic output.

6.3   (LA)TEX Usage

The most likely scenario for (LA)TEX users is using the Greek babel package, and adding the $\mu o\nu o 2\pi o\lambda\upsilon$ 7-bit polytonic output text into the source .tex file. See figures 7 and 8.

The 7-bit output from $\mu o\nu o 2\pi o\lambda\upsilon$ could presumably also be inserted into .fo files, and processed through PassiveTEX, but this has not yet been tested. Likewise, the ISO 10646-1 output could presumably be processed directly with Ω/Λ, but this has not been tested, either.

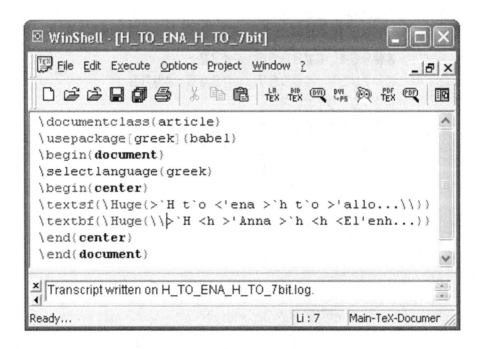

Fig. 7. Example of polytonic TEX output, either from $\mu o\nu o 2\pi o\lambda\upsilon$ or Writer2LATEX.

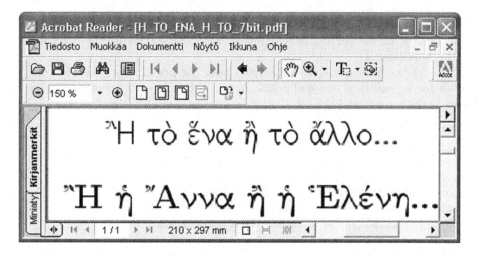

Fig. 8. Polytonic PDF output from TeX.

7   Technologies Used in *μονο2πολυ*

After some evaluation, we chose to focus on Java, Unicode and XML, due to their flexibility in processing non-Latin strings, obviously a critical requirement of *μονο2πολυ*.

7.1   Programming Language

Two major reasons for choosing Java (J2SE) as the implementation language of *μονο2πολυ* were the capabilities for handling XML and Unicode through widely-available and well-documented libraries. The Java SDK provides extremely useful internationalization features, with the ability to easily manipulate string values and files containing wide characters.

In order to concentrate on *μονο2πολυ*'s essential features, no graphical user interface has been designed.

7.2   Character Set

The choice of Unicode/ISO 10646-1 for the character set should be clear. It combines monotonic and polytonic Greek letters, is known worldwide and standardized on most platforms, and contains most (though not all) variations of Greek vowels and consonants, in the Greek and the Greek Extended tables[2].

For further information on writing polytonic Greek text using Unicode, see http://www.stoa.org/unicode/.

---

[2] http://www.unicode.org/versions/Unicode4.0.0/ch07.pdf

7.3   Text Parsing Libraries

Most helpful for the parsing of XML-based database entries are the SAX and DOM Java libraries.

The following Java source code, taken from the $\mu o\nu o2\pi o\lambda\upsilon$ class DBparse, serves to demonstrate usage of SAX and DOM. The code counts and then outputs the total amount of all available entries in the XML database file.

```
[\scriptsize]
import java.io.*;
import org.xml.sax.SAXException;
import org.xml.sax.SAXParseException;
import javax.xml.parsers.DocumentBuilder;
import javax.xml.parsers.DocumentBuilderFactory;
import javax.xml.parsers.FactoryConfigurationError;
import javax.xml.parsers.ParserConfigurationException;
import org.w3c.dom.*;
public class DBparse{
  static Document document;
  String warn="No XML database filename given...";
    public static void main(String param[]){
        if (param.length!=1){
            System.out.println(warn);
            System.exit(1);}
        File mydbfile=new File(param[0]);
        boolean load=mydbfile.canRead();
        if (load){
          try{
            DocumentBuilderFactory fct
               = DocumentBuilderFactory.newInstance();
            DocumentBuilder builder
               = fct.newDocumentBuilder();
            document = builder.parse(mydbfile);}
          catch (SAXParseException error){
            System.out.println("\nParse error at line: "
                + error.getLineNumber() + " in file: "
                + error.getSystemId());
            System.out.println("\n" + error.getMessage() );}
          catch (ParserConfigurationException pce)
                  {pce.printStackTrace();}
            catch (IOException ioe){ioe.printStackTrace();}
            catch (Throwable t){t.printStackTrace();}}
        else{System.out.println("XML database missing!");}
      String mytag='\u03C3'+"";
      NodeList taglist=document.getElementsByTagName(mytag);
      int amount=taglist.getLength();
      System.out.println("amount of entries:\n" + amount );}}
```

Notice particularly the fourth-last line, where `mytag` is assigned '`\u03C3`', namely the character σ, used as the search string.

8   Database Structure

The XML standard from the W3C has proven to be a simpler choice for storing either monotonic or polytonic Unicode text than the alternatives, such as spreadsheets or even SQL databases. The quality of the final polytonic result depends on the precision of the XML content, where ambiguities have to be marked with special symbols for manual post-processing.

Currently, the entries of the basic database consist of tags with parameters and values. The tag name indicates the type of the expression: a single character, a prefix, a suffix, a substring, a word or a chain of words. The five parameters are as follows:

1. The monotonic ISO 8859-7 encoded source expression to be converted.
2. The Unicode output text.
3. A 7-bit output text for (L^A)T_EX usage with the Greek babel package.
4. The equivalent numeric value according to the *Extended Greek* Unicode table for HTML usage.
5. An explanatory comment or example, in case of ambiguities or linguistic conflicts.

Here, I have built on the work of prior Greek T_EX packages, such as GreekT_EX (K. Dryllerakis), Scholar T_EX (Y. Haralambous), and `greektex` (Y. Moschovak-is and G. Spiliotis), for techniques of using the iota subscript, breathings and accents in 7-bit transliterated `.tex` source files.

In the following examples, note carefully the different bases used: '074 is octal, #8172 is decimal and '03D1' is hexadecimal.

8.1   Data Type Definition

The required basic *Data Type Definition* is currently located in the experimental namespace `xmlns:`β` = http://koti.welho.com/ilikos/TeX/LaTeX/mono2poly/mono2poly.dtd`. It contains the following information:

```
<!ELEMENT  β  (σ+)>
<!ELEMENT  σ (#PCDATA)>
<!ATTLIST  σ
   μ  CDATA  #REQUIRED
   π  CDATA  #REQUIRED
   τ  CDATA  #REQUIRED
   δ  CDATA  #REQUIRED
   ξ  CDATA  #REQUIRED>
```

Thus, we have one element, called β (βάση δεδομένων = *database*). It contains multiple element sets, called σ (στοιχε ια συλλαβ ης = *syllable data*). Each element set has, at present, five attributes, namely μ for monotonic expressions, π for polytonic expressions, τ for 7-bit (LA)TEX code, δ for HTML code, and finally ξ for comments.

The DTD can be overridden by a local `.dtd` file, which must be specified in the header of the `.xml` database file; for example:

```
<!DOCTYPE β SYSTEM "my_own_mono2poly.dtd">
```

Both the `.dtd` and `.xml` must reside in the same directory.

8.2   Data Entries

Here is an example database entry, showing the only Greek capital consonant with spiritus asper:

```
<σ
    μ="Ρ"
    π="‘Ρ"
    τ="\char'074 R"
    δ="&#8172;"
    ξ="‘Ρόδος"
></σ>
```

The *slash* symbol indicates the closing element tags in XML, while the *backslash* symbol is used for (LA)TEX commands. Both appear in the `.xml` database file.

8.3   Header and Body

Although not explicitly documented, exotic characters may be used in `.dtd` and `.xml` files as long as the appropriate encoding is declared:
```
<?xml version="1.0" encoding="UTF-16"?>
```
The header should include other information as well. Schematically:

```
<?xml version="1.0" encoding="UTF-16"?>
<!DOCTYPE β SYSTEM "mono2poly.dtd">
<!-- author: ... -->
<!-- affiliation: ... -->
<!-- creation date: ... -->
...
<!-- notes: ... -->
<β>
  <σ μ="..." π=".." τ=".." δ=".." ζ=".."></σ>
  ...
  <σ μ="..." π=".." τ=".." δ=".." ζ=".."></σ>
</β>
```

For quality assurance, after database creation and after each update a validation and verification test should be run, to detect XML syntax errors and linguistic content mistakes.

This concept of the database as a lookup/mapping table allows differentiating between initial and intermediate consonants. For example:

ϐ (03D0) ↔ β (03B2)
ϑ (03D1) ↔ θ (03B8)
ϱ (03F1) ↔ ρ (03C1)
ϕ (03D5) ↔ φ (03C6)

Therefore, by updating the XML file, post-processing may be reduced. Experienced linguists may wish to use different tools for the correcting and the updating of the flat database. Rows with multiple columns from spreadsheets can be inserted directly into XML data files, as long as the columns are sorted in the expected order.

8.4   Expression Types

In each database entry, there is one source expression, at least three target expressions, and possibly one explanation. The ISO 8859-7 encoded source expression and the first ISO 10646-1 encoded target expression may be a:

- single uppercase or lowercase character with or without spiritus and/or accent
- partial word, such as prefix, intermediate syllable, suffix
- complete word
- chain of combined words
- combination of partial word pairs, such as a suffix followed by a prefix
- mixture of complete and partial words, such as a complete word followed by a prefix or a suffix, followed by a complete word

The rest of the target expressions represent the same information as the first in other output formats, namely for 7-bit Greek (LA)TEX and HTML as well. The intelligence of the μονο2πολυ system currently lies in the database, so while creating and editing entries, it is crucial to write them correctly.

8.5   Editing Tools

One of the most powerful Unicode editors is the Java-based Simredo 3.x by Cleve Lendon, which has a configurable keyboard layout, and is thus suitable for this sort of task. The latest version of Simredo, 3.4 at this writing, can be downloaded from `http://www4.vc-net.ne.jp/~klivo/sim/simeng.htm`, and installed on any platform supporting JDK 1.4.1 from Sun. Simredo can be started by typing `java Simredo3` or perhaps `java -jar Simredo3.jar` in the shell window (Linux) or in the command window (Windows). Unicode/XML with Simredo has been successfully tested on Windows XP and on SuSE Linux 8.1 Professional Edition.

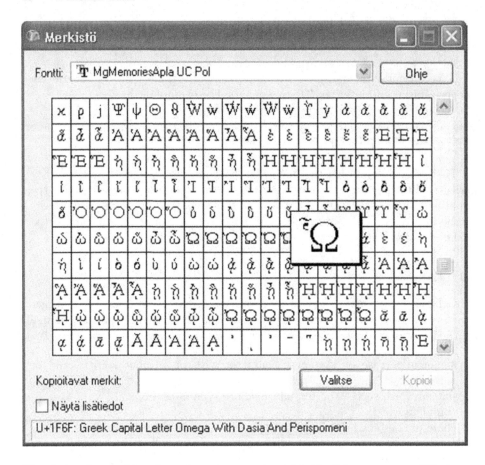

Fig. 9. Another useful tool is a character mapping table like this accessory on Windows XP, which displays the shape and the 16-bit big endian hexadecimal code of the selected character.

The author would be happy to assist in the preparation of a polytonic Greek keymap file (`.kmp`) for Simredo, but the manual may prove sufficient. The creation of such a keymap file is easily done by simply writing one line for each key sequence definition. For instance, given the sequence `2keys;A"A` using the desired Unicode character, or the equivalent sequence `2keys;A\u1F0D` with the big endian hexadecimal value, one can produce an uppercase *alpha with spiritus asper and acute accent* by pressing the ⌗ ; ⌗ and ⌗ A ⌗ keys simultaneously. According to the Simredo manual, other auxiliary keys such as `Alt` can be combined with vowel keys, but not `Ctrl`.

Some other Unicode editors:

- For Windows: http://www.alanwood.net/unicode/utilities_editors. html.
- For Linux: http://www.unicodecharacter.com/unicode/editors.html.
- For Mac OS: http://free.abracode.com/sue/.

Unfortunately, XMLwriter and friends neither support configurable keyboard layouts nor display 16-bit Unicode.

8.6 Polytonic Keyboard Drivers

Instant interactive multi-accenting while editing Greek documents is available either through plug-ins for some Windows applications, such as SC Unipad (`http://www.unipad.org/main/`) and Antioch (`http://www.users.dircon.co.uk/~hancock/antioch.htm`), or with the help of editable keyboard mapping tables, such as the Simredo Java program described above. Regrettably, the *Hellenic Linux User Group* (HEL.L.U.G., `http://www.hellug.gr` and `http://www.linux.gr`) has no recommendations for polytonic Greek keybord support.

Whatever polytonic keyboard driver has been installed and activated may be useful for new documents, but does not much help the author who is not familiar with the complicated rules of polytonism!

8.7 Auxiliary Tables

Preparation and periodic updates of auxiliary tables can of course be done with any software supporting Unicode. Spreadsheets have the advantage of putting the entries into cells row-by-row and thus organizing the parameters by column. This may prove easier than directly writing the XML file. See figure 10.

A row in such a `.csv` file looks like this:
```
"P","'P","\char'074 R","&#8172;","'Ρόδος"
```
Of course it then must be re-shaped with element and attribute tags to make an XML-syntax database entry.

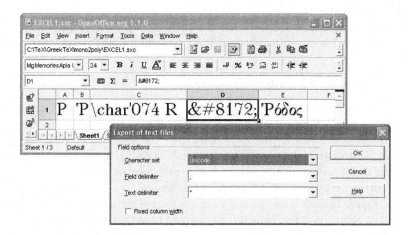

Fig. 10. Using a spreadsheet to produce a long extendable list with five columns, which then can be saved as a `.csv` file. Be careful with the parametrization!

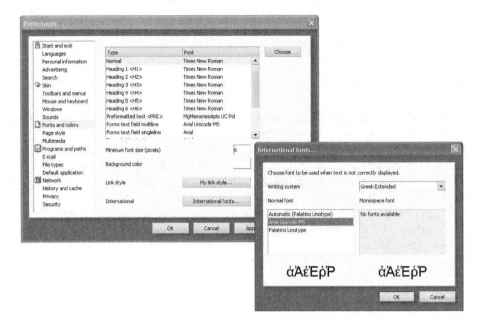

Fig. 11. Choosing the Unicode font for viewing in a browser.

8.8   Viewing Tools

Users without any programming knowledge may find it useful to open and inspect the header and the body of the XML database before using it in polytonic documents. Here is a procedure for doing that.

First, set the Unicode font in the preferences of the desired browser (Figure 11). These days, most browsers support this, including Internet Explorer, Konqueror, Netscape Navigator and Opera.

Then, select Unicode UTF-16 as the default encoding (Figure 12). The browser can now detect syntax errors, giving immediate feedback (Figure 13).

8.9   Priorization of Database Entries

Polytonic exceptions (e.g., οὔτε and ὥστε without circumflex) and especially ambiguities (e.g., που → ποὺ or πού, ποὺ → ποῦ; πως → πὼς or πώς, πὼς → πῶς) have the highest priority in the database, then the special expressions, while the simple, casual and obvious accented syllables or particles have the lowest priority. In order to avoid mis-accented and mis-spirited syllables as much as possible, entries must be in the appropriate order.

For example, Table 3 shows lexical rules defining eight variations of the Greek interrogative pronoun τί (= "which") as a single monotonic expression:

– with and without neutral accent
– with and without Greek question mark

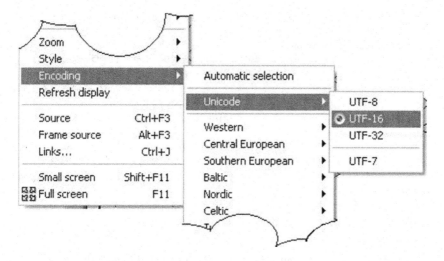

Fig. 12. Selecting UTF-16 for the default encoding.

Fig. 13. Example error message from browser.

- standalone
- leading word in the sentence
- intermediate word in the sentence
- trailing word in the sentence

Database entries like these are needed to account for the variations shown in Table 4. As a rough analogy in English, it is as if Table 3 shows variations on "I": Initial position ("I went to the store"); after a verb ("What do I know?"); etc., and then Table 4 shows that "I" isn't always capitalized: "It looks good" vs. "Can you see it?"

The above does not cover all cases related to τί. The monotonic text γιατι may be accented in two different ways in polytonic Greek (namely, γιατὶ and γιατί); additional entries would be required to handle this.

9   Polytonic Printing Press

The author has found several Greek newspapers, magazines, and books, including university presses, using polytonic Greek:

Table 3. Eight variations of τί as a monotonic expression.

```
<!--   ἐρωτηματικὲς ἀντωνυμίες   -->
<σ μ="Τι;" π="Τί;" τ="T'i;" δ="&#932;&#8055;&#894;" ξ="Τί;"> </σ>
<σ μ="Τι " π="Τί " τ="T'i " δ="&#932;&#8055;&#32;" ξ="Τί λές;"> </σ>
<σ μ=" τι;" π=" τί;" τ=" t'i;" δ="&#32;&#964;&#8055;&#894;" ξ="Κι ' ἔγραψε
τί;"> </σ>
<σ μ=" τι " π=" τί " τ=" t'i " δ="&#32;&#964;&#8055;&#32;" ξ="Καὶ τί
ἔγραψε;"> </σ>
<σ μ="Τί;" π="Τί;" τ="T'i;" δ="&#932;&#8055;&#894;" ξ="Τί;"> </σ>
<σ μ="Τί " π="Τί " τ="T'i " δ="&#932;&#8055;&#32;" ξ="Τί λές;"> </σ>
<σ μ=" τί;" π=" τί;" τ=" t'i;" δ="&#32;&#964;&#8055;&#894;" ξ="Κι ' ἔγραψε
τί;"> </σ>
<σ μ=" τί " π=" τί " τ=" t'i " δ="&#32;&#964;&#8055;&#32;" ξ="Καὶ τί
ἔγραψε;"> </σ>
```

Table 4. Similar but unrelated syllables treated differently.

Position	Syllable	Polytonic examples
leading	τι-, Τι-	τιμή, Τισσαφέρνης
intermediate	-τι-	ἀδυνάτισμα
trailing	-τι	κάτι, πράγματι
leading	τί-, Τί-	τίποτα, Τίγρης
intermediate	-τί-	ἐκτίμηση
trailing	-τί	γατί, ψωμί, τυρί

- daily newspapers:
  - *Η ΚΑΘΗΜΕΡΙΝΗ*
  - *ΕΣΤΙΑ*
- monthly magazines:
  - *ΝΕΜΕΣΙΣ*
- book publishers:
  - *ΕΚΔΟΤΙΚΗ ΑΘΗΝΩΝ*
  - *ΚΥΡΙΑΚΙΔΗΣ*
  - *ΓΕΩΡΓΙΑΔΗΣ*
  - *ΠΑΠΑΝΙΚΟΛΑΟΥ*
  - *ΙΝΔΙΚΤΟΣ*
  - *ΓΝΩΣΗ*
  - *ΚΑΛΟΦΩΛΙΑΣ*
- academic, polytechnic and university presses:
  - Academy of Athens
  - Polytechnics of Athens
  - University Publications of Crete
  - University of Ioannina
  - Democritian University of Thrace

– private educational organizations:
  • *ΚΟΡΕΛΚΟ*
  • *ΜΩΡΑΪΤΗ*
– others:
  • Hellenic Parliament
  • military press
  • Orthodox Church

10 Testing

The following testing procedure was used for μονο2πολυ development. The author worked on SuSE Linux and Windows XP, but any platform (Linux, Unix, Mac or Windows) should work as well, as long the JDK is installed.

1. Visit any web site with rich Modern Greek content, for example, news sources such as http://www.pathfinder.gr.
2. Open a new document with a word processor supporting spell checking of monotonic Greek.
3. Copy a long excerpt of continuous text from the web site.
4. Paste the selected and copied text into the word processor window.
5. Correct any misspelled words, but do not use any style or font effects.
6. Save the document as plain ISO 8859-7 encoded text file.
7. Process the document with μονο2πολυ, as a Java application from a console window.
8. Take the 7-bit TEX result and add it to the LATEX template file in your favourite environment (LyX, Kile, MiKTEX, etc.).
9. Produce a .ps or a .pdf file and check the final result with GSview or some other reader.

The results improve as the database is enriched. However, some manual editing is inevitable, depending on the complexity of the document to be multi-accented, because authors may mix Ancient Greek phrases into Modern Greek sentences.

11 Future Developments

One important improvement would be to relocate some of the intelligence to external script files, for defining and modifying the polytonic grammar rule sets.

Another avenue is to integrate μονο2πολυ with the source and data files of the open source Writer2LATEX project (by Henrik Just, http://www.hj-gym.dk/~hj/writer2latex/). That would provide a reverse conversion, from UTF-16BE/LE encoded Greek documents into 7-bit (LA)TEX.

12   Related Links

Here we list some further readings on the complexity of Greek multiple accenting and related subjects. First, these articles (mainly written in Greek) on the importance of the spiritus lenis and especially of the spiritus asper:

- http://www.typos.com.cy/nqcontent.cfm?a_id=4681
- http://www.kairatos.com.gr/polytoniko.htm
- http://www.krassanakis.gr/tonos.htm
- http://www.mathisis.com/nqcontent.cfm?a_id=1767

  Further general sources are the following:

- Ministry of National Education and Religion Affairs – http://www.ypepth. gr/en_ec_home.htm
- Institute for Language and Speech Processing – http://www.ilsp.gr
- http://www.ekivolos.gr

References

1. Blomqvist, J., Toivanen, A., *Johdatus Uuden testamentin Kreikkaan.* Yliopistopaino: Helsinki (1993), 15–25.
2. Bornemann, E., Risch, E., *Griechische Grammatik.* Verlag Moritz Diesterweg: Frankfurt a./M. (1978), 1–25.
3. Deitsch, A., Czarnecki, D., *Java Internationalization.* O'Reilly: Beijing, Cambridge, Köln, Paris, Sebastopol, Taipei, Tokyo (2001), 171–198.
4. Harold, E.R., *Java I/O.* O'Reilly: Beijing, Cambridge, Köln, Paris, Sebastopol, Taipei, Tokyo (1999), 387-413
5. Kaegi, A., Bruhn, E., *Griechische Schulgrammatik.* Verlag Weidmann: Zürich, Hildesheim (1989), 2–10.
6. Dr.Maier, F., Weiss, M., Zeller, A., *OPΓANON Grammatik I+II.* Bayerischer Schulbuch-Verlag: München, C.C. Buchners Verlag, Salzburg (1979), 1–12.
7. Οἰκονόμου, Μ.Χ., *ΓΡΑΜΜΑΤΙΚΗ ΤΗΣ ΑΡΧΑΙΑΣ ΕΛΛΗΝΙΚΗΣ. ΙΝΣΤΙΤΟΥΤΟ ΝΕΟΕΛΛΗΝΙΚΩΝ ΣΠΟΥΔΩΝ:* Θεσσαλονίκη (1993), 12–21.
8. Pakarinen, W., *Kreikan kielioppi.* Suomalaisen Kirjallisuuden Seura: Helsinki (1993), 1–13.
9. Seeboerger-Weichselbaum, M., *Java/XML.* DAS *bhv* TASCHENBUCH. verlag moderne industrie: Bonn Landsberg (2002), 181–208.
10. Syropoulos, A., Tsolomitis, A., Sofroniou, N., *Digital Typography Using LATEX.* Springer Professional Computing, Springer-Verlag: Berlin, Heidelberg, New York (2003), 315–319.
11. Τσάρτζανος, Α., *ΓΡΑΜΜΑΤΙΚΗ ΤΗΣ ΑΡΧΑΙΑΣ ΕΛΛΗΝΙΚΗΣ ΓΛΩΣΣΗΣ. ΕΚΔΟΤΙΚΟΣ ΟΙΚΟΣ ΑΔΕΛΦΩΝ ΚΥΡΙΑΚΙΔΗ:* Θεσσαλονίκη, (1993), 9–14.
12. Τσολάκης, Χρ. Λ., *ΝΕΟΕΛΛΗΝΙΚΗ ΓΡΑΜΜΑΤΙΚΗ. ΕΚΔΟΣΕΙΣ ΚΩΔΙΚΑΣ,* Θεσσαλονίκη: (1988), 28–35.
13. Dr. Wendt, H.F., *Langenscheidts Praktisches Lehrbuch Neugriechisch. Ein Standardwerk für Anfänger,* Langenscheidt: Berlin, München, Wien, Zürich, New York (1993), 20–35.

Using LATEX to Typeset
a Marāṭhī-English Dictionary

Manasi Athale and Rahul Athale

Research Institute for Symbolic Computation
Johannes Kepler University
Linz
Austria
{manasi,athale}@risc.uni-linz.ac.at

Abstract. We are using LATEX to typeset an old Marāṭhī-English dictionary, dated 1857. Marāṭhī is the official language of Mahārāshtra, a western state of India. Marāṭhī (मराठी) is written using the Devanāgarī script. The printed edition of the dictionary contains approximately 1000 Royal Quarto size ($9\frac{1}{2}'' \times 12\frac{2}{3}''$) pages with around 60,000 words. The roots of the words come from many languages including Sanskrit, Arabic and Persian. Therefore the original dictionary contains at least *three* different scripts along with many esoteric punctuation marks and symbols that are not used nowadays.

We have finished typesetting 100 pages of the original dictionary. We present our experiences in typesetting this long work involving Devanāgarī and Roman script. For typesetting in Devanāgarī script we used the **devnag** package. We have not yet added the roots in other scripts but that extension can be achieved with the help of ArabTEX. We want to publish the dictionary in electronic format, so we generated output in PDF format using pdfLATEX. The bookmarks and cross-references make navigation easy. In the future it would be possible to design the old punctuation marks and symbols with the help of METAFONT.

1 Introduction

Marāṭhī is a language spoken in the Western part of India, and it is the official language of Mahārāshtra state. It is the mother tongue of more than 50 million people. It is written in the Devanāgarī script, which is also used for writing Hindi, the national language of India, and Sanskrit. The script is written from left to right. A consonant and vowel are combined together to get a syllable, in some cases consonants can be combined together to get conjuncts or ligatures. While combining the vowel and a consonant one might have to go to the left of the current character – which is a big problem for a typesetting program.

We are typesetting a Marāṭhī-English dictionary compiled by J. T. Molesworth and published in 1857. The dictionary is old so there is no problem about copyright. This will be the first Marāṭhī-English dictionary in an electronic format.

A. Syropoulos et al. (Eds.): TUG 2004, LNCS 3130, pp. 55–58, 2004.

2 Devanāgarī Script

There are 34 consonants, 12 vowels, and 2 vowel-like sounds in Marāṭhī. Table 1 gives the consonants along with some common English words to illustrate the sounds. In some cases, there is no exact equivalent English sound, and we give those with standard philological transliteration. The *h* in this table designates aspiration, and a dot under a consonant designates retroflexion. Although Hindi and Marāṭhī use the same Devanāgarī script, the consonant ळ, which is used in Marāṭhī is not used in Hindi. Similarly some characters used in Sanskrit are not used in Marāṭhī. All the consonants have one inherent vowel अ (*a*), and in order to write the consonant itself without the vowel, a special "cancellation" character ( ) called *virāma*, must be used. For example, स् , is स् + अ, where अ is a vowel.

Table 1. Devanāgarī consonants.

क	ख	ग	घ	ङ
*c*ar	*kh*	*g*o	*gh*	nasal
च	छ	ज	झ	ञ
*ch*air	*cch*	*j*ail	*z*ebra	nasal
ट	ठ	ड	ढ	ण
ṭ	*ṭh*	*ḍ*	*ḍh*	*ṇ*
त	थ	द	ध	न
*T*ehran	*th*	*d*ark	*dh*	*n*ew
प	फ	ब	भ	म
*p*air	*f*ail	*b*at	*bh*	*m*an
य	र	ल	व	
*y*ellow	*r*oad	*l*ove	*w*ay	
श	ष	स	ह	ळ
*sh*are	*ṣ*	*s*un	*h*appy	

Table 2. Devanāgarī vowels.

अ	आ	इ	ई	उ	ऊ
*a*bout	*ca*r	s*i*t	s*ea*t	p*u*t	r*oo*t
ऋ	ऌ	ए	ऐ	ओ	औ
und*er*	bott*le*	s*ay*	*by*	r*oa*d	l*ou*d
अं	अः				

Table 2 lists the vowels and the two vowel-like sounds. The first two rows give the vowels and the last row gives the vowel-like sounds, called *anuswāra* and *visarga*, respectively. In general, the vowels are paired with one member short, the other long. For ऋ, make the *r* into a syllable by itself.

A vowel is added to a consonant to produce a syllable, for example all the consonants written above already have the vowel अ. Suppose we want to get the sound, *S*arah, with a long *a*. We add the second vowel आ to स् to get सा, where we can see a bar added behind the consonant स.

Now to write *sit* we add the third vowel इ to स्, and here it gets difficult, because although the *i* is pronounced after the *s*, it is written before the consonant. We get सि, where a bar is added before the character स.

Syllables can even be formed using more than one consonant and a vowel. For example, द्वितीया, here we add द्, व् and इ. It can also be written as द्वितीया. There are many such variations when two or more consonants are combined, and some conjunct characters look nothing like their constituent parts. For example, र or *r* is written in *four* different ways depending on the other consonant in the conjunction.

The first vowel-like sound, *anuswāra*, is the nasal consonant at the end of each of the first five consonant rows in the consonant table. For example, गंगा (Ganges), here the " ˙ " on the first character is the *anuswāra* but it is pronounced as the nasal sound in the row of the next character, which is गा. The sound is like ङ. *Visarga* is more or less a very brief aspiration following the inherent vowel (and for this reason it is usually written *ḥ* in philological transcription).

3   Problems

We tried many approaches before choosing LATEX. Scanning the pages was out of question as the printed quality is very poor. Also many of the consonant conjuncts are written in a different way nowadays, so it would be difficult for the average modern reader to decipher the old dictionary. There are some Web sites that have dictionaries in two scripts using Unicode. But in many cases it does not show the correct output, and it is difficult to find suitable viewers. We thank referees for mentioning an XML approach, but we did not try that. We also tried Omega, but there was hardly any information available when we started our work more than two years ago and also the setup was very difficult.

The first problem was having two scripts in the text, and typesetting it such that both scripts mesh well. Molesworth uses Marāṭhī words to explain the concepts so Devanāgarī script text appears also in the meaning. Also there are couplets of a poem in places to explain the usage. Many Marāṭhī words have roots in Sanskrit, Hindusthani, Arabic and Persian. Arabic, Persian, and the Urdu variant of Hindusthani are written using the Arabic script, which is the third script used in the dictionary. In Marāṭhī, a word is spoken – and also written – in a slightly different way depending on the region of the publication. Therefore in the dictionary, the most used form usually has the meaning listed for it, and all other forms have a note pointing to the most used form. This requires cross-referencing for faster use.

The dictionary has a long preface giving the details of how the words were chosen, which meanings were added, and so on. It contains different symbols and punctuation marks. Also in the meaning of some words, symbols are used to show the short form used during that period, which is obsolete now.

The printed dictionary is heavy, so carrying it everywhere is out of question. We wanted to give the user the possibility to carry the dictionary on a compact disc or computer. Therefore the next question was, which is the most user-friendly and/or popular output format?

4   Solution

In a single word: pdfLATEX. We mainly used two packages to do the typesetting: lexikon for dictionary style, and devnag for Devanāgarī script. It is a two step process to typeset in Devanāgarī script. A file, usually with extension .dn, is processed with devnag, a program written in the C language, to get a .tex file. The preprocessing step is necessary due to the problem of vowel placement, complex conjunct characters, and so on, as mentioned in the introduction. The style file dev is used to get the Devanāgarī characters in the output PDF file after compiling using pdfLATEX.

Once we have a .tex file we can get output in many formats, DVI, PS, PDF, etc. We chose PDF as there are free readers for almost all platforms and pdfLATEX makes it easy to go from TEX to PDF. The hyperref package solved the problem of cross-referencing and bookmarks. The user can click on a hyperlinked word to go to the form of the word that has the complete meaning, and come back to the original word with the back button in his favourite reader. In addition to the hyperlinks, bookmarks make navigation much easier; for example, bookmarks point to the first words starting with *aa*, *ab*, *ac*, etc. An additional nested level of bookmarks is chosen if there are many words starting with the character combination. For example, if there are many words starting with *ac* then we also have bookmarks for *aca*, *acc* and so on. Usually there are fewer than five pages between two bookmarks, so finding a word is not time consuming.

The preface contains characters like आ॒, which is not part of the modern Marāṭhī character set, but which was used as a short form a hundred years ago. To typeset this character we directly edited the .tex file after preprocessing to get the required result.

We have attached at the end of this article an annotated sample page from the typeset dictionary. At the top of the page the first entry is the first word on the page, then the copyright information with our name for the dictionary, शब्दविश्व, simply translated as "the world of words", followed by the entry of the last word on the page. On the right hand side is the page number. At the bottom, the page number is given in Devanāgarī script.

5   Future Work

After completing the typesetting the whole dictionary we will add the roots of the words in Hindusthani, Arabic and Persian. Currently we denote this using [H], [A] or [P], respectively. We have tried typesetting in three secripts on some small examples and did not find any conflicts between ArabTEX and devnag. We have not yet created new symbols but it is possible with the help of the pstricks package or METAFONT.

References

1. Devanāgarī for TEX, http://www.ctan.org/tex-archive/language/devanagari/velthuis/doc/devnag/manual.ps

Hyphenation Patterns
for Ancient and Modern Greek

Dimitrios Filippou

Kato Gatzea
GR-385 00 Volos
Greece
dfilipp@hotmail.com

Abstract. Several files with Greek hyphenation patterns for TEX can be found on CTAN. However, most of these patterns are for use with Modern Greek texts only. Some of these patterns contain mistakes or are incomplete. Other patterns are suitable only for some now-outdated "Greek TEX" packages. In 2000, after having examined the patterns that existed already, the author made new sets of hyphenation patterns for typesetting Ancient and Modern Greek texts with the greek option of the babel package or with Dryllerakis' GreeKTEX package. Lately, these patterns have found their way even into the ibycus package, which can be used with the *Thesaurus Linguae Graecae*, and into Ω with the antomega package.

The new hyphenation patterns, while not exhaustive, do respect the grammatical and phonetic rules of three distinct Greek writing systems. In general, all Greek words are hyphenated after a vowel and before a consonant. However, for typesetting Ancient Greek texts, the hyphenation patterns follow the rules established in 1939 by the Academy of Athens, which allow for breaking up compound words between the last consonant of the first constituent word and the first letter of the second constituent word, provided that the first constituent word has not been changed by elision. For typesetting polytonic (multi-accent) Modern Greek texts, the hyphenation rules distinguish between the nasal and the non-nasal double consonants μπ, ντ, and γχ. In accordance with the latest Greek grammar rules, in monotonic (uni-accent) Modern Greek texts, these double consonants are not split.

1   Introduction

Before 2000, one could find on CTAN four different files with hyphenation patterns for Modern Greek only, namely

- rgrhyph.tex by Yannis Haralambous [1],
- grkhyphen.tex by Kostis Dryllerakis [2],
- gehyphen.tex by Yiannis Moschovakis [3], and
- grhyph.tex by Claudio Beccari [4].

A. Syropoulos et al. (Eds.): TUG 2004, LNCS 3130, pp. 59–67, 2004.
© Springer-Verlag Berlin Heidelberg 2004

The first two hyphenation-pattern files [1,2] are almost identical. The only difference is that the patterns by Dryllerakis contain an \endinput command several lines before the end-of-file. (Probably, Dryllerakis cut down Haralambous' patterns to reduce memory usage, at a time when memory space was still rather limited.) The patterns by Moschovakis [3] are not only limited to Modern Greek, but they have been "frozen" based on an obsolete mixed US-Greek codepage for DOS and an equally obsolete LaTeX 2.09. The end result is that some words containing vowels with combined diacritical marks (e.g., εἶδος, θεῷ, etc.) are not hyphenated at all.

Haralambous' patterns [1] do not provide for the correct hyphenation of combinations of three or more consonants. In addition, they do not allow for the hyphenation of the nasal consonant combinations μπ (*mb*), ντ (*nd*) and γκ (*ng*), which must be split in polytonic Modern Greek. Haralambous' patterns erroneously split the combination τμ and prohibit the hyphenation of all final two-letter combinations for no apparent reason.

Beccari's patterns [4], which are commonly used with the greek option of babel, contain a number of mistakes and are also incomplete. For example, the word πυκνότητα is hyphenated as πυκ-νό-τη-τα. According to some rules outlined further in this text, that word should have been hyphenated as πυ-χνό-τη-τα. Similar bad hyphenations include ισ-θμός (it should be ἰ-σθμός), Ἀλκ-μή-νη (it should be Ἀλ-χμή-νη), etc. Beccari's patterns also allow for separation of the consonant combinations δμ, δν and τλ. These combinations should not be split, because one can find some Ancient Greek words that start with such combinations (δμώς, δνοφερός, τλημωσύνη).

In 2000, while typesetting a large volume in polytonic Modern Greek, the author of the present article noticed the mishaps in Beccari's hyphenation patterns and the inadequacy of all other Greek hyphenation patterns. He noticed also that hyphenation patterns for Ancient Greek, although they had been discussed by Haralambous back in 1992 [5], were not available at all in the public domain. That was the incentive for the author to revise the existing hyphenation patterns for Modern Greek and to provide in the public domain a set of hyphenation patterns for Ancient Greek.

The author has already presented these patterns in the newsletter of the Greek TeX Friends [6,7], but this communication is the first (and long overdue) presentation of the patterns to the global TeX community. The patterns were created for the 1988 *de facto* Levy Greek encoding [8], which later became the Local Greek (LGR) encoding.

2   Creation of Patterns

One way to produce hyphenation patterns is by using PATGEN [9]. PATGEN scans a given database with hyphenated words and prepares a set of hyphenation patterns based on observations the programme has made. Another way of using PATGEN is modular [10]: first one creates a limited set of hyphenated words, then runs PATGEN on these words, checks the produced hyphenation patterns and expands the list of hyphenated words with those words that were badly hyphenated. The whole cycle *create word list-run* PATGEN-*check bad hyphenations-expand word list* is repeated until an acceptable set of hyphenation patterns is produced. To the author's knowledge, an electronic dictionary with hyphenated words does not exist for Greek. Given the excessive morphology of the Greek words, even the modular use of PATGEN would be a daunting task. A less time-consuming effort is the translation of the simple grammatical rules for the hyphenation of Greek into patterns for the TEX machine as it has already been done [1,3,4]. This is the solution chosen also by the author of the present article.

Each language has its rules and exceptions that must be duly respected. It is not rare for one language to have different hyphenation rules for different dialects, or to have different hyphenation rules for texts written in different eras. The best-known example is English, where some words are hyphenated differently depending on the continent (e.g., *pre-face* in British English and *pref-ace* in American English).

In the case of Greek, one has to distinguish – grossly – between three "dialects" that demand separate sets of hyphenation patterns:

1. Ancient Greek and old-style literate Modern Greek (*katharevousa*),
2. polytonic Modern Greek, and
3. monotonic Modern Greek.

Ancient Greek is considered essentially every text that has been written in Greek from Homeric times (8th century B.C.) to about the end of the Byzantine Empire (15th century A.D.). *Katharevousa* (literally, *the purifying*) is a formal written language (almost never spoken) conceived by Greek scholars in the period of the Enlightenment as a way to purify Modern Greek from foreign influences. It was used in Greek literature of the 19th and early 20th century, and by the Greek state from its creation in 1827 until 1976. It is still used by the Greek Orthodox Church.

Polytonic and monotonic Modern Greek are essentially the same language. The only difference is that polytonic (literally, *multi-accent*) Modern Greek uses all accents, breathings and diacritics of Ancient Greek and *katharevousa*, while monotonic (literally, *uni-accent*) Modern Greek, which was adopted officially in Greece in 1982, has just one accent mark (much to the dismay of some classicists).

The hyphenation rules for Ancient Greek and *katharevousa* have special provisos for compound words [11]. The hyphenation rules for polytonic Modern Greek make a distinction between nasal μπ, ντ and γκ (pronounced as *mb*, *nd* and *ng* respectively) and non-nasal μπ, ντ and γκ (pronounced as *b*, *d* and *g*) [12]. The hyphenation rules for monotonic Modern Greek do not distinguish between nasal and non-nasal μπ, ντ and γκ, nor do they make any special demand for compound words [13].

2.1   Patterns for Modern Greek

Monotonic Texts. The grammatical rules for the hyphenation of monotonic Modern Greek [13] and the corresponding hyphenation patterns are:

1. *One consonant between two vowels always remains together with the second vowel.* This rule can be seen slightly differently: a word is hyphened after each vowel, for example, τη-λε-ό-ρα-ση. With the Levy character encoding [8], the corresponding hyphenation patterns are: a1 e1 h1 i1 o1 u1 w1.

2. *Double vowels* (diphthongs *in Ancient Greek*) *that are pronounced as one are not hyphenated.* Hence the double vowels αι, αί, αυ, etc. should not be split apart. The corresponding hyphenation patterns are: a2i a2'i a2u ... u2i u2'i. However, when the first vowel is accented, the two vowels are to be pronounced separately and they can be hyphenated. Hence, we include some exceptions: 'a3u 'e3u 'o3u 'u3i.

3. *Semi-vowels are not hyphenated.* Vowels, simple and double, that are usually pronounced as *i* are sometimes semi-vowels, i.e., they are not pronounced totally separately from the preceding or following vowel. Hence some vowel combinations involving semi-vowel sounds (*j*) should not be split apart. The most common semi-vowel combinations are: *aj* (νε-ράι-δα), *ej* (ζεï-μπέ-κης) and *oj* (κο-ρόι-δο) when they are accented on the first vowel or when they are not accented at all, and the combinations *ja* (δια-βάζω), *je* (ε-λιές) and *jo* (Μα-ριώ) when they are accented on the second vowel or when they are not accented at all. The resulting hyphenation patterns are: a2h a2"i ... i2a i2'a ... u2w u2'w. Some notable exceptions are: 'a3h ... 'u3w.

   It is worth noting that there is an inherent difficulty in distinguishing between vowels and semi-vowels. Sometimes, two words are written the same, but they are pronounced with or without a semi-vowel, thus completely changing their meaning, e.g., δό-λια (the adjective *devious* in feminine singular) and δό-λι-α (the adverb *deviously*). Distinguishing between a semi-vowel and a true vowel is very difficult and requires textual analysis [14]. For the purpose of TEX, all such suspicious semi-vowel combinations are treated as semi-vowels. The end result is that the word απόηχος will be hyphenated as α-πόη-χος. But it is better seeing some words hyphenated with one less syllable, than seeing extra syllables in other words, e.g., βό-η-θα Πα-να-γι-ά! (Apparently, Liang took the same approach, disallowing some valid hyphenations for the sake of forbidding definitely invalid ones [15].)

4. *Single or double consonants at the end or the beginning of a word do not constitute separate syllables.* The corresponding patterns are 4b. 4g. ... 4y. .b4 .g4 ... .y4. To these patterns, one must add some other ones for the case of elision: 4b'' 4g'' ... 4y''.

5. *Double consonants are hyphenated.* The patterns for this rule are: 4b1b 4g1g ... 4q1q 4y1y.

6. *Consonant combinations that cannot be found at the beginning of Greek words must be split after the first consonant.* The patterns are: 4b1z 4b1j ... 4y1f 4y1q. No distinction is made between nasal and non-nasal μπ (*mb/b*), ντ (*nd/d*) and γκ (*ng/g*); these consonant combinations are not to be split. However, some other patterns are inserted to deal with some thorny combinations of three or more consonants:

```
4r5g2m    ἔρ-γμα (Anc. Gr.)
tz2m      μάνα-τζμεντ
4r5j2m    πορ-θμός
...
4m5y2t    λάμ-ψτε
4g1kt     ελεγ-κτής
4n1tz     νεραν-τζιά
4n1ts     βιολον-τσέλο
```

More patterns could have been inserted here to deal with non-Greek proper names with sequences of three or more consonants transliterated into Greek. For example, the pattern `4r512s` could have been added to hyphenate the transliterated name *Carlson* as Κάρ-λσον and not as Κάρλ-σον (the latter is not allowed according to Greek grammar rules). However, the number of such words is infinite and the effort most likely worthless.

7. *Two or more consonants at the end of a word do not constitute separate syllables.* Such endings are mostly found in Ancient Greek words, or words of non-Greek origin which have became part of the Modern Greek vocabulary: `4kl.` (πι-νάκλ) ... `4nc.` (ἔλ-μινς, Anc. Gr.) ... Such words can be found easily in reverse dictionaries of Modern Greek [16].

8. *Combinations of double consonants are separated.* These are some rare combinations of non-nasal μπ with ντ and/or γκ in words of non-Greek origin which are now part of the Modern Greek vocabulary, e.g., `4mp1nt` (ρομπ-ντεσάμπρ = *robe-de-chambre*).

Polytonic Texts. The hyphenation rules that apply to monotonic Modern Greek texts apply also to polytonic Modern Greek texts. Of course, the patterns for polytonic Modern Greek had to be expanded to include all possible combinations of vowel and diacritic (breathing, accent and/or iota subscript).

As mentioned above, polytonic Modern Greek has another notable difference in hyphenation: The nasal μπ, ντ and γκ, which are pronounced as *mb*, *nd* and *ng* respectively, are to be separated. On the contrary the non-nasal μπ, ντ and γκ, which are pronounced as *b*, *d* and *g*, must not be separated. In general, μπ, ντ and γκ are nasal, thus the patterns: `4m1p`, `4n1t`, and `4g1k`. These consonant combination are non-nasal when they follow another consonant: ἄλ-μπου-ρο, σεβ-ντάς, ἀρ-γκό, etc., or in words of non-Greek origin: Ἰ-μπραήμ, μπι-ντές, etc.

For the creation of hyphenation patterns, the non-nasals μπ, ντ and γκ can be treated in the same way Haralambous treated Ancient Greek compound words [5]. Hence, with the help of Andriotis' etymological dictionary [17], a list of *exceptions* was built such as:

```
.giou5g2k    Γιου-γκοσλάβος
5g2krant.    Βόλγκο-γκραντ
...
.qa5n2to     χα-ντούμης
.qa5n2tr     χα-ντρῶν
.q'a5n2tr    χά-ντρα
```

The list of all these exceptions is quite lengthy and covers five printed pages of *Eutypon* [6].

2.2   Patterns for Ancient Greek

The grammatical rules for hyphenation of Ancient Greek are mostly the same as those for polytonic Modern Greek. Apparently, the Ancient Greeks hyphenated following the simple rule that a single consonant between two vowels in one word belongs with the second vowel: σο-φί-ζω, κα-θά-περ. The Ancient Greeks also considered non-accented words as being part of the following word [18]. For example, the Ancients would hyphenate ἐκ τούτου as ἐ-κτού-του. Nonetheless, rules introduced by later scholars do not allow for such extravagant hyphenations.

A very tricky rule introduced by modern scholars states that "[Ancient Greek] compound words divide at the point of union" [18]. This rule has been extended to *katharevousa* and some typographers are still using it for polytonic Modern Greek (most likely mistakenly). That rule also appears in two variations. In one variation, which has been adopted by *The Chicago Manual of Style* [19], compound words are divided into their original parts irrespective of whether those original parts have been modified or not. Therefore, one should hyphenate στρατ-ηγός (στρατὸν + ἄγω), Διόσ-κουρος (Διὸς + κοῦρος), etc. This is the rule followed by Haralambous for the creation of Ancient Greek hyphenation patterns for the commercial package ScholarTEX [5]. In another variation, adopted by some 19th-century scholars [20] and the Academy of Athens [21], compound words are divided into their original constituent words *only* when the first word has not lost its last vowels by elision. According to that rule variation, the word στρατηγός should be hyphenated as στρα-τηγός, because the first word (στρατόν) has lost its final ον.

For the creation of hyphenation patterns for Ancient Greek, the author chose to follow the rule adopted by the Academy of Athens, because this rule has also been adopted in the manuals used in the Greek high schools and lycées [11]. Thus, with the help of two widely-used dictionaries [22,23], a list of *exceptions* for compound words was incorporated into the list of patterns for Ancient Greek:

>adi'e2x1	ἀδιέξ-οδος
>adie2x1	ἀδιεξ-όδου
>adu2s1'w	ἀδυσ-ώπητος
>adu2s1w	ἀδυσ-ωπήτου
. . .	
i2s1qili'akic.	δισ-χιλιάκις, etc.
i2s1muri'akic.	δισ-μυριάκις, etc.

This list is quite extensive; it includes 1555 patterns and covers twenty-eight printed pages [24].

It is worth mentioning here that special care has been taken not to confuse Ancient and Modern Greek exceptions for the division of consonants. For example, there are no Ancient Greek words that start with the Modern Greek double consonants μπ, ντ, γκ, τζ and τσ. Therefore, all these combinations are divided in Ancient Greek texts, with no exception. Also, combinations of stopped consonants (π, β, φ / τ, δ, ϑ / χ, γ, χ) and the nasals μ or ν are not divided [20].

3 Putting the Patterns to Work

The patterns have been archived in three files, which have already found their way onto CTAN [24]:

- GRMhyph?.tex for monotonic Modern Greek,
- GRPhyph?.tex for polytonic Modern Greek, and
- GRAhyph?.tex for Ancient Greek.

(The ? is a number indicating the current version.)

The first two patterns for Modern Greek were tested on a sample text created by the author, after building a new bplain format [6]. (Incidentally, bplain is just an extension of Knuth's plain format for the use of several languages with babel.) The result showed considerable improvement in comparison to hyphenation results obtained by earlier set of patterns (Table 1). With another bplain format, the hyphenation patterns for Ancient Greek were tested on five classic texts in their original:

- Herodotus, *The Histories* A, I–III;
- Xenophon, *Anabasis* A, 1.IV.11–13;
- Plutarch, *Lives* Themistocles, II.1–5;
- Strabo, *Geography*, 7.1.1–5; and
- Lysias, *Defence against a Charge for Taking Bribes.*

Surprisingly, TEX correctly hyphenated *all* Ancient Greek words found in these texts, which cover about seven printed pages [7,24].

The author, however, does not believe that his patterns are error-free. The Ancient Greek adjective προσκοπή has two different etymologies and meanings: "looking out for" hyphenated as προ-σκοπή (πρὸ + σκοπέω), or "an offence" hyphenated as προσ-κοπή (πρὸς + κόπος). Unfortunately, TEX does not do textual analysis and will not understand the difference. Syllables with vowel synizesis may be erroneously split apart, e.g., χρυ-σέ-ω instead of χρυ-σέω. Again, TEX does not do textual analysis and it is impossible for a typesetting system to capture such small details. Finally, the use of the same patterns for typesetting a mixed Ancient and Modern Greek text will bring a few surprises. For the purpose of TEX, Ancient and Modern Greek are better treated as two different \languages.

4 Creation of Patterns for **ibycus** and Ω

The patterns created by the author have already been picked up by other people who are working on other packages or systems that use different font encodings. Using a Perl script, Apostolos Syropoulos adapted the hyphenation patterns for

Table 1. Results from hyphenation tests with three different sets (files) of hyp henation patterns available in the public domain. Mistakes represent erroneous h yphenations. Misses represent missed hyphenation points.

Patterns	Mistakes (%)	Misses (%)
`rgrhyph.tex` [1]	25	13
`grhyph.tex` [4]	3	16
`GRPhyph.tex` (this work)	–	3

monotonic Modern Greek and Ancient Greek for usage with Ω [25]. Using another Perl script, Peter Heslin [26] adapted the hyphenation patterns for Ancient Greek for the ibycus package, which can be used for typesetting texts obtained from the *Thesaurus Linguae Graecae.*

5   Conclusions

The hyphenation patterns created by the author for Ancient and Modern Greek are indeed superior to those previously found on CTAN. Nonetheless, the patterns are presently under revision to eliminate a few minor mistakes. The author anticipates that the improved patterns will be released in CTAN very soon – probably before the TUG 2004 conference. Hopefully, these patterns will shortly after migrate into ibycus and Ω, and they will become the default Greek hyphenation patterns in whatever system/package becomes the successor of TEX.

Acknowledgements

The author would like to thank Dr Spyros Konstandatos, former lecturer of Classics at McGill University, Montreal, Canada, for giving him access to his collection of Greek dictionaries. The author would like also to express his gratitude to Karl Berry (president, TEX Users Group, USA), Baden Hughes (University of Melbourne, Australia) and Steve Peter (TEX Users Group/Beech Stave Press, USA) for meticulously reviewing and editing this paper.

References

1. Y. Haralambous. `rgrhyph.tex`, vers. 1.1. CTAN: fonts/greek/yannis, 1990.
2. K. J. Dryllerakis. `grkhyphen.tex`, GREEKTEX, vers. 4.0α. ftp://laotzu.doc.ic.ac.uk/pub/tex, 1994.
3. Y. Moschovakis. `gehyphen.tex`. CTAN: fonts/greek/greektex, 1994.
4. C. Beccari. `grhyph.tex`. CTAN: fonts/greek/cb, 1997.
5. Y. Haralambous. Hyphenation patterns for Ancient Greek and Latin. *TUGboat*, 13:459–467, 1992.

6. D. Filippou. Beltiomenoi kodikes syllabismou polytonikon kai monotonikon keimenon gia to TEX kai to LATEX (Improved hyphenation patterns for polytonic and monotonic Modern Greek texts typeset by TEX and LATEX). *Eutypon*, (4):1–16, 2000. In Greek.

7. D. Filippou. Kodikes sullabismou gia ten stoicheiothesia archaion hellenikon keimenon me to TEX kai to LATEX (Hyphenation patterns for typesetting Ancient Greek texts by TEX and LATEX). *Eutypon*, (5):7–15, 2000.

8. S. Levy. Using Greek fonts with TEX. *TUGboat*, 9:20–24, 1988.

9. F. M. Liang, P. Breitenlohner, and K. Berry. `PATGEN` – PATtern GENeration Program, vers. 2.3. CTAN: systems/knuth/unsupported/texware/patgen.web, 1996.

10. P. Sojka. Hyphenation on demand. *TUGboat*, 20:241–247, 1999.

11. M. Oikonomou. *Grammatike tes Archaias Hellenikes (Grammar of Ancient Greek)*. Organismos Ekdoseos Didaktikon Biblion, Athena, 5th edition, 1987. In Greek.

12. M. Triantafyllides. *Mikre Neoellenike Grammatike (Abridged Modern Greek Grammar)*. Aristoteleion Panepistemion Thessalonikes, Hidryma Manole Triantafyllide, Thessalonike, 2nd edition, 1975. In Greek.

13. *Neoellenike Grammatike (Modern Greek Grammar)*. Organismos Ekdoseos Didaktikon Biblion, Athena, 8th edition, 1985. In Greek.

14. G. Orphanos, Ch. Tsalides, and A. Iordanidou. Hoi hellenoglossoi hypologistes emathan na syllabizoun? (Have the Greek-speaking computers learned how to hyphenate?). In *Praktika tes 23es Synanteses Ergasias tou Tomea Glossologias*, pages 1–8, Thessalonike, 2002. Aristoteleio Panepistemio Thessalonikes. In Greek.

15. F. M. Liang. *Hy-phen-a-tion by Com-put-er*. PhD thesis, Department of Computer Science, Stanford University, 1983.

16. G. Kourmoulakes. *Antistrophon Lexikon tes Neas Hellenikes (Reverse Dictionary of Modern Greek)*. Athenai, 1967. In Greek.

17. N. P. Andriotes. *Etymologiko Lexiko tes Koines Neoellenikes (Etymological Dictionary of Common Modern Greek)*. Aristoteleion Panepistemion Thessalonikes, Hidryma Manole Triantafyllide, Thessalonike, 1967. In Greek.

18. H. W. Smyth. *Greek Grammar*. Harvard University Press, Cambridge, Massachusetts, USA, 1956. Revised by G. M. Messing.

19. *The Chicago Manual of Style*. The University of Chicago Press, Chicago and London, 1982.

20. W. W. Goodwin. *A Greek Grammar*. Ginn and Company, Boston, 1892.

21. I. Kallitsounakes. Orthographikon diagramma tes Akademias Athenon (The Academy of Athens Dictation Diagramm). *Praktika tes Akademias Athenon*, 14, 1939. In Greek.

22. H. G. Liddell and R. Scott. *A Greek-English Lexicon*. Oxford University Press, Clarendon Press, Oxford, 1968.

23. I. Dr. Stamatakos. *Lexikon tes Archaias Hellenikes Glosses (Dictionary of the Ancient Greek Language)*. Ekdotikos Organismos "O Phoinix" EPE, Athenai, 1972.

24. D. Filippou. CTAN: fonts/greek/package-babel/hyphenation/filippou, 2000.

25. A. Kryukov. ANTOMEGA language support package, vers. 0.7. CTAN: systems/omega/contrib/antomega/, 2003.

26. P. Heslin. CTAN: fonts/greek/package-babel/ibycus-babel/, 2003.

Typesetting the Deseret Alphabet
with LaTeX and METAFONT

Kenneth R. Beesley

Xerox Research Centre Europe
6, chemin de Maupertuis
F-38240 Meylan
France
Ken.Beesley@xrce.xerox.com
http://www.xrce.xerox.com/people/beesley/

Abstract. The Deseret Alphabet was an orthographical reform for English, promoted by the Church of Jesus Christ of Latter-day Saints (the Mormons) between about 1854 and 1875. An offshoot of the Pitman phonotypy reforms, the Deseret Alphabet is remembered mainly for its use of non-Roman glyphs. Though ultimately rejected, the Deseret Alphabet was used in four printed books, numerous newspaper articles, several unprinted book manuscripts, journals, meeting minutes, letters and even a gold coin, a tombstone and an early English-to-Hopi vocabulary. This paper reviews the history of the Deseret Alphabet, its Unicode implementation, fonts both metal and digital, and projects involving the typesetting of Deseret Alphabet texts.

1 Introduction

The Deseret Alphabet was an orthographical reform for English, promoted by the Church of Jesus Christ of Latter-day Saints (the Mormons) between about 1854 and 1875. While the Deseret Alphabet is usually remembered today as an oddity, a strange non-Roman alphabet that seemed doomed to failure, it was in fact used on and off for 20 years, leaving four printed books (including *The Book of Mormon*), numerous newspaper articles, several unprinted book manuscripts (including the entire *Bible*), journals, meeting minutes, letters and even a gold coin and a tombstone. There is also growing evidence that the Deseret Alphabet was experimentally used by some Mormon missionaries to transcribe words in Spanish, Shoshone, Hopi and other languages.

A number of historians [19, 11, 20, 21, 4, 1, 22, 6] have analyzed the Deseret Alphabet, which was justly criticized by typographers [21, 31], but what is often overlooked is the corpus of phonemically written documents, which are potentially interesting to both historians and linguists. Because few people, then or now, can be persuaded to learn the Alphabet, the majority of the documents have lain unread for 140 years. For example, in December of 2002, an "Indian Vocabulary" of almost 500 entries, written completely in the Deseret Alphabet,

A. Syropoulos et al. (Eds.): TUG 2004, LNCS 3130, pp. 68–111, 2004.

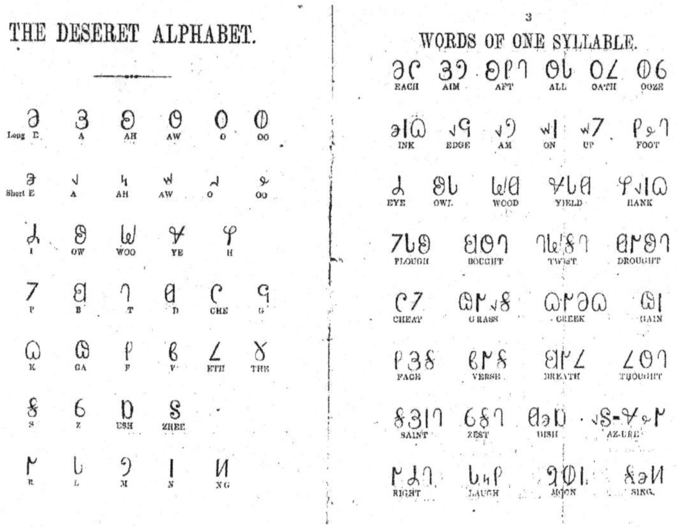

Fig. 1. On 24 March 1854 the newly adopted Deseret Alphabet was first printed, probably using wooden type, and presented to the Board of Regents of the Deseret University. Although this rare flier is undated, it matches the 38-letter Alphabet as copied into the journal of Regent Hosea Stout on that date [30]. Utah State Historical Society.

was finally identified as being English-to-Hopi, being perhaps the oldest written record of the Hopi language.

This paper will proceed with a short history of the Deseret Alphabet, putting it in the context of the Pitman phonotypy movement that inspired it from beginning to end[1]; special emphasis will be placed on the variants of the Alphabet used over the years, and on the cutting and casting of historical fonts. Then I will review some modern digital fonts and the implementation of the Deseret Alphabet in Unicode, showing how some honest mistakes were made and how the results are still awkward for encoding and typesetting some of the most interesting historical documents. Finally, I will show how I have used a combination of XML, LaTeX, the TIPA package and my own METAFONT-defined [16, 10] desalph font to typeset a critical edition of the English-to-Hopi vocabulary, and related documents, from 1859–60.

2   The Pitman Reform Context

2.1   The Pitman Reform Movements

To begin, it is impossible to understand the Deseret Alphabet without knowing a bit about two nineteenth-century orthographic reformers, Isaac Pitman (1813–1897) and his younger brother Benn (1822–1910). The Mormon experiments in

---

[1] Parts of this paper were first presented at the 22nd International Unicode Conference in San Jose, California, 11-13 September 2002 [6].

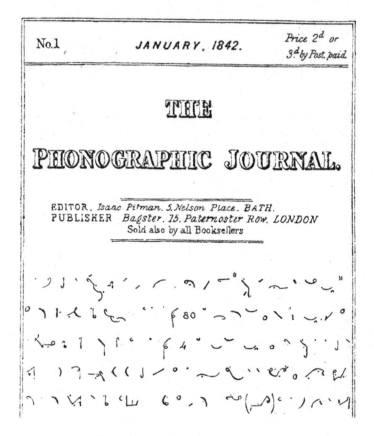

Fig. 2. Early Pitman phonography.

orthographical reform, too often treated as isolated aberrations, were in fact influenced from beginning to end by the Pitman movements, at a time when many spelling reforms were being promoted.

Pitman Shorthand or Phonography. There have been hundreds of systems of stenography, commonly called shorthand, used for writing English; but Isaac Pitman's system, first published in his 1837 *Stenographic Sound-hand* and called "phonography"[2], was soon a huge success, spreading through the English-speaking world and eventually being adapted to some fifteen other languages. Modern versions of Pitman shorthand are still used in Britain, Canada, and in most of the cricket-playing countries; in the USA it was taught at least into the 1930s but was eventually overtaken by the Gregg system.

The main goal of any shorthand system is to allow a trained practitioner, called a "reporter" in the Pitman tradition, to record speech accurately at

---

[2] In 1839 he wrote *Phonography, or Writing by Sound, being also a New and Improved System of Short Hand.*

speed, including trial proceedings[3], parliamentary debates, political speeches, sermons, etc. Pitman's phonography, as the name implies, differs from most earlier systems in representing the distinctive sounds of English (what modern linguists call phonemes) rather than orthographical combinations. Simplicity and economy at writing time are crucial: consonants are reduced to straight lines and simple curves (see Figure 2). The "outline" of a word, typically just a string of consonants, is written as a single connected stroke, without lifting the pen. Voiced consonants are written as thick lines, their unvoiced counterparts as thin lines, which requires that a Pitman reporter use a nib pen or soft pencil. Vowels are written optionally as diacritical marks above and below the consonant strokes; one is struck by the similarities to Arabic orthography. In advanced styles, vowels are left out whenever possible, and special abbreviation signs are used for whole syllables, common words, and even whole phrases.

Pitman Phonotypy. Pitman became justifiably famous for his phonography. With help from several family members, he soon presided over a lecturing and publishing industry with a phenomenal output, including textbooks, dictionaries, correspondence courses, journals, and even books published in shorthand, including selections from Dickens, the tales of Sherlock Holmes, *Gulliver's Travels*, *Paradise Lost*, and the entire *Bible*. But while phonography was clearly useful, and was both a social and financial success, Pitman's biographers [25, 24, 2] make it clear that his real mission in life was not phonography but *phonotypy*[4], his philosophy and movement for reforming English orthography, the everyday script used in books, magazines, newspapers, personal correspondence, etc.

The first Pitman phonotypy alphabet for which type was cast was Alphabet No. 11, demonstrated proudly in *The Phonotypic Journal* of January 1844 (see Figure 3). Note that this 1844 alphabet is bicameral, sometimes characterized as an alphabet of capitals; that is, the uppercase and lowercase letters differ only in size. The letters are stylized, still mostly recognizable as Roman, but with numerous invented, borrowed or modified letters for pure vowels, diphthongs, and the consonants /θ/, /ð/, /ʃ/, /ʒ/, /ʧ/, /ʤ/ and /ŋ/[5].

---

[3] In modern parlance we still have the term *court reporter*.

[4] According to one of Pitman's own early scripts, which indicates stress, he pronounced the word /foˈnɒtipi/.

[5] To provide a faithful representation of original Pitman and Deseret Alphabet texts, I adopt a broad phonemic transcription that uses, as far as possible, a single International Phonetic Alphabet (IPA) letter for each English phoneme [12]. Thus the affricates C and 9 are transliterated as the rarely used IPA /ʧ/ and /ʤ/ letters, respectively, rather than the sequences /tʃ/ and /dʒ/ or even the tied forms /t͡ʃ/ and /d͡ʒ/. The diphthongs are shown in IPA as a combination of a nucleus and a superscript glide. The Deseret Alphabet, and the Pitman-Ellis 1847 alphabet which was its phonemic model, treat the /ʲu/ vowel in words like *mule* as a single diphthong phoneme; see Ladefoged [17] for a recent discussion and defense of this practice. Although in most English dialects the vowels in *mate* and *moat* are diphthongized, the Deseret Alphabet follows Pitman in treating them as the simple "long vowels" /e/ and /o/.

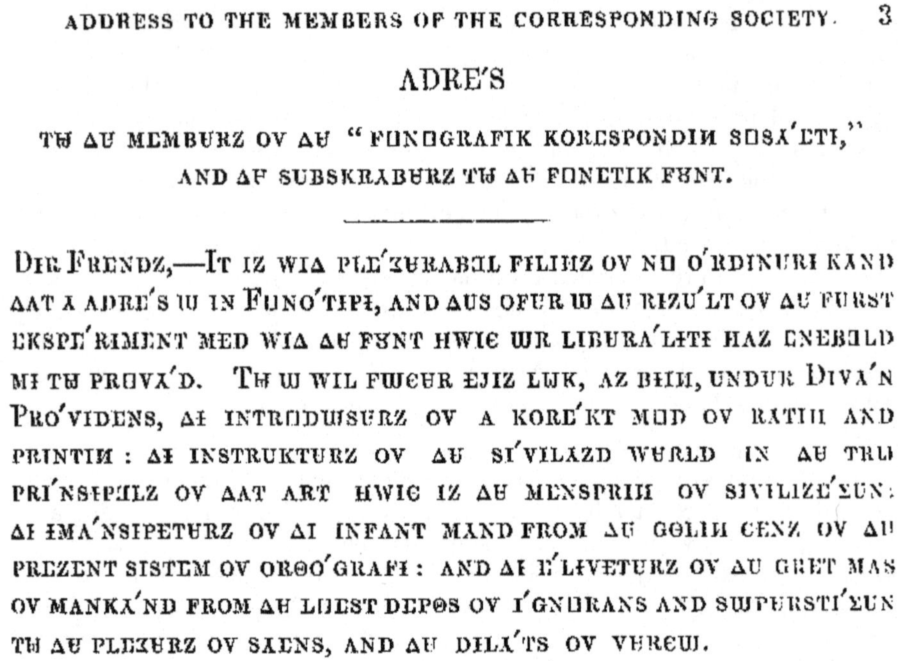

ADDRESS TO THE MEMBERS OF THE CORRESPONDING SOCIETY.   3

ADRE'S

TW ΔU MCMBUKZ OV ΔU " FUNOGRAFIK KOKCSPONDIM SOSX´CTI,"
AND ΔF SUBSKRΔBUKZ TW ΔH FONCTIK FUNT.

DIK FKENDZ,—IT IZ WIΔ PLC´ZUKABΟL FILIHZ OV NO O´RDINUKI KAND
ΔAT X ΔDKE´S IW IN FUNO´TIPI, AND ΔUS OFUK W ΔU KIZU´LT OV ΔU FUKST
CKSPC´KIMENT MED WIΔ ΔU FUNT HWIC WK LIBUKA´LITI HAZ CNEBΟLD
MI TW PKOVX´D.   TW W WIL FWCUK EJIZ LWK, AZ BIII, UNDUK DIVΔ´N
PKO´VIDCNS, ΔI INTKΟDWISUKZ OV A KOKC´KT MOD OV KΔTIII AND
PKINTIM : ΔI INSTKUKTUKZ OV ΔU SI´VILΔZD WUKLD IN ΔU TKU
PKI´NSIPΟLZ OV ΔAT AKT HWIC IZ ΔU MCNSPKIII OV SIVILIZC´ZUN;
ΔI IMA´NSIPETUKZ OV ΔI INFANT MXND FKOM ΔU GΟLIII CEN% OV ΔU
PKCZCNT SISTCM OV OKΘΟ´GKAFI : AND ΔI H´LIVETUKZ OV ΔU GKET MAS
OV MANKX´ND FKOM ΔU LΟJCST DCPOS OV I´GNΟKANS AND SWPUKSTI´ZUN
TW ΔU PLCZUKZ OV SXCNS, AND ΔU DILX´TS OV VUKEUJ.

Fig. 3. In January 1844, Isaac Pitman proudly printed the first examples of his phonotypy. This Alphabet No. 11, and the five experimental variants that followed it, were bicameral, with uppercase and lowercase characters distinguished only by size.

The goals of general spelling reform, to create a new "book orthography", are quite different from those of shorthand. While shorthand is intended for use by highly trained scribes, a book orthography is for all of us and should be easily learned and used. Where shorthand requires simplicity, abbreviation and swiftness of writing, varying with the reporter's skill, a book orthography should aim for orthographical consistency, phonological completeness and ease of reading. Finally, a book orthography must lend itself to esthetic typography and easy typesetting; Pitman's phonographic books, in contrast, had to be engraved and printed via the lithographic process[6].

Pitman saw his popular phonography chiefly as the path leading to phonotypy, which was a much harder sell. His articles in the phonographic (shorthand) journals frequently pushed the spelling reform, and when invited to lecture on phonography, he reportedly managed to spend half the time talking about phonotypy. Throughout the rest of his life, Pitman proposed a long succession of alphabetic experiments, all of them Romanic, trying in vain to find a winning formula.

---

[6] Starting in 1873, Pitman succeeded in printing phonography with movable type, but many custom outlines had to be engraved as the work progressed.

Pitman's phonotypic publications include not only his phonotypic journals but dozens of books, including again the entire *Bible* (1850). But in the end, phonotypy never caught on, and the various phonotypic projects, including the constant cutting and casting of new type, were "from first to last a serious financial drain" [2]. In 1894, a few years before his death, Pitman was knighted by Queen Victoria for his life's work in phonography, with no mention made of his beloved phonotypy.

Today Pitman phonotypy is almost completely forgotten, and it has not yet found a champion to sponsor its inclusion in Unicode. But Pitman was far from alone – by the 1880s, there were an estimated 50 different spelling reforms under consideration by the English Spelling Reform Association. This was the general nineteenth-century context in which the Deseret Alphabet was born; lots of people were trying to reform English orthography.

2.2   The Mormons Discover the Pitman Movement

The Church of Jesus Christ of Latter-day Saints was founded in 1830 in upstate New York by Joseph Smith, a farm boy who claimed to have received a vision of God the Father and Jesus Christ, who commanded him to restore the true Church of Christ. He also claimed that he received from an angel a book, engraved on golden plates, which he translated as *The Book of Mormon*. His followers, who revered him as a prophet, grew rapidly in number, and soon, following the western movement and spurred by religious persecution, they migrated from New York, to Ohio, to Missouri and then to Illinois, where in 1839 they founded the city of Nauvoo on the Mississippi River.

Missionary work had started immediately, both at home and abroad, and in 1837, the same year that Pitman published his *Stenographic Sound-hand*, a certain George D. Watt was baptized as the first Mormon convert in England. Despite an unpromising childhood, which included time in a workhouse, young George had learned to read and write; and between the time of his baptism and his emigration to Nauvoo in 1842, he had also learned Pitman phonography. The arrival of Watt in Nauvoo revolutionized the reporting of Mormon meeting minutes, speeches and sermons. Other converts flowed into Nauvoo, so that by 1846 it had become, by some reports, the largest city in Illinois, with some 20,000 inhabitants.

But violence broke out between the Mormons and their "gentile" neighbors, and in 1844 Joseph Smith was assassinated by a mob. In 1845, even during the ensuing confusion and power struggles, Watt gave phonography classes; one notable student was Mormon Apostle Brigham Young. Watt was also President of the Phonographic Club of Nauvoo [1]. In addition to phonography, Watt was almost certainly aware of the new phonotypy being proposed by Pitman, and it is likely that he planted the idea of spelling reform in Brigham Young's mind at this time.

In 1846, Watt was sent on a mission back to England. The majority of the Church regrouped behind Brigham Young, abandoned their city to the mobs, and crossed the Mississippi River to spend the bleak winter of 1846–47 at Winter

Quarters, near modern Florence, Nebraska. From here Brigham Young wrote to Watt in April 1847[7]:

> It is the wish of the council, that you procure 200 lbs of phonotype, or thereabouts, as you may find necessary, to print a small book for the benefit of the Saints and cause same to be forwarded to Winter Quarters before navigation closes, by some trusty brother on his return, so that we have the type to use next winter.

The "phonotype" referred to is the actual lead type used for Pitman phonotypy. The Saints, meaning the members of the Church, were still in desperate times – 600 would die from exposure and disease at Winter Quarters – and while there is no record that this type was ever delivered, it shows that the Mormons' first extant plans for spelling reform involved nothing more exotic than an off-the-shelf Pitman phonotypy alphabet.

It is not known exactly which version of Pitman phonotypy Young had in mind; Pitman's alphabets went through no fewer than 15 variations between January 1844 and January 1847, and the isolated Mormons were likely out of date. In any case, Pitman's alphabets had by this time become more conventionally Roman. Alphabet No. 15 (see Figure 4), presented in *The Phonotypic Journal* of October 1844[8], marked Pitman's abandonment of the bicameral "capital" alphabets, and his adoption of alphabets that had distinguished uppercase vs. lowercase glyphs, which he called "lowercase" or "small letter" alphabets.

The Mormons started leaving Winter Quarters as soon as the trails were passable, and the first party, including Brigham Young, arrived in the valley of the Great Salt Lake in July of 1847, founding Great Salt Lake City. Mormon colonists were soon sent throughout the mountain west. They called their new land Deseret, a word from *The Book of Mormon* meaning honey bee. In response to Mormon petitions to found a State of Deseret, Congress established instead a Territory of Utah, naming it after the local Ute Indians. In spite of this nominal rebuff, Brigham Young was appointed Governor, and the name Deseret would be applied to a newspaper, a bank, a university, numerous businesses and associations, and even a spelling-reform alphabet. The name Deseret, and the beehive symbol, remain common and largely secularized in Utah today.

3 The History of the Deseret Alphabet

3.1 Deliberations: 1850–1853

Education has always been a high priority for the Mormons, and on 13 March 1850 the Deseret University, now the University of Utah, was established under a Chancellor and Board of Regents that included the leading men of the new society. Actual teaching would not begin for several years, and the first task given to the Regents was to design and implement a spelling reform.

---

[7] *The Latter-day Saints' Millennial Star*, vol. 11, 1847, p. 8.

[8] *The Phonotypic Journal*, vol. 3, no. 35, Oct. 1844.

PHONOTYPIC ALPHABET.—No. 15.

VOWELS.				CONSONANTS.		
No.	Type.	Example of its sound.	Name in Phonotypes.	Type.	Example of its sound.	Name in Phonotypes.
1	Ɪ i	feet	i	P p	pay	pi
	I i	fit	it	B b	bay	bi
2	Ɛ ɛ	mate	ɛ	T t	toe	ti
	E e	met	et	D d	doe	di
3	Ӕ ɑ	psalm	ɑ	Ҫ ç	chew	çɛ
	A a	Sam	at	J j	jew	jɛ
4	Ɵ ɔ	caught	ɔ	K k	call	kɛ
	O o	cot	ot	G g	gall	gɛ
5	Ɛ c	cur	c	F f	few	ef
	U u	curry	ut	V v	view	vɛ
6	Ω o	bone	o	Ꞇ t	thigh	it
7	Ꝋ o	fool	o	đ d	thy	đi
	℧ u	full	ut	S s	seal	es
COMPOUND VOWELS.				Z z	zeal	zɛ
	Ɨ i	high	i	Σ ʃ	mesh	iʃ
	Φ q	hoy	q	Ƨ ʒ	measure	ʒi
	Ӈ u	how	u	L l	bail	el
	Ɯ ɯ	hew	ɯ	R r	bare	ɛr
COALESCENTS.				M m	sum	am
	Y y	yea	yɛ	N n	sun	en
	W w	way	wɛ	Ŋ ŋ	sung	iŋ
BREATHING.						
	H h	hay	hɛ			

Fig. 4. Alphabet No. 15 appeared in October 1844 and was the first of Pitman's "lowercase" or "small letter" alphabets, employing separate glyphs for uppercase and lowercase letters.

Although serious discussion of spelling reform began in 1850, I will jump ahead to 1853, when the Regency met regularly in a series of well-documented meetings leading to the adoption of the Deseret Alphabet. Throughout that year, the Regents presented to each other numerous candidate orthographies ranging from completely new alphabets, to Pitman shorthand, to minimal reforms that used only the traditional 26-letter Roman alphabet with standardized use of digraphs. The discussion was wide open, but by November of 1853, it was clear that the "1847 Alphabet" (see Figure 5), a 40-letter version backed jointly by Isaac Pitman and phonetician Alexander J. Ellis [15], was the recommended model. The 1847 Alphabet was presented to the Board in a surviving chart (see Figure 6) and the meeting minutes were even being delivered by reporter George D. Watt in the longhand form of this alphabet.

THE PHONETIC ALPHABET.

The phonetic letters in the first column are pronounced like the italic letters in the words that follow. The last column contains the names of the letters.

Long Vowels.					Explodents.				
Ɛ	ɛ	*ease*		ɛ	P	p	*pole*		pɛ
Ꭺ	a	*age*		a	B	b	*bowl*		bɛ
A	q	*alms*		q	T	t	*toe*		tɛ
O	ɵ	*awning*		ɵ	D	d	*doe*		dɛ
O	ɷ	*ope*		ɷ	Ɛ	ɕ	*cheer*		ɕa
Ɯ	ɯ	*ooze*		ɯ	J	j	*jeer*		ja
					C	c	*came*		ca
Short Vowels.					G	g	*game*		ga
I	i	*is*		it					
E	e	*egg*		et	*Continuants.*				
A	u	*am*		at	F	f	*fear*		ef
O	o	*on*		ot	V	v	*veer*		va
U	u	*up*		ut	Ꞇ	t̵	*thigh*		it̵
Ʋ	u	*sugar*		ut	ꝺ	d̵	*thy*		d̵ɛ
					S	s	*seal*		es
Diphthongs.					Z	z	*zeal*		za
ᵻ	i̵	*ice*		i̵	Ʃ	ʃ	*shall*		iʃ
Ơ	ơ	*oyster*		ơ	Ʒ	ʒ	*vision*		ʒɛ
Ȣ	s	*ounce*		s					
Ʉ	ꭀ	*use*		ꭀ	*Liquids.*				
					R	r	*rare*		ur
Coalescents.					L	l	*lull*		el
Y	y	*yea*		ya					
W	w	*way*		wa	*Nasals.*				
					M	m	*mum*		am
Breathing.					N	n	*nun*		en
H	h	*hay*		haɕ	Ŋ	ŋ	*sing*		iŋ

(ˈ) *Vocal, as in ab'l, siz'm, hev'n, &c.*

Fig. 5. The 1847 Alphabet of Alexander J. Ellis and Isaac Pitman as it appeared in Pitman's 1850 *Bible*. This alphabet was the main phonemic model for the Deseret Alphabet in late 1853. The Board of Regents of the Deseret University almost adopted a slightly modified form of this alphabet, but they were persuaded, at the very last moment, to change to non-Roman glyphs. Compare the layout of this chart to that of the Deseret Alphabet charts in the books of 1868–69 (see Figure 17).

Brigham Young, President of the Church of Jesus Christ of Latter-day Saints and Governor of the Territory of Utah, took a personal interest in the 1853 meetings, attending many and participating actively. On the 22nd and 23rd of November, he and the Regents adopted their own modified version of the 1847 Alphabet, with some of the glyphs modified or switched, and names for the letters were adopted. A couple of Pitman letters were simply voted out, namely those for the diphthongs /ɔʲ/ and /ʲu/, which are exemplified with the words *oyster* and *use* in the 1847 chart. The result was a 38-letter alphabet, still very fɷnetic   ɑlfɑbet.

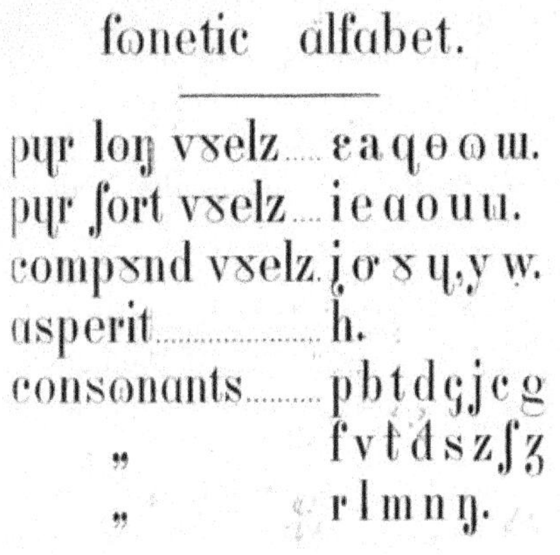

pʉr loŋ vꞇelz.... ɛ a q ɵ ɷ ɯ.
pʉr ʃort vꞇelz.... i e ɑ o u ɯ.
compꞇnd vꞇelz. ȷ ơ ꞇ ʮ͑,y w.
ɑsperit.................. h.
consɷnɑnts........ p b t d ꞔ j c g
     „   f v t̆ d s z ʃ ʒ
     „   r l m n ŋ.

Fig. 6. In November 1853, Parley P. Pratt presented "Pitman's Alphabet in Small Letters" to the Board of Regents in the form of this chart. These are in fact just the lowercase letters of the famous 1847 Alphabet devised by Isaac Pitman and Alexander J. Ellis. More stable than Pitman's other alphabets, it lasted several years and was used to print a short-lived newspaper called *The Phonetic News* (1849), the *Bible* (1850), and other books. LDS Church Archives.

Pitmanesque and Romanic. For the second time – the first was in 1847 – the Mormons were about to embark on a Pitman-based spelling reform.

However, all plans were turned upside-down by the sudden arrival of Willard Richards at the meeting of 29 November 1853. Richards, who was Second Counselor to Brigham Young, was gravely ill, had not attended the previous meetings, and was not up to date on the Board's plans. But when he saw the Board's new Romanic alphabet on the wall, he could not contain his disappointment. The following excerpts, shown here in equivalent IPA to give the flavor of George D. Watt's original minutes, speak for themselves:

wi wɒnt e nju ka^jnd ɒv ælfæbɛt, dɪfɛrɪŋ frɒm ði kɒmpa^wnd mɛs ɒv stʌf ʌpɒn ðæt ʃit.... ðoz kæræktɛrz me bi ɛmplɔɪd ɪn ɪmpruvɪŋ ði ɪŋglɪʃ ɒrθɒgræfɪ, ðo æt ði sem ta^jm, ɪt ɪz æz a^j hæv sʌmta^jmz sɛd, ɪt simz la^jk pʌtɪŋ nju wa^jn ɪntu old bɒtlz.... a^j æm ɪnkla^jnd tu θɪŋk hwɛn wi hæv rɪflɛktɛd lɒŋɛr wi ʃæl stɪl mek sʌm ædvæns ʌpɒn ðæt ælfæbɛt, ænd prhæps θro æwe ɔl kæræktɛrz ðæt ber mʌtʃ rɪzɛmblɛns tu ði ɪŋglɪʃ kæræktɛrs, ænd ɪntrodjus æn ælfæbɛt ðæt ɪz ɒrɪʤɪnæl, so far æz wi no, æn ælfæbɛt ɛnta^jrlɪ dɪfɛrɛnt frɒm ɛnɪ ælfæbɛt ɪn jus[9].

---

[9] "We want a new kind of alphabet, differing from the compound mess of stuff upon that sheet. ... Those characters may be employed in improving the English orthography, though at the same time, it is as I have sometimes said, it seems like putting new wine into old bottles. ... I am inclined to think when we have reflected longer we shall still make some advance upon that alphabet, and perhaps throw away all characters that bear much resemblance to the English characters, and introduce an alphabet that is original, so far as we know, an alphabet entirely different from any alphabet in use."

Some objections were tentatively raised. It was pointed out that the key committee had been instructed to keep as many of the traditional Roman letters as possible, and that Brigham Young himself had approved the alphabet and had already discussed ordering 200 pounds of type for it. Richards then attenuated his criticism a bit, but renewed his call for a complete redesign, waxing rhetorical:

> whɒt hæv ju gend baʲ ði ælfæbɛt ɒn ðæt kɑrd aʲ æsk ju. ʃo mi wʌn aʲtɛm, kæn ju pɒɪnt aᵂt ði fɛrst ædvæntɛʤ ðæt ju hæv gend ovɛr ði old wʌn? ... hwɒt hæv ju gend, ju hæv ði sem old ælfæbɛt ovɛr ægɛn, onlɪ a fju ædiʃnæl mɑrks, ænd ðe onlɪ mɪstɪfaʲ ɪt mor, ænd mor.[10]

Richards believed fervently that the old Roman letters varied too much in their values, that no one would ever agree on their fixed use, and that keeping them would just be a hindrance; a successful, lasting reform would require starting with a clean slate. He also argued for economy in writing time, paper and ink. These arguments anticipated those advanced by George Bernard Shaw in the 20th century to support the creation of what is now known as the Shaw or Shavian Alphabet [28, 18][11].

Brigham Young and the Board of Regents were persuaded, the Board's modified Pitman alphabet was defenestrated, and the first version of a new non-Roman alphabet was adopted 22 December 1853, with 38 original glyphs devised by George D. Watt and perhaps also by a lesser-known figure named John Vance. The Deseret Alphabet was born.

3.2   Early Deseret Alphabet: 1854–1855

In Salt Lake City, the *Deseret News* announced the Alphabet to its readers 19 January 1854:

> The Board of Regents, in company with the Governor and heads of departments, have adopted a new alphabet, consisting of 38 characters. The Board have held frequent sittings this winter, with the sanguine hope of simplifying the English language, and especially its Orthography. After many fruitless attempts to render the common alphabet of the day subservient to their purpose, they found it expedient to invent an entirely new and original set of characters.
>
> These characters are much more simple in their structure than the usual alphabetical characters; every superfluous mark supposable, is wholly excluded from them.
>
> The written and printed hand are substantially merged into one.

---

[10] "What have you gained by the alphabet on that card I ask you. Show me one item, can you point out the first advantage that you have gained over the old one? ... What have you gained, you have the same old alphabet over again, only a few additional marks, and they only mystify it more, and more."

[11] http://www.shavian.org/

Type of some kind, almost certainly wooden[12], was soon prepared in Salt Lake City, and on 24 March 1854 a four-page folded leaflet with a chart of the Deseret Alphabet was presented to the Board (see Figure 1). In this early 1854 version of the Alphabet, we find 38 letters, the canonical glyphs being drawn with a broad pen, with thick emphasis on the downstrokes, and light upstrokes and flourishes. The short-vowel glyphs are represented smaller than the others.

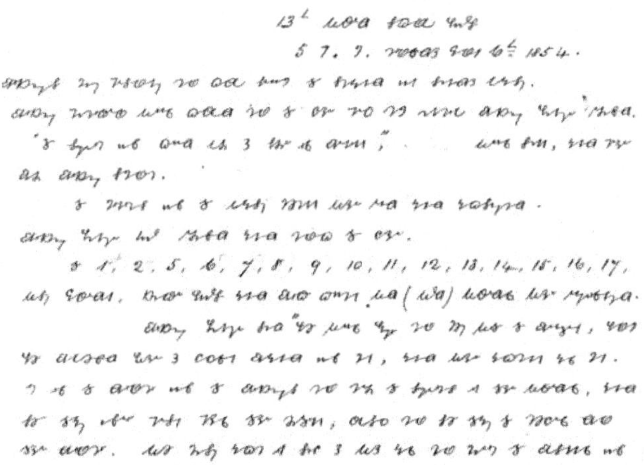

Fig. 7. Extract from the minutes of a Bishops' meeting, 6 June 1854, concerning the support of the poor. These minutes, written in a cursive, stenographic style, were prepared by George D. Watt and addressed directly to Brigham Young. LDS Church Archives.

George D. Watt was the principal architect of the Deseret Alphabet and, judging by surviving documents, was also the first serious user. Watt was a Pitman stenographer, and the early documents (see Figure 7) are written in a distinctly stenographic style[13]. Watt drew the outline of each word cursively, without lifting the pen. Short vowels, shown smaller than the other glyphs in the chart, were incorporated into the linking strokes between the consonants; thus vowels were usually written on upstrokes, which explains their canonical thin strokes and shorter statures in the first chart. The writer had to go back and cross the Ɩ vowels after finishing the outline; and often short vowels were simply left out.

The demands of cursive writing seem to have influenced the design of several of the letters. In particular, the fussy little loops on the ɑ (/d/), 8 (/s/), ℚ (/g/), Ɵ (/ɔ/) and ℬ (/aʷ/) were used to link these letters with their neighbors. Watt also combined consonants together with virtuosity, "amalgamating" them together to save space, but at the expense of legibility. Another lamentable

---

[12] *Deseret News*, 15 August 1855.

[13] James Henry Martineau was another early cursive writer.

Fig. 8. Rémy and Brenchley almost certainly copied this chart from an almost identical one in W.W. Phelps' *Deseret Almanac* of 1855. With the addition of letters for /ɔʲ/ and /ʲu/, this 40-letter version of the Deseret Alphabet had the same phonemic inventory as the Pitman-Ellis 1847 Alphabet.

characteristic of the early style was the inconsistent use of letters, sometimes to represent their phonemic value and sometimes to represent their conventional name. Thus Watt writes *people* as the equivalent of /ppl/, expecting the reader to pronounce the first p-letter as /pi/, that being the letter's conventional name when the alphabet is recited. Similarly, Watt can spell *being* as the equivalent of just /bŋ/, the letters having names pronounced /bi/ and /ɪŋ/, respectively. While probably seen by shorthand writers as a clever way to abbreviate and speed their writing, the confusion of letter names and letter values is a mistake in any book orthography.

Like Isaac Pitman, the Mormons could not resist experimenting with their new alphabet, changing both the inventory of letters and the glyphs. The 1854 alphabet was almost immediately modified, substituting new glyphs for /ɪ/ and /aʷ/ and adding two new letters for the diphthongs /ɔʲ/ and /ʲu/, making a 40-letter alphabet as printed in the 1855 *Deseret Almanac* of W.W. Phelps. This chart was almost certainly the one copied by Rémy and Brenchley [27] who visited Salt Lake City in 1855 (see Figure 8)[14].

---

[14] For yet another chart of this version of the Alphabet, see Benn Pitman's *The Phonographic Magazine*, 1856, pp. 102–103.

Watt apparently believed that the same basic alphabet could serve for both stenography and everyday orthography, or as the *Deseret News*, cited above, put it, "The written and printed hand are substantially merged into one." This was in fact an early goal of phonotypy, but it was soon abandoned by Pitman as impractical [15]. The retention of this old idea contributed to making the Deseret Alphabet an esthetic and typographical failure.

One of the fundamental design problems in the Alphabet was the elimination of ascenders and descenders. This was done in a well-intentioned attempt to make the type last longer – type wears out during use, and the ascenders and descenders wear out first – but the lamentable result was that all typeset words have a roughly rectangular shape, and lines of Deseret printing become very monotonous. Some of the glyphs, in particular 𐐝 and 𐐘, are overly complicated; and in practice writers often confused the pairs 𐐘 vs. 𐐚 and 𐐘 vs. 𐐔. These fundamental design problems need to be distinguished from the font-design problems, which will be discussed below.

3.3   The 1857 St. Louis Font

The reform was moving a bit slowly. On 4 February 1856 the Regents appointed George D. Watt, Wilford Woodruff, and Samuel W. Richards to prepare manuscripts and arrange for the printing of books. The journals of Richards and Woodruff show that they went at it hammer and tongs, working on elementary readers and a catechism intended for teaching religious principles to children. The next step was to get a font made.

There are references to an attempt, as early as 1855, to cut Deseret Alphabet punches right in Utah, by a "Brother Sabins"[15], but there is as yet no evidence that this project succeeded. In 1857, Erastus Snow was sent to St. Louis to procure type, engaging the services of Ladew & Peer, which was the only foundry there at the time [31]. But Snow abandoned the type and hurried back to Utah when he discovered that President Buchanan had dispatched General Albert Sydney Johnston to Utah with 2500 troops from Fort Leavenworth, Kansas, to put down a reported Mormon rebellion and install a new non-Mormon governor. The news of "Johnston's Army" reached Salt Lake City 24 July 1857, when the alleged rebels were gathered for a picnic in a local canyon to celebrate the tenth anniversary of their arrival in Utah. In the ensuing panic, Salt Lake City and the other northern settlements were abandoned, and 30,000 people packed up their wagons and moved at least 45 miles south to Provo. The territorial government, including records and the printing press, were moved all the way to Fillmore in central Utah. While this bizarre and costly fiasco, often called the Utah War or Buchanan's Blunder, was eventually resolved peacefully, it was another setback to the Deseret Alphabet movement.

By late 1858, the Utah War was over, the St. Louis type had arrived in Salt Lake City, and work recommenced. It is very likely that only the punches

---

[15] *The Latter-day Saints' Millennial Star*, 10 November 1855. The reference is probably to John Sabin (not Sabins), who was a general mechanic and machinist.

and matrices were shipped to Utah[16], and that the Mormons did the actual type casting themselves. The children's texts prepared by the committee of Woodruff, Richards and Watt had been lost; unfazed, Brigham Young told Woodruff to "take hold with Geo. D. Watt and get up some more"[17]. The first use of the new type was to print a business card for George A. Smith, the Church Historian. The stage was now set for the revival of the Deseret Alphabet reform in 1859–60.

3.4   The Revival of 1859–1860

Sample Articles Printed in the *Deseret News*. The period of 1859–60 was a busy and productive one for the Deseret Alphabet. The type was finally available, and on 16 February 1859 the *Deseret News* printed a sample text from the Fifth Chapter of Matthew, the Sermon on the Mount. Similar practice texts, almost all of them scriptural, appeared almost every week to May 1860. Despite this progress, everyone involved was extremely disappointed with the St. Louis font, which was crudely cut and ugly by any standards. Young felt that the poor type did as much as anything to hold back the reform.

The 1859 Alphabet as printed in the *Deseret News* (see Figure 9) had reverted to 38 letters, lacking dedicated letters for the diphthongs $/ɔ^j/$ and $/^ju/$, which had to be printed with digraphs; but the *Deseret News* apologized for the lack of a $/^ju/$ letter and promised a correction as soon as a new punch could be cut[18].

In 2002 I found the punches for the 1857 St. Louis font in the LDS Church Archives (see Figure 10). There proved to be only 36 punches in each of three sizes, but investigation showed that they were originally intended to support a 40-letter version of the Alphabet. The trick was the double use of four of the punches, rotating them 180 degrees to strike a second matrix. Thus the punch for ٦ also served to strike the matrix for Ⴑ; the punch for ٦ also served for Ⴑ; and similarly for the pairs Ⴢ–Ⴒ and Ⴑ–ľ. The sets include punches for the $/ɔ^j/$ and $/^ju/$ diphthongs, being Ꮎ and Ꮎ, respectively, but these glyphs had apparently fallen out of favor by 1859 and were not used in the *Deseret News*.

Handwritten Deseret Alphabet in 1859–60. Brigham Young directed his clerks to use the Alphabet, and the history or biography of Brigham Young was kept in Deseret Alphabet at this time. Another surviving text from this period is the financial "Ledger C", now held at Utah State University (see Figure 12). This ledger was probably kept by clerk T.W. Ellerbeck who later wrote [19], "During one whole year the ledger accounts of President Young were kept by me in those characters, exclusively, except that the figures of the old style were used, not having been changed."

The Ledger C alphabet has 39 letters, including the glyph ? for $/^ju/$ but using a digraph for $/ɔ^j/$. The Ledger abandons the Alphabet in May of 1860, at

---

[16] *Deseret News*, 16 February 1859.

[17] Journal History, 20 November 1858. The journal of Wilford Woodruff for 22 November 1858 indicates that the manuscripts were soon found.

[18] The *Deseret News* also promised a new letter for the vowel in *air*, which was a highly suspect distinction made in some Pitman alphabets.

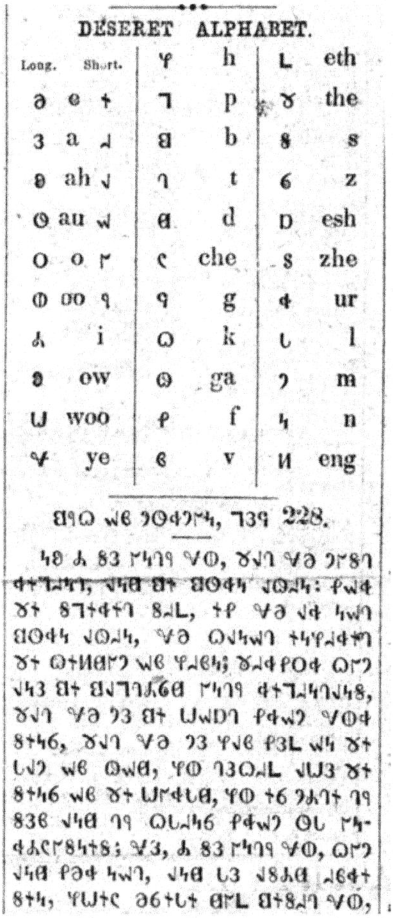

Fig. 9. The *Deseret News* printed sample articles in the Deseret Alphabet in 1859–60, and again in 1864, using the crude St. Louis type of 1857. This article, of which only a portion is shown here, appeared in the issue of 30 November 1864, vol. XIV, no. 9, which also included reports of the fall of Atlanta, Georgia to General Sherman during the American Civil War.

the same time that the *Deseret News* stopped printing sample articles, and the Deseret text was at some point given interlinear glosses in standard orthography.

My own favorite document from this era is the Deseret Alphabet journal of Thales Hastings Haskell [29], kept from 4 October 1859 to the end of that year while he and Marion Jackson Shelton[19] were serving as Mormon missionaries

---

[19] Shelton also kept a journal in 1858–59, in a mix of standard orthography, Pitman shorthand, and some Deseret Alphabet. LDS Church Archives.

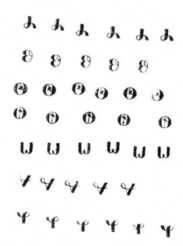

Fig. 10. Some smoke proofs of the 1857 St. Louis punches, found in 2002 in the LDS Church Archives. The ⊖ and ⊕ glyphs, representing /ɔʲ/ and /ʲu/, respectively, were not used when the *Deseret News* finally started printing sample articles with the type in 1859.

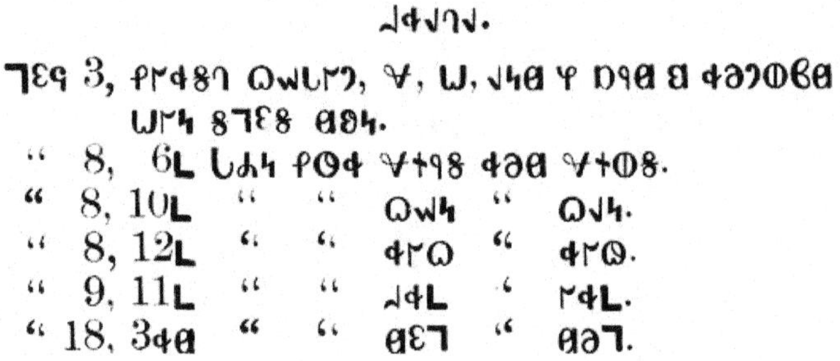

⌐d𝈩𝈩·

⅂Ɛ٩ 3, Ᵽ𝈩48٦ ⵀwⵏ𝈩, ∀, Ⱳ, ⌐ꞝꞕ ꝑ ⵀꝗꝺ ꝑ ꝺꝏⵀꝺ
Ⱳꞃꞕ 8⅂ᵽ8 ꝺꝺꞕ.
" 8, ⵀⵏ ⵏꝺꞕ Ᵽⵀⴸ ꝑ+٦8 ꝺꝺꝺ ꝑ+ⵀ8·
" 8, 10ⵏ " " ⵀwꞕ " ⵀꝺꞕ·
" 8, 12ⵏ ' ' ⴸꞃⵀ " ⴸꞃⵀ·
" 9, 11ⵏ " " ⌐ⴸⵏ ' ꞃⴸⵏ·
" 18, 3ⴸꝺ " " ꝺꝗⵏ " ꝺꝺⵏ.

Fig. 11. A portion of the errata sheet, printed in Utah using the St. Louis type of 1857, for *The Deseret First Book* of 1868. A much better font was cut for printing the readers (see Figure 15), but it was left in the care of Russell Bros. in New York City.

to the Hopi[20]. They were staying in the Third-Mesa village of Orayvi (also spelled Oribe, Oraibi, etc.), now celebrated as the oldest continuously inhabited village in North America. Haskell used a 40-letter version of the alphabet, like the contemporary *Deseret News* version, but adding ? for /ʲu/ and, idiosyncratically, ⊕ for /ɔʲ/. The original manuscript is faint and fragile; the following is a sample in typeset Deseret Alphabet and equivalent IPA:

---

[20] The original journal is in Special Collections at the Brigham Young University Library. At some unknown time after the mission, Haskell himself transcribed the Deseret text into standard orthography, and this transcription was edited and published by Juanita Brooks in 1944 [9].

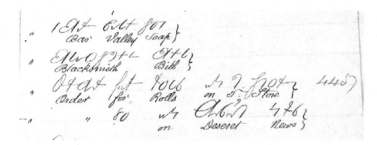

Fig. 12. *Ledger C* of 1859-60, probably kept by T.W. Ellerbeck, illustrates an idiosyncratic 39-letter version of the Deseret Alphabet. There are still cursive links and "amalgamations" in this text, but far fewer than in George D. Watt's early texts of 1854–55. Interlinear glosses in traditional orthography were added later. Utah State University.

ᏰᎫ᛭ ᏒᎷ ᏢᏒ ᎯᏝᎤᏢᏒᏚᏒ ᏨᏳᏰ ᏚᏒᎴᏒᏢᏰ ᏢᏱᏲᏒᏒᏙ ᏲᏒ ᎤᏘᏝᏰ ᏰᏘᏝᏒᏚ ᏲᎤ ᏘᏝ ᏱᏢᏒ ᏱᏝᏒ ᏲᎤ ᏲᏘᏘ ᏲᏝᏘ ᎤᏒᏚᏘᏝ

gʊt ʌp tʊk bɛkfʌst [sic] ænd stɑtɪd ɪndɪʌn wɛnt æhɛd tu oraʲb vɪlɪʤ tu tɛl ðɛm ðæt wi wæːr kʌmɪŋ

In standard orthography, this reads, "Got up, took b[r]eakfast and sta[r]ted [;] Indian went ahead to Oribe village to tell them that we were coming." The missing *r* in *breakfast* is just an isolated error, but the spelling of /stɑtɪd/ for *started* is characteristic; Haskell was from North New Salem, Franklin Country, Massachusetts, and he dropped his *r*s after the /ɑ/ vowel [5]. Other writers similarly leave clues to their accents in the phonemically written texts.

Marion J. Shelton was a typical 40-letter Deseret writer from this period, using the more or less standard glyphs Ꙩ for /ɔʲ/ and Ꙅ for /ʲu/, as in the following letter[21], written shortly after his arrival in Orayvi.

ᎤᏘᏝᏰ ᏰᏘᏝᏒᏚ. ᏱᏲ ᏲᏝᎤᏚᏘᎤᎤ.
ᏝᎤᏰ. 13, 1859.

ᏰᏘᏝᏒᏰᎯ ᏰᏘᏒᏲᏘᏰ,
Ꮭ ᏒᏲ ᏚᏲᎤᏘᏝ ᏲᏘ ᏲᏝᏒ ᏲᏰ ᏲᏘ ᎯᏳᏲᏝᏘᏝ ᏲᏘᏲᏘᏝ. Ᏺ ᏳᏚᏚ ᏳᏰ ᏰᏲᏒ ᏲᏲᏒᏒ ᏰᏲ ᏲᎯᏰ ᏲᏘ ᏝᏲᎤ ᏚᎤᏳᏲᏘ ᏲᎤᏝ ᏲᏲ Ᏺ ᏲᎤᏲ. ᏳᏰ ᏰᎤ ᏰᏰᏲ Ꮪ ᏝᏝᏲᏘ ᏲᏰᏒ ᏲᏳᏝᏲ ᏳᏰ ᏰᏲᏒ ᏰᏰᏲ ᏳᏰ ᏲᏝᏰ ᏲᏲ ᏚᏲᏝᏰᎤ ᏚᏲᎤᏘᏲᏘᎤ ᏲᏲ ᏰᏒᏢᏲ ᏰᏲ ᏲᏝᏰᎤ. ᏲᏚᏚᏲᏝᏲᏰᏚ ᏲᏒᏲᏲᎤ Ꮭ ᏲᏲᎤ ᏰᏲᎯᎤᏢᏝᏒᏲ ᏳᏒᏲ ᏳᏒᏲ ᏲᏰ ᏲᎤ ᏲᏝᎤ ᏲᏲᏝᏰᎤ. Ꮭ ᏳᏝᏲᏒ ᏒᏲ ᏲᏲᏒᏒ Ᏺ ᏝᏲᏲᎤ ᏚᏲᎤᏲᏲ ᏲᏲᎤ ᏰᏲᏝᎤ ᏲᏰᏲᏚᏝᎤ ᏲᏒ Ᏺ ᎯᏝᎤᏲ ᏰᏲᏝᎤᏲ ᏲᎤ ᎤᏲᏝᏲᏰ. Ᏻ ᏝᏲᏲᏲ ᏲᏰ Ᏺ ᏲᏲᏚ ᏲᏲᎤᏝ 3 "ᏨᏰᎤᏰᏘᏲᏝ", ᏲᏲ ᏝᏲᏝᏒ ᎤᏲᏲᏲ, ᏲᏝᏘ ᏲᏰ ᏰᎤᏘᎴ, ᏲᏲᎤ Ꭿ ᏰᏲᏰᎤᎤᏝ ᏲᏲᏱ ᏲᏰ "ᏲᏰᏰᎤ". (Ꮄ ᏲᏲᏝᎤ ᏲᏒᏰᎴᏲᏰᏝᎤᏰ ᏰᏝᏚ ᏲᎫᏲᏒᎤ ᏲᏲᎴᏲᏳᏲ ᎤᏲᏝᏰᏒᎴᏲ) Ᏻ ᏲᏝᏰ ᏝᎴᏲᏲ ᏰᏲᏲᏝᏰ ᎤᏲᎯᏲᎴᏝᎤ, Ꮄ ᏝᏲᏝᏝ ᏰᏲ ᏲᏝᏰᏲ ᏲᏲᏰ ᏝᎴᏲᏝᏲᏲ Ᏺ ᏰᏲᏒ ᏲᏲ ᏲᏲᏰ ᏲᏝᏰᏲ ᏳᏲᏲᏙ ᏲᏲᏰ ᏲᏝᏰ ᏲᏲ Ᏺ ᏰᏲᏲᏝ ᏲᏲᏰ ᏲᏲᏰ. ᏲᏝᏒ ᎴᏲᏲ ᏒᏝ Ᏺ ᏲᏰᎴ. 80 ᏳᏰ ᏰᏲᎤᎤ ᏒᎴᎴᎤ ᏰᏲᎤᎤ ᏲᏲ ᎯᏲᏝᏰᏲᏲᏲᎤ ᏲᏲᎤ ᏰᏝᏰ Ꮄ ᎤᏲᎤᏲ ᏰᏲᎯᎤᏢᏝᏒᏲ.

<hr />

[21] Marion Jackson Shelton to George A. Smith and others, 13 November 1859, George A. Smith Incoming Correspondence, LDS Church Archives.

Ɏɑ6 Oɟ⅃ɑ16 ɑɑ1 Ɏ Ͻ⅃ɟϽΓɅ6 ⴼ⅃ɟ CɟLɑɟ⅃Ʌ, 3 ⴼϽ ɑ⅃ɑ6 ⅃Ʌɑ ɑ⅃18 ⅃Ʌɑ ⴼ⅃ɟ8⅃6, 3 ⵔ1ɑ Ͻ⅃ɅꞀ Dɑ1, 1Γɟɑ16, ⅃Ʌɑ CɟɑɅ6 ⱳ1Ɏ L⅃18 ⅃8 1ɑC⅃6, ɑ⅃ɟⱳ, ɑɑɅ6, Ͻ⅃LΓⱳ6, ɟ⅃ɑ 1Ⅎ1⅃ɟ, 8ɑⱳⱳ⅃0⅃6 &c. Ɏɑ6 LΓⱳ6 Ɏ3 ɟ36.

Ɏ⅃ɟ ⱳΓɟɑ0⅃∩18 0ɟ Γⱳ⅃⅃ɟ Oɟɑⱳɑ. Ɏ⅃ɟ ⱳΓɟɑ 16 CϽⴼLɟ ϽϽϽ1ɴ ɑL⅃∩ɑ⅃18 ⅃Ʌɑ ɑ⅃L18 ⅃8 ⱳⵔL − Ɏ3 ɟ36 8Γϧ ɑ⅃Ꞁⱳ, ⅃Ʌɑ 0ɟ ⅃⅃1 ⅃ɑ1ɑꞀ⅃0 11 ɑ⅃ɑ1ⱳ, ɑꞀ1 0ɟ 6⅃ɟɟ ⵏⱳϽ⅃L1ϧ⅃⅃1 ⅃Ʌɑ ⅃Ʌɑ ɟⱳɑꞀ81ɟ1Γ8 ɟⱳɑ1⅃Ʌ6

⅄ ɟ⅃1 ϧO⅃1ⱳLɟ ɑꞀ1 1ɟϽⴼϧLɟ. 8Ꞁ1, 8ɟΓⱳ6, ⅄ D⅃L 8ɑ Ɏϧ ⅃10817 ⴼOL ⅃Ʌɑ ⱳΓL ⴼ⅃8 LΓɟɑ ϽOɟ ⅃881 Ɏɑ6 ⴼOɑ8 ɑ⅃ Ɏ⅃1 1⅃Ͻ ⅃Ʌɑ Ɏ⅃⅃ ⱳɑ'L ⴼ⅃8 ɑ1ɑ 1ɑ08 11ɑ⅃Ɏɟ.   Ɏϧɟ6.

Ͻ.Ϥ.D⅃LⱳꞀ.

11 Ϥ.L. 8ϽɟL, ɟ. 8⅃ⱳ1Lɟ, ɟ. ⵔ⅃Ͻ8L, Ϥ.Ϥ, Ϥ.6. ⅃Ʌɑ Γɏɟ6.

Here is the same letter transcribed into traditional orthography.

Oribe Village   New Mexico.
Nov. 13. 1859.
Beloved Brothers,

            I am sitting on top of my dwelling writing. The way
we get into our house is through a little square hole in the top. We go down a
ladder and when we get down we have to stand stooping or bump our heads.
Yesterday morning I took breakfast with one of my red friends. I went up into
the third story and seated myself on the floor beside my friend. The lady of
the house brought a "chahkahpta" [*tsaqapta*], or earthen jar, full of soup, and
a basket full of "peek". (a bread resembling blue wrapping paper folded) The
old lady seated herself, a little boy also and lastly the cat to its place with its
head in the soup and its tail on the peek. So we broke peek dipped soup with
our fingers and had a merry breakfast.

These Oribes beat the Mormons for children. a few dogs and cats and horses,
a good many sheep, turkeys, and chickens with lots of peaches, corn, beans,
melons, and pepper, squashes &c. These things they raise.

Their workshops [kivas] are underground. Their work is chiefly making blan-
kets and belts of wool – they raise some cotton, and are not addicted to begging,
but are very intelligent and industrious indians.

I write jokingly but truefully [sic]. But, brothers, I shall see you next fall and
will have learned more about these folks by that time and then we'll have big
talks together. Yours,

M.J.Shelton.

To G.L.[sic] Smith, R. Bentley, R. Campbell, J.J, J.V. and others.

Over the years, Shelton proposed a number of modifications to the Deseret
Alphabet, including the addition of the letter ⵏ; its use in the following text[22]
shows that it was intended to represent the schwa, or neutral vowel, a phoneme
missing from the standard Deseret Alphabet and from the 1847 Ellis-Pitman
Alphabet that was its principal model.

---

[22] Marion J. Shelton to Brigham Young, 3 April 1860, Brigham Young Incoming
   Correspondence, LDS Church Archives.

𐐼 𐐶𐐮𐐼 𐑌𐐱𐐻 𐑅𐐪𐐿𐑅𐐮𐐼 𐐮𐑌 𐑊𐐪𐑉𐑌𐐮𐑍 𐑄𐐯𐑋 𐐻𐐭 𐑉𐐩𐐾𐐻 𐐰𐑆 𐑄 𐐼𐐰𐑌𐑅𐐮𐑍 𐐿𐐱𐑋𐐯𐑌𐑅𐐻 𐑅𐐬𐑉𐑃 𐐰𐑁𐐻𐐲𐑉 𐐪𐐶𐑉
𐐱𐑉𐐩𐐾𐑂𐐲𐑊 𐑄𐐯𐑉 𐐰𐑌𐐼 𐐿𐐱𐑌𐐻𐐮𐑌𐐾𐐲𐐼 𐐲𐑌𐐻𐐮𐑊 𐐶𐐮 𐑊𐐯𐑁𐐻. 𐐺𐐰𐐻 𐐴 𐐰𐑋 𐑅𐐰𐐻𐐮�𐑅𐑁𐐩𐐼 𐑄𐐰𐐻 𐐶𐐮𐑄 𐐹𐑉𐐱𐐹𐐲𐑉 𐐿𐐪𐑉𐐼𐑆 𐐴 𐐿𐐰𐑌 𐑊𐐪𐑉𐑌 𐑄𐐯𐑋 𐐻𐐭 𐑉𐐩𐐾𐐻 𐐮𐑌 𐐶𐐪𐑌 𐐶𐐮𐑌𐐻𐐲𐑉 𐑋𐐱𐑉. 𐐴 𐐸𐐰𐑂 𐑄 𐐴𐑆 𐐻𐐱𐑊𐐲𐑉𐐲𐐺𐑊𐐮 𐐶𐐯𐑊 𐐺𐑉𐐬𐐿𐐲𐑌.

This experiment, which never caught on, resulted in a 41-letter Deseret Alphabet. The text in equivalent phonemic IPA is the following:

aʲ dɪd nɒt sʌksɪd ɪn lʌrnɪŋ ðɛm tʊ raʲt æz ð dænsɪŋ kɒmɛnst ʃɔrtlɪ aftər aʷr əraʲvəl ðer ænd kɒntɪnjəd ʌntɪl wi lɛft. bʌt aʲ æm sætɪsfaʲd ðæt wɪð prɒpər kɑrdz aʲ kæn lʌrn ðɛm tʊ raʲt ɪn wʌn wɪntər mor. aʲ hæv ð aʲs tɒlərəblɪ wɛl brokən.[23]

3.5   The 1860s and the Printed Books

Most of the enthusiasm for the Deseret Alphabet collapsed in 1860, and by 1862 it was dead, except in the determined mind of Brigham Young. When Superintendent of Common Schools Robert L. Campbell presented Brigham Young with a manuscript of a "first Reader" in standard orthography, Young rejected it emphatically, insisting that "he would not consent to have his type, ink or paper used to print such trash"[24].

In 1864, the Regents considered adopting the phonotypy of Benn Pitman, the brother of Isaac who had established his own Phonographic Institute in Cincinnati in 1853, but the ultimate response was a recommitment to the Deseret Alphabet; sample Alphabet articles reappeared defiantly in the *Deseret News* 11 May 1864 and continued to the end of the year.

There were in fact several attempts during the 1860s to abandon the Deseret Alphabet. In December of 1867[25], the Board of Regents, with Brigham Young, resolved unanimously to adopt "the phonetic characters employed by Ben [sic] Pitman of Cincinnati, for printing purposes, thereby gaining the advantage of the books already printed in those phonetic characters." However, on 3 February 1868[26], the Board once again did an about-face, recommitted to the Deseret Alphabet and started the serious and expensive work of getting books prepared for publication. Apostle Orson Pratt was hired to transcribe *The Deseret First Book* and *The Deseret Second Book* into the Deseret Alphabet.

After the disappointment with the crude St. Louis type, the Regents in 1868 sent their agent D.O. Calder to New York to get better workmanship. Calder engaged the firm of Russell Bros[27], which cut and cast an English (14-point) font for the project. The new school books (see Figures 14 and 15) were delivered to

---

[23] "I did not succeed in learning them to write as the dancing commenced shortly after our arrival there and continued until we left, but I am satisfied that with proper cards I can learn them to write in one winter more. I have the ice tolerably well broken."

[24] Journal History, 22 May 1862.

[25] *Deseret News*, 19 December 1867.

[26] *Deseret News*, 3 February 1868.

[27] Russell's American Steam Printing House, located at 28, 30 and 32 Centre Street, New York City, Joseph and Theodore Russell, Props.

Fig. 13. The 1855 Benn Pitman or American Pitman Alphabet. In 1852, Benn Pitman carried the Pitman phonography and phonotypy movement to the United States, setting up The Phonographic Institute in Cincinnati in 1853. Whereas Isaac Pitman was an incurable tinkerer, constantly modifying his alphabets, brother Benn recognized the virtues of stability.

Salt Lake City in late 1868, at which time Orson Pratt had already turned his dogged energy to the transcription of *The Book of Mormon*.

In 1869, Pratt was sent as the agent to New York, to supervise the printing of *The Book of Mormon*. He too chose Russell Bros. and had a font of Long Primer (10-point) type cut and cast for the body of the text[28]. The bicameral

---

[28] Small Pica (11-point) type was also considered and, unfortunately, rejected. With the inherent design problems of the Deseret Alphabet, the Long Primer type is too small for comfortable reading.

Fig. 14. In 1868, *The Deseret First Book*, shown here, and *The Deseret Second Book* were printed by Russell Bros. of New York and shipped to the Territory of Utah. The print run for each book was 10,000 copies.

nature of the Deseret Alphabet allowed him to save some money by using the lowercase letters of the existing English (14-point) font as the uppercase letters of the Long Primer (10-point) font. Pratt also had fonts prepared in the Great Primer (18-point) and Double English (28-point) sizes to serve in headings and titles. Not surprisingly, Pratt complained that the three unlucky compositors assigned to the project were making "a great abundance of mistakes in setting

90   Kenneth R. Beesley

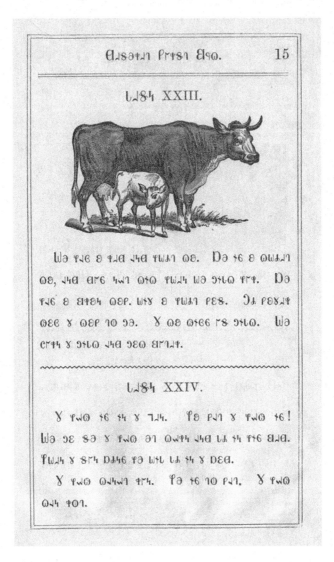

Fig. 15. A page from *The Deseret First Book*.

type", and he had to give the proofs four good readings and supervise many corrections before the pages could be stereotyped[29].

The Book of Mormon (see Figure 16) was published in two formats. *The Book of Mormon Part I*, intended to serve as an advanced reader, consisted of The First Book of Nephi, The Second Book of Nephi, The Book of Jacob, The Book

[29] Orson Pratt to Robert L. Campbell, 12 June 1869, Deseret Alphabet Printing Files 1869, LDS Church Archives.

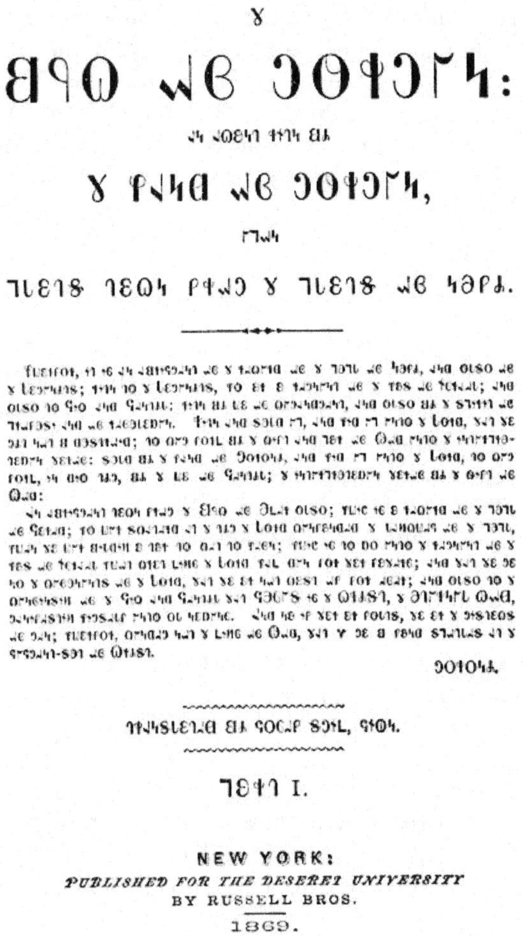

ঽ

ଡ଼୧ୠ ୶୧ ୦୦ୱଡ଼୮୳:

ঀ୪ ୰୦୧ঽ୩ ୲୲୲୳ ୠ୪

ঽ ୮୴୶ଡ଼ ୶୧ ୦୦ୱଡ଼୮୳,

୮୳ঀ୪

୳୪୧୲ଃ ୩୧ଡ଼୪ ୮୴୶୦ ঽ ୳୪୧୲ଃ ୶୧ ୳୦୮୴.

[facsimile text in the Deseret Alphabet]

୦୦ୱଡ଼୳.

ঀ୮ঀ୳୪୧୲ঀ୦ ଃঀ ୦୦୦ঀ୮ ୦୦ঀ୪, ୯୳୦୪.

୳୧୲୳ I.

NEW YORK:
PUBLISHED FOR THE DESERET UNIVERSITY
BY RUSSELL BROS.
1869.

Fig. 16. In 1869, *The Book of Mormon*, a book of Mormon scripture, was published in two formats: the first third of the book, which cost 75 cents, and the full text, which cost $2. Part I had a print run of 8000 copies, and a good specimen today sells for perhaps $250 to $300. Only 500 copies of the full *Book of Mormon* were printed, and in 2004 an average copy sells for about $7000 or $8000.

of Enos, The Book of Jarom, The Book of Omni and The Words of Mormon[30]. The entire *Book of Mormon* was also printed on better paper, and was more expensively bound.

---

[30] *The Book of Mormon Part I* is usually known, inaccurately, among used-book dealers as "The First Book of Nephi". The Regents' plan was eventually to offer the whole book in three parts, printing Parts II and III with proceeds from the sale of the first four books.

Receipts from 1868 and 1869[31] show that the punches, matrices, type and other printing paraphernalia remained the property of the Board of Regents of the Deseret University, but they were left in the care of Russell Bros. in expectation of future work, which in fact never materialized. Although a large collection of nineteenth-century punches survives at Columbia University in New York City, attempts to locate the Russell Bros. Deseret Alphabet punches have so far been unsuccessful.

3.6   The 1868–69 "Book" Alphabet and Fonts

After the disappointing debut of the St. Louis type, used reluctantly to print sample articles in the *Deseret News* in 1859–60 and 1864, Brigham Young had vowed to go to England the next time to get better workmanship[32]. But in fact in 1868 and 1869 the Mormons went only as far as New York City, engaging Russell Bros. to cut new punches, strike matrices, cast type, typeset and print the books.

This time they did get professional workmanship, but the resulting book font is still somewhat bizarre, partly because of the inherent awkwardness of the basic shapes, and partly because of choices in font design that now seem old-fashioned. A look at the book font (see Figures 15, 16 and 17) shows that the glyphs, compared to the earlier charts, have been Bodonified: made rigidly vertical, symmetrical wherever possible, and with extreme contrasts of thick and thin. Thom Hinckley, an expert typographer and printer (personal communication), has pointed out that the extreme thins of the font reveal the punch cutter as a master; at the same time, these thin lines would have caused the type to wear quickly, which was one of the very problems the Regents were trying to avoid; printing the extreme thins also required the use of unusually high-quality paper. The 38 glyphs of the 1868–69 book font were basically the same as the 38 glyphs used in printing articles in the *Deseret News* in 1859–60 and 1864; the only significant difference was that the old 3 glyph was mirror-imaged to Ɛ.

Nash [21, pp. 23–29] lays out in devastating detail how the Deseret Alphabet type violates principle after principle of good book type, including the catas-trophic lack of ascenders and descenders. In the words of printing historian Roby Wentz [31], "The result was a very monotonous-looking line of type." Hinckley has emphasized the problems of "weight" and "color" in the book font, resulting from the extreme contrast of thicks and thins and the uniformly thin short vowels.

I believe that the problems of weight and color, including the thin repre-sentation of short vowels, the fussy loops that overcomplicate some glyphs, and the overall inharmonious collection of glyphs, go all the way back to the original amateur conception of the Deseret Alphabet as being suitable for both shorthand and everyday orthography. It was awkward enough as shorthand, and the translation to type was a failure that no amount of good type design

---

[31] Deseret Alphabet Printing Files 1868 and 1869, LDS Church Archives.
[32] Journal History, 16 February 1859.

ⴤ ⴃⵊ⠁⠕ⵑⵊⵑ ⵎⵊⵃⵝⴝⵑⵊⵑ.

Long Sounds.				Letter.	Name.		Sound.

Letter.	Name.		Sound.
Ә	e	as in	eat.
Ɛ	a	"	ate.
Ȣ	ah	"	art.
O	aw	"	aught.
O	o	"	oat.
O	oo	"	ooze.

	Short Sounds of the above.		
†	as in		it.
⌐		"	et.
↲		"	at.
↵		"	ot.
⌐		"	ut.
৭		"	book.

⌡	i	as in	ice.
Ȣ	ow	"	owl.
ⱳ	woo		
Ɣ	ye		
ſ	h		

Letter.	Name.		Sound.
٦	p		
Ⴙ	b		
٦	t		
ⵁ	d		
C	che	as in	cheese.
Ϙ	g		
Ꝺ	k		
ꝺ	ga	as in	gate.
Ρ	f		
Ɛ	v		
L	eth	as in	thigh.
ⴤ	the	"	thy.
ȣ	s		
6	z		
Ꝺ	esh	as in	flesh.
S	zhe	"	vision.
Ψ	ur	"	burn.
Ⴑ	l		
Ͽ	m		
٦	n		
Ϻ	eng	as in	length.

Fig. 17. The 1868–69 Book Version of the Deseret Alphabet consisted of 38 letters, with uppercase and lowercase characters distinguished only by size. Aside from the strange glyphs, the inventory, grouping and alphabetical order of the Alphabet are based solidly on the 1847 Alphabet of Alexander J. Ellis and Isaac Pitman (see Figure 5).

can really cure. One need only compare the Deseret Alphabet to the Shavian Alphabet (see Figures 19 and 18) to see the difference between an amateur and a professional design.

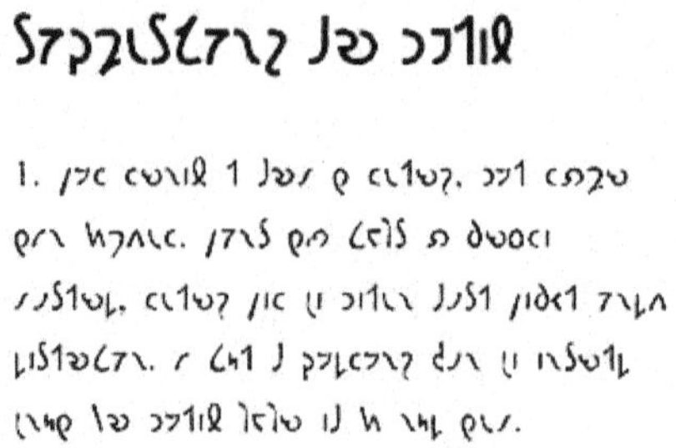

𐑕𐑹𐑿𐑕𐑤𐑮𐑰𐑟 𐑤𐑩 𐑩𐑛𐑒𐑦𐑚

1. /𐑮𐑒 𐑒𐑳𐑮𐑦𐑤 1 𐑤𐑩/ 𐑐 𐑒𐑦𐑤�3� �'1 𐑒𐑩𐑟𐑳
𐑐𐑮 𐑣𐑮𐑨𐑤𐑒. /𐑮𐑤𐑕 𐑐𐑮 𐑤𐑗𐑤𐑕 𐑩 𐑛�3𐑒𐑦
𐑮𐑕1�3𐑤, 𐑒𐑦𐑤�3� /𐑦𐑒 𐑘 𐑩1𐑦𐑒 𐑤𐑮51 /𐑦𐑛𐑒1 7𐑦𐑤𐑩
𐑤𐑦51𐑩𐑒7𐑒. 𐑮 𐑤𐑤1 𐑤 𐑐𐑮𐑤𐑒7𐑒𐑮 𐑛𐑮𐑤 𐑘 𐑦𐑕𐑳1𐑦
𐑤𐑦𐑤𐑐 𐑤𐑩 𐑩𐑛𐑒𐑦𐑚 𐑣𐑮𐑤𐑳 𐑦𐑘 𐑤 𐑦𐑤 𐑐𐑮/.

Fig. 18. In this extract of Shavian script, the title is set in the Ghoti (pronounced "fish") font, and the body in the Androcles font, both by Ross DeMeyere. Copyright © 2002 DeMeyere Design Incorporated. All rights reserved. Reproduced by permission.

3.7   The 1870s: Decline and Fall

The Deseret First Book and *The Deseret Second Book* had print runs of 10,000 copies each and sold for 15 and 20 cents, respectively. The first third (in actual quantity about a fourth) of the *Book of Mormon*, intended as an advanced reader, had a print run of 8,000 copies, and sold for 75 cents. Only 500 copies of the full *Book of Mormon* were printed, and they sold for $2. Or more to the point, the books did not sell.

By the mid 1870s, the Deseret Alphabet was recognized as a failure even by Brigham Young. The bottom line was that books were expensive to produce, and not even loyal Mormons could be persuaded to buy and study them. On 2 October 1875 *The Juvenile Instructor*, a magazine for Mormon youth, laid the Deseret Alphabet to rest.

> The Book of Mormon has been printed in the Deseret Alphabet, but President Young has decided that they are not so well adapted for the purpose designed as it was hoped they would be. There being no shanks [ascenders or descenders] to the letters, all being very even, they are trying to the eye, because of their uniformity. Another objection some have urged against them has been that they are entirely new, and we should have characters as far as possible with which we are familiar: and they have felt that we should use them as far as they go and adopt new characters only for the sounds which our present letters do not represent. There is a system known as the [Benn] Pitman system of phonetics which possesses the advantages alluded to. Mr. Pitman has used all the letters of the alphabet as far as possible and has added seventeen new characters to them, making an alphabet of forty-three letters. The Bible, a dictionary and a number of other works, school books, etc., have been printed in these new characters, and it is found that a person familiar with our present method of reading can learn in a few minutes to read those works printed after this system. We think it altogether likely that the regents of the University will upon further examination adopt this system for use in this Territory.

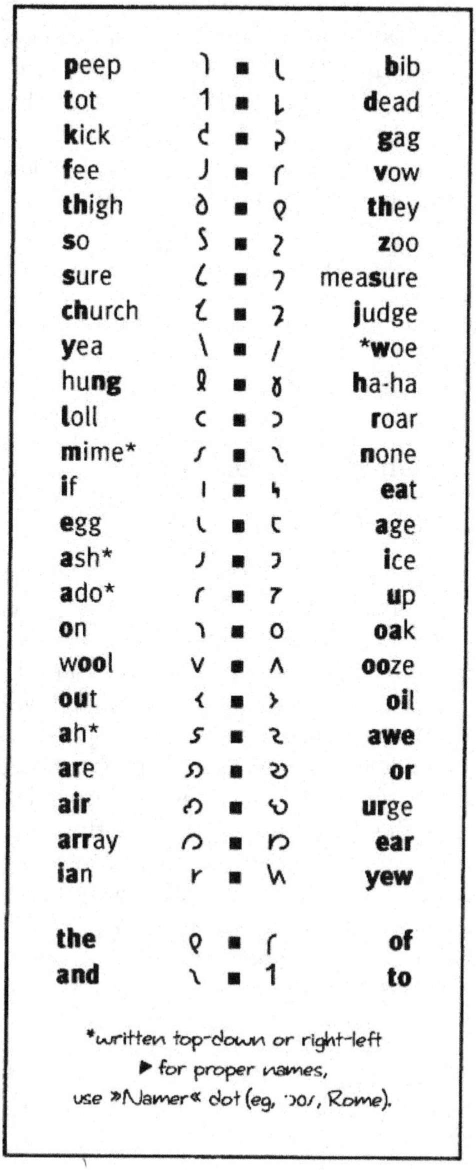

peep	⑂	■	⑃	bib
tot	1	■	Ⳑ	dead
kick	ⳇ	■	⳵	gag
fee	⌡	■	⌠	vow
thigh	ð	■	℺	they
so	∫	■	ⳡ	zoo
sure	Ⳙ	■	ⳗ	measure
church	ⳍ	■	ⳋ	judge
yea	\	■	/	*woe
hung	ℓ	■	℧	ha-ha
loll	⟨	■	⟩	roar
mime*	ʃ	■	⟍	none
if	I	■	⅂	eat
egg	⌞	■	⌜	age
ash*	⌡	■	⌐	ice
ado*	⌐	■	7	up
on	⌐	■	○	oak
wool	⋁	■	⋀	ooze
out	⟨	■	⟩	oil
ah*	ʂ	■	⳶	awe
are	℘	■	℘	or
air	⌒	■	ʋ	urge
array	⌒	■	⌒	ear
ian	ɾ	■	⋀	yew
the	℘	■	⌠	**of**
and	\	■	1	**to**

*written top-down or right-left
▶ for proper names,
use »Namer« dot (eg, ⌐⌐/, Rome).

Fig. 19. The Shaw or "Shavian" Alphabet was designed by typographer Kingsley Read and has inspired a number of other professional typographers, including Ross DeMeyere (http://www.demeyere.com/shavian/). The glyphs are simple and harmonious; ascenders and descenders give words distinctive shapes and avoid monotony. Copyright © 2002 DeMeyere Design Incorporated. All rights reserved. Reproduced by permission.

So while the Deseret Alphabet was dead, the Mormons hadn't yet given up on spelling reform. In July of 1877, Orson Pratt was sent to Liverpool to arrange to have *The Book of Mormon* and *The Book of Doctrine and Covenants*, another book of Mormon scripture, printed in the Benn Pitman orthography, "with the exception of two or three characters"[33]. But in August of that year, after most of the specially ordered phonotype had arrived from London, Brigham Young died; Orson Pratt was called back home, and the Mormons never dabbled in orthographical reform again.

It has been written, and repeated numerous times, that "the Deseret Alphabet died with Brigham Young"; however, the Deseret Alphabet had already been dead for at least a couple of years, and what died with Brigham Young was a very serious project, well in progress, to print Mormon scripture in a slight modification of Benn Pitman's "American phonotypy".

4   The Deseret Alphabet in Unicode

4.1   The Character Inventory and Glyphs

The Deseret Alphabet was first added to the Unicode 3.1 standard[34] in 2001, in the surrogate space 10400–1044F, mostly through the efforts of John H. Jenkins of Apple Computer[35]. It holds some distinction as the first script proposed for the surrogate space; as Jenkins describes it, "Nobody started to implement surrogates because there were no characters using them, and nobody wanted their characters to be encoded using surrogates because nobody was implementing them"[36]. The Deseret Alphabet, being a real but pretty dead script, was chosen as a pioneer – or sacrificial lamb – to break the vicious circle.

The Unicode 3.1 encoding handled only the 38-letter version of the Deseret Alphabet (this made 76 characters, including uppercase and lowercase) used in the printed books of 1868–69. The implementors were honestly unaware that earlier 39- and 40-letter versions of the Alphabet had been seriously used, and so might need to be encoded. I later argued vigorously[37] for the addition of the /ɔj/ and /ju/ letters used in several earlier versions of the Alphabet, including the one used in the Haskell journal and Shelton letters that I have transcribed. John Jenkins backed me up[38] and again deserves the credit for dealing with most of the paperwork and bureaucracy.

The two new letters were included in Unicode 4.0, but unfortunately I could not persuade them to use the 1859–60 glyphs Θ and ? as the citation glyphs; instead they went all the way back to the primitive glyphs of the 1854–55 charts. Unicode fonts based on the current heterogeneous collection of glyphs will be useless for any practical typesetting of 40-letter Deseret Alphabet documents.

---

[33] *Journal of Discourses*, vol. XIX, p. 112.

[34] http://www.unicode.org/

[35] http://homepage.mac.com/jenkins/

[36] http://homepage.mac.com/jenkins/Deseret/{Unicode.html,Computers.html}

[37] Unicode discussion document N2474 2002-05-17.

[38] Unicode discussion document N2473 2002-05-17.

Fig. 20. The Deseret Alphabet as it appears in Unicode 4.0. Copyright © 1991–2003 Unicode, Inc. All rights reserved. Reproduced by permission of Unicode, Inc.

4.2 Unicode Character Names

The Unicode implementation of the Deseret Alphabet is also flawed by some changes to the letter names. Not to criticize anyone personally, but just for the record, there are several reasons why the name changes were ill-advised:

Table 1. The Deseret Alphabet was added to Unicode by General American English speakers who honestly misunderstood the ꙃ (/ɒ/) and Ө (/ɔ/) vowels, which have collapsed to /ɑ/ in their dialect, and renamed them confusingly as SHORT AH and LONG AH.

Char.	IPA	Original Name	Unicode Name
ə	/i/	e as in eat	LONG I
Ɛ	/e/	a as in ate	LONG E
ꟁ	/ɑ/	ah as in art	LONG A
Ө	/ɔ/	aw as in aught	LONG AH
Ο	/o/	o as in oat	LONG O
ⵔ	/u/	oo as in ooze	LONG OO
⊦	/ɪ/	i as in it	SHORT I
⊣	/ɛ/	e as in et	SHORT E
⊥	/æ/	a as in at	SHORT A
ꙃ	/ɒ/	o as in ot	SHORT AH
ſ	/ʌ/	u as in ut	SHORT O
٩	/ʊ/	oo as in book	SHORT OO

1. The Deseret Alphabet had a traditional set of letter names already established and available. Arbitrary changes in the names make it more difficult to compare the original charts and the Unicode charts.
2. Some early Deseret Alphabet writers, including George D. Watt, consciously or unconsciously confused the traditional letter names and their phonological values. Some of their spellings make sense only if the letters are read with their original names.
3. Some letter-name changes were made because the implementors simply did not hear and understand some of the vowel distinctions provided in the Deseret Alphabet; they were speakers of General American English, a dialect that has lost some of the vowel distinctions still present in English and New England dialects.

The last point is the most unfortunate. Consider Table 1: The original name for the Deseret ꟁ letter, which is /ɑ/ in IPA, was "ah", using a common convention in English romanization whereby "ah" represents an unrounded low-back vowel. Most English speakers use this vowel in the words *father*, *bah* and *hah*. In England, and in much of New England, this vowel is distinct from the first vowel in *bother*, represented in Deseret Alphabet as ꙃ or in IPA as /ɒ/, which is a rounded low-back vowel; thus for these speakers the words *father* and *bother* do not rhyme. But the rounded /ɒ/ has collapsed into unrounded /ɑ/ in General American English, so the words do rhyme for most Americans. Similarly, the Deseret Ө letter, IPA /ɔ/, represents a mid-low back rounded vowel that has also collapsed into /ɑ/ for many American speakers. It can still be heard quite distinctly in the speech of many New Yorkers, Philadelphians, and New Englanders in general. The original Deseret name for the Ө, "aw", used a common convention for representing this rounded vowel, which occurs in words like *law*, *flaw*, *paw*, *aught*, *caught*, etc. The equivalent letter in the Shaw

Alphabet is appropriately named AWE. Not understanding the phonological distinctions involved, the implementors of Unicode renamed ꚍ as SHORT AH and ꚟ as LONG AH, giving precisely the wrong clues to the pronunciation of these rounded vowels. Unfortunately, Unicode policy values consistency over accuracy, and it's almost impossible to change character names once they have been adopted.

$$\text{ЈᎯᏟᎾᏗᏢᏩᎩᏖᎷᎧᏞᎣ}$$
$$\text{ᏂᏗᎢᎤᏌᎣᏞᎶᏔᏞᏤᎶ}$$
$$\text{ЈᎯᏟᎾᏗᏢᏩᎩᏖᎷᎧᏞᎣ}$$
$$\text{ᏂᏗᎢᎤᏌᎣᏞᎶᏔᏞᏤᎶ}$$
$$\textbf{1234567890}$$

Fig. 21. Kearney's Deseret font.

5   Digital Fonts for the Deseret Alphabet

5.1   Non-METAFONT Fonts

Kearney's Deseret Font. A number of digital fonts have been designed for the Deseret Alphabet, most of them based on the 38-letter inventory and glyphs of the book font of 1868–69. The following is a very preliminary survey of fonts that I was able to find and test in early 2004[39].

The prize for the first digital font would seem to go to Greg Kearney, whose Deseret font was created about 1991 using Fontographer. Kearney (personal communication) says that his font, now in the public domain, was created for the LDS Church History Department, now the LDS Church Archives, as a display font for an exhibit.

I had difficulty testing this font[40] to input specific texts on my Mac OS X system, but see Figure 21 for a sample of the glyphs as displayed by the FontBook application.

Bateman's Deseret Font. Edward Bateman, a graphic designer in Salt Lake City, scanned the Russell Bros. fonts from a copy of *The Deseret Second Book*,

---

[39] The world of fonts, and especially amateur fonts, is woefully lacking in documentation. I would be extremely grateful for corrections and additions to the information in this section.

[40] http://www.fontage.com/pages/deseret.html; http://funsite24.com/fo/d/

cleaned them up electronically using Fontographer, and created his font, also called Deseret, in August 1995 [3]. The font came out of his graphics work on the delightfully tongue-in-cheek 1995 science-fiction film *Plan 10 from Outer Space*[41], with a plot that revolves around a mysterious plaque written by aliens in the Deseret Alphabet. The font (see Figure 22) is still available from Bateman[42], in both a TrueType version for Windows and a PostScript version for Macintosh[43]. He has plans (personal communication) to repackage the font on a CD-ROM for modern Mac owners who no longer have a floppy-disk drive.

An unusual feature of the Bateman font is that it contains only lowercase letters, or perhaps only uppercase – you really can't tell the difference in the Deseret Alphabet. This font is notable for reproducing the extreme contrast of thicks and thins seen in the original Russell Bros. font.

Jenkins' Zarahemla and Sidon Fonts. John Jenkins of Apple has created two fonts. The first, named Zarahemla, was created about 1995, originally using Fontographer (personal communication). Jenkins scanned the 1868–69 Russell Bros. glyphs, traced them, and cleaned them up digitally. This font is still available stand-alone and was part of Jenkins' DLK[44] (Deseret Language Kit) for typing Deseret Alphabet in Apple operating systems up to OS 9. The Zarahemla glyphs (see Figure 23) are now included in the Apple Symbols font distributed with OS X. Real Unicode Deseret Alphabet text can be typed using the Character Palette or the Unicode Hex Keyboard.

A second Jenkins font, called Sidon, was created about 1999, originally using METAFONT, with the glyphs later copied into FontLab. "The idea was to have a Deseret Alphabet font which was *not* intended to just slavishly copy what the Church did in the 1860s." Sidon is not yet available stand-alone, but the glyphs (see Figure 24) are now incorporated into the Apple Simple font used to demonstrate the Apple Font Tools[45].

Brion Zion's Beehive Font. A certain Brion Zion (perhaps a pseudonym) at some point created a font named Beehive. As far as I can tell, it is no longer available, and numerous Internet links to Zion pages are dead. A webpage[46] dedicated to Deseret Alphabet fonts is a virtual cemetery of dead links.

Kass's Code2001 Font. The freely available Code2001 font[47] by James Kass is a Plane 1 Unicode-based font, providing glyphs for the characters in the surrogate space, including Old Persian Cuneiform, Deseret, Tengwar, Cirth, Old Italic,

---

[41] http://www.cc.utah.edu/~th3597/kolob1.htm

[42] http://www.xmission.com/~capteddy/

[43] Macintosh OS X can now handle Windows TrueType fonts.

[44] http://homepage.mac.com/jenkins/Deseret/

[45] http://fonts.apple.com/

[46] http://cgm.cs.mcgill.ca/~luc/deseret.html

[47] http://home.att.net/~jameskass/code2001.htm

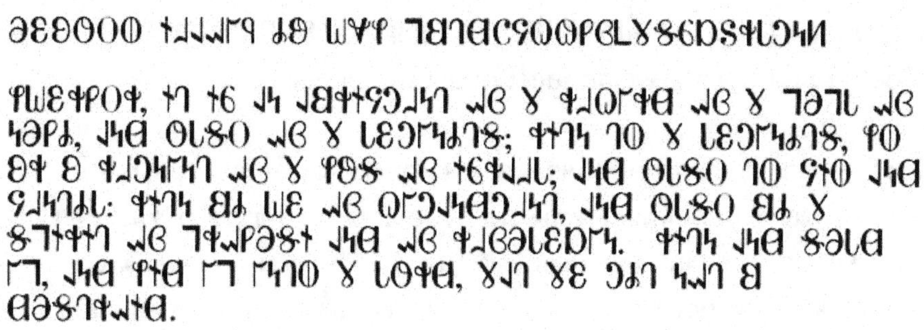

Fig. 22. Bateman's Deseret font.

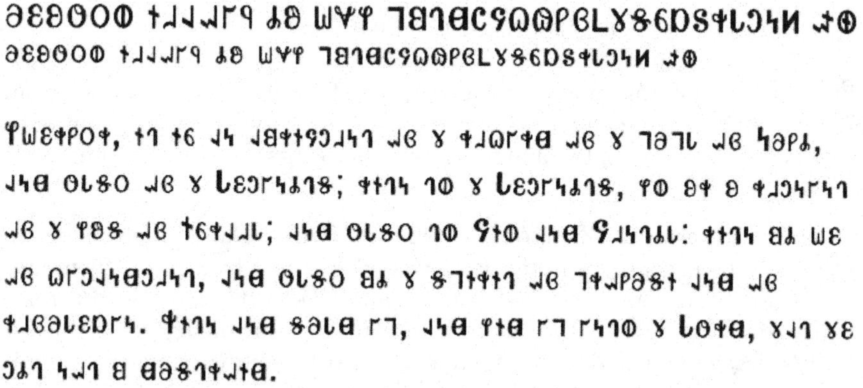

Fig. 23. Jenkins' Zarahemla font.

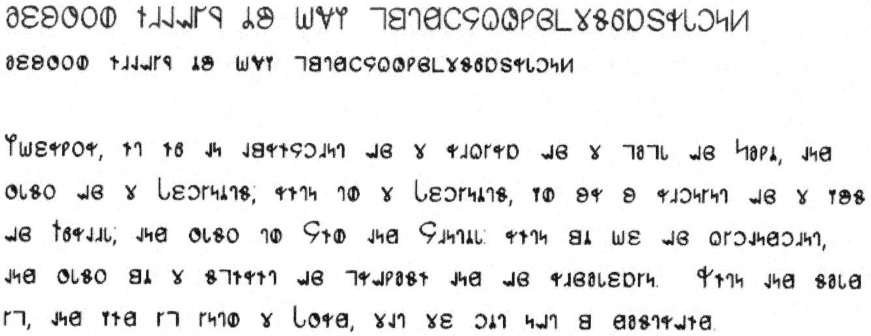

Fig. 24. Jenkins' Sidon font.

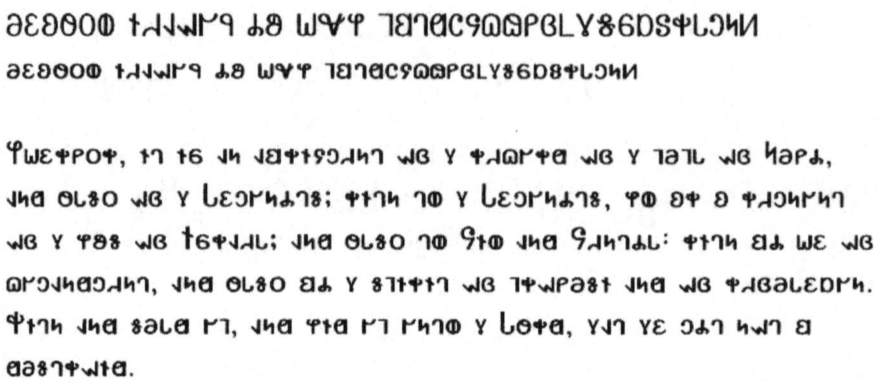

𐐔𐐯𐑅𐐲𐑉𐐯�𐻁 𝙩𐐲𐑅𐐲𐑉𐐲� 𐑊𐐲 𐐎𐐴𐐻 𝖳𐐯𐑌𐐴𐑅𐐻𐑉𐐴...

𐐔𐐯𐑅𐐲𐑉𐐯𐻏 𝙩𐐲𐑅𐐲𐑉𐐲� 𐑊𐐲 𐐎𐐴𐐻 𝖳𐐯𐑌𐐴𐑅𐐻𐑉𐐴...

(Deseret Alphabet sample text — Figure 25)

Fig. 25. Kass's Code2001 font.

Gothic, etc. Kass informs me that the glyphs (see Figure 25) were designed from scratch and resided originally in the Private Use Area of the Code2000 font until Deseret was officially accepted and assigned code points in the surrogate space.

Thibeault's Deseret and Bartok's HuneyBee Fonts. Daniel Thibeault took the Deseret Alphabet glyphs from the Code2001 font and transposed them into the ANSI range to make yet another font named Deseret[48]. Stephen Bartok's HuneyBee font[49] was created in September 2003 by rearranging the glyphs in Thibault's Deseret font to effect a different keyboard layout (personal communication). In both fonts the glyphs are ultimately from the Code2001 font, already illustrated in Figure 25.

Elzinga's Brigham Font. Dirk Elzinga of the Department of Linguistics and English Language at Brigham Young University is working on a new font called Brigham (see Figure 26), using FontForge, that is largely mono-width but judiciously uses thinner strokes for the loops.

Robertson's Fonts. Graphic designer Christian Robertson is working on two fonts, "trying to make the Deseret Alphabet look good in type" (personal communication), which is quite a challenge. In his first font, Robertson is not afraid to "take out some of the curly queues that really mucked things up", to rethink the representation of the short vowels, to add serifs, and even to introduce something like ascenders. The sample in Figure 27, kindly provided by Robertson, does not represent the latest version of his font, and the text is gibberish, but it illustrates his innovative approach. Robertson's next font will be even more challenging, designed for typesetting the early cursive manuscripts from 1854–55.

---

[48] http://www.angelfire.com/pq/Urhixidur/Fonts/Fonts.html

[49] http://home.earthlink.net/~slbartok/projects/fonts.htm

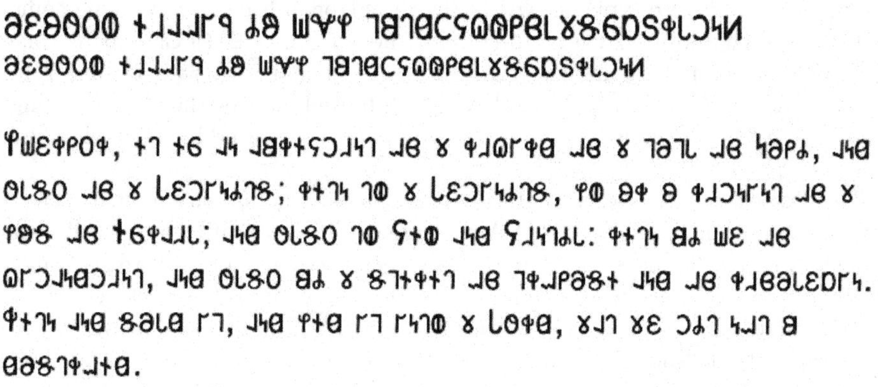

𝟃Ɛ𝟄𝟘𝟘𝟘 ⊦⌋⌋⌋⌐𝟫 ⅃𝟠 ꟿⱯꟳ ꟽ𝟠ꟼ𝟘Cꟻ𝟘𝟘ꟼ𝟠Ɫꓯ𝟪𝟞𝟞ꓷⱾꟼⱢꟷꓱ ꟽⱵCⱢꟷ𝟆꓿𝟫𝟪Ɫꓯꓱ𝟞ꓷⱾꟼⱢꟷꓱ

(Deseret Alphabet display text — top specimen)

(Deseret Alphabet body paragraph — Fig. 26 specimen)

Fig. 26. Elzinga's Brigham font.

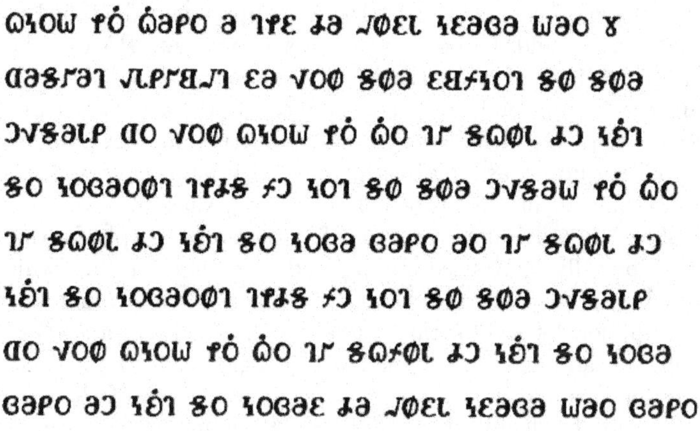

(Deseret Alphabet body text — Fig. 27 specimen)

Fig. 27. Robertson's experimental font.

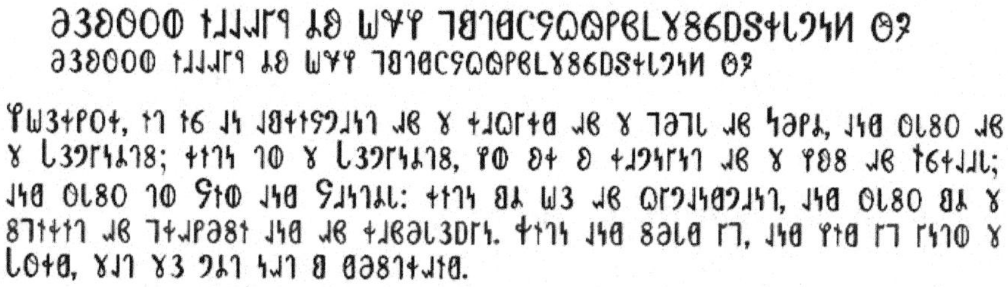

(Deseret Alphabet display and body text — Fig. 28 specimen)

Fig. 28. Beesley's desalph font.

5.2   Beesley's METAFONT desalph Font and LᴬTEX Package

My own desalph font (see Figure 28) was created with METAFONT for the specific purpose of typesetting 40-letter Deseret Alphabet manuscripts from 1859–60.

These documents were typically written with narrow nib pens, producing some thick-thin distinction, so the coding relies heavily on METAFONT penstroke commands. I took my inspiration from the pre-book charts of 1854–55, and from real handwriting. The penstrokes follow the path used to draw the glyphs, giving a hint of the original handwriting that is completely obscured in the Bodonified book font of 1868–69.

The desalph font is made available in a desalph package, which can be used in a LATEX document much like the TIPA package[50]. The input of Deseret Alphabet characters can be done somewhat clumsily using commands like \dalclongi (Deseret Alphabet lowercase long i) for 𐐇 or \dauclongi (Deseret Alphabet uppercase long i) for 𐐀. Inside \textda{} commands, a more convenient system of transliteration "shortcuts" can be used. As I was already somewhat comfortable with the shortcuts of the TIPA package, for entering IPA letters, I laid out the desalph font internally so that the same shortcuts could be used wherever possible. Simple commands were defined to enter diphthongs and affricates, which have no shortcuts in TIPA. A simply defined \ipa{} command allows the same commands to be used to enter equivalent IPA diphthongs and affricates. The principal entry commands are summarized in Table 2, and some extra commands for unusual and idiosyncratic glyphs are shown in Table 3. Uppercase letters, found in Deseret Alphabet but not in IPA, can be entered with corresponding uppercase "uc" commands with names like \dauclongi, or by placing the shortcut in the \uc{} command, e.g. \uc{i}.

The use of METAFONT allowed me to define the proper glyphs for the 1859–60 manuscripts, especially the ⊖ used for /ɔʲ/ and the ꝗ used for /ʲu/, which I have never seen in a printed chart or document[51]. When I found a manuscript with the experimental new letter I for the neutral vowel called schwa (/ə/), making a 41-letter alphabet, adding it to my METAFONT font was a simple exercise.

The skeleton example in Figure 29 illustrates the use of the desalph and tipa packages, and the definition of the \ipa{} command. This file yields the following output:

A sample of Deseret Alphabet entered using shortcuts:

𐐀 𐐁 𐐂 𐐃 𐐄 𐐅 𐐆 𐐇 𐐈 𐐉 𐐊 𐐋 𐐌 𐐍 𐐎 𐐏 𐐐 𐐑 𐐒 𐐓 𐐔 𐐕 𐐖 𐐗 𐐘 𐐙 𐐚 𐐛 𐐜 𐐝 𐐞 𐐟 𐐠 𐐡 𐐢 𐐣 𐐤

Parallel phonemic IPA entered using the same shortcuts:
i e ɑ ɔ o u i ɛ æ ɒ ʌ ʊ aʲ ɔʲ aʷ ʲu w j h p b t d ʧ ʤ k g f v θ ð s z ʃ ʒ r l m n ŋ

6   Current and Future Projects

6.1   The Deseret Alphabet and Native American Languages

Although the Deseret Alphabet was intended for writing English, there was some hope and expectation that it could be used to transcribe other languages, that it

---

[50] http://tooyoo.l.u-tokyo.ac.jp/~fkr/

[51] An ⊖ punch appears in the set of St. Louis punches of 1857, but it was not used when printing finally started in 1859.

Table 2. Commands from the desalph package to insert 1859–60 Deseret Alphabet glyphs into running text, and shortcuts that can be used in desalph environments. The single-letter shortcuts are parallel to the input transliteration for the TIPA package. The commands defined for diphthongs and affricates can also be used inside \ipa{} commands, allowing the same entry method to be used for both the Deseret Alphabet and equivalent phonemic IPA.

Deseret	Command	Shortcut	IPA
∂	\dalclongi	i	i
3	\dalclonge	e	e
8	\dalclonga	A	ɑ
ϴ	\dalclongaw	O	ɔ
0	\dalclongo	o	o
◍	\dalclongu	u	u
↑	\dalcshorti	I	ɪ
↲	\dalcshorte	E	ɛ
↓	\dalcshorta	\ae	æ
↲	\dalcshortaw	6	ɒ
Γ	\dalcshorto	2	ʌ
۹	\dalcshortu	U	ʊ
↓	\dalcay	\aI or \aJ	aʲ
ϴ	\dalcoi	\OI or \OJ	ɔʲ
8	\dalcow	\aU or \aW	aʷ
ʔ	\dalcyu	\ju or \Ju	ʲu
ɯ	\dalcwu	w	w
Y	\dalcye	j	j
Ƴ	\dalch	h	h
٦	\dalcpee	p	p
ठ	\dalcbee	b	b
٦	\dalctee	t	t
ठ	\dalcdee	d	d
ɾ	\dalcchee	\tS	t͡ʃ
ϛ	\dalcjee	\dZ	d͡ʒ
ϙ	\dalckay	k	k
ϙ	\dalcgay	g	ɡ
ρ	\dalcef	f	f
ϵ	\dalcvee	v	v
ʟ	\dalceth	T	θ
Ɣ	\dalcthee	D	ð
8	\dalces	s	s
ϛ	\dalczee	z	z
ᴅ	\dalcesh	S	ʃ
ϟ	\dalczhee	Z	ʒ
ɬ	\dalcer	r	r
ɭ	\dalcel	l	l
ϡ	\dalcem	m	m
ɥ	\dalcen	n	n
и	\dalceng	N	ŋ

Table 3. Extra commands used to enter rare and idiosyncratic Deseret Alphabet glyphs.

𐐀	\daucslju	St. Louis 1857 font, unused glyph for /ʲu/
𐐀	\dauchaskoi	Haskell's idiosyncratic glyph for /ɔʲ/
ǀ	\daucschwa	Shelton's proposed glyph for schwa /ə/
ꝫ	\daucspellerow	Deseret Phonetic Speller glyph for /aʷ/

```
\documentclass[]{article}
\usepackage{times}
\usepackage{desalph}
\usepackage{tipa}
% commands used in \ipa{}, parallel to commands in \textda{}, to get
% an equivalent phonemic IPA transliteration of Deseret Alphabet
\newcommand{\ipa}[1]{{\tipaencoding%
\providecommand{\aI}{}\renewcommand{\aI}{a\textsuperscript{j}\xspace}%
\providecommand{\aJ}{}\renewcommand{\aJ}{a\textsuperscript{j}\xspace}%
\providecommand{\OI}{}\renewcommand{\OI}{O\textsuperscript{j}\xspace}%
\providecommand{\OJ}{}\renewcommand{\OJ}{O\textsuperscript{j}\xspace}%
\providecommand{\aU}{}\renewcommand{\aU}{a\textsuperscript{w}\xspace}%
\providecommand{\aW}{}\renewcommand{\aW}{a\textsuperscript{w}\xspace}%
\providecommand{\ju}{}\renewcommand{\ju}{\textsuperscript{j}u\xspace}%
\providecommand{\Ju}{}\renewcommand{\Ju}{\textsuperscript{j}u\xspace}%
\providecommand{\dZ}{}\renewcommand{\dZ}{\textdyoghlig\xspace}%
\providecommand{\tS}{}\renewcommand{\tS}{\textteshlig\xspace}#1}}

\begin{document}
\begin{center}
A sample of Deseret Alphabet entered using shortcuts:\\
\textda{i e A O o u I E \ae{} 6 2 U \aI{} \OI{} \aU{} \ju{}
w j h p b t d \tS{} \dZ{} k g f v T D s z S Z r l m n N}
\smallskip
Parallel phonemic IPA entered using the same shortcuts:\\
\ipa{i e A O o u I E \ae{} 6 2 U \aI{} \OI{} \aU{} \ju{}
w j h p b t d \tS{} \dZ{} k g f v T D s z S Z r l m n N}
\end{center}
\end{document}
```

Fig. 29. A skeleton LATEX example using the TIPA and desalph packages.

could serve as a kind of international phonetic alphabet[52]. The Deseret Alphabet reform coincided with a period of intense Mormon interest in Native Americans, and there is growing evidence that missionaries tried to use the Alphabet in the field. For example, Isaac Bullock wrote a Shoshone vocabulary that includes

---

[52] Parley P. Pratt to Orson Pratt, 30 January 1854, Orson Pratt Incoming Correspondence, LDS Church Archives. Journal History, 4 June 1859.

Deseret Alphabet pronunciations for at least some of the Shoshone words[53]. In 1859, Marion J. Shelton tried to teach the Deseret Alphabet to the Paiutes in the area of Santa Clara, Utah, and there are hints that missionaries may have tried to introduce Deseret-Alphabet-based literacy to the Navajo, the Zuñi, the Creeks, and other tribes. Much research remains to be done in this area.

6.2   The Second Mormon Mission to the Hopi: 1859–60

In the last couple of years, it has become clear that there was a serious attempt to introduce Deseret-Alphabet-based literacy to the Hopi. In 1859, President Brigham Young personally chose Marion J. Shelton, instructed him to go to Hopi-land, stay a year, learn the language and try to "reduce their dialect to a written language" using the Deseret Alphabet[54]. This was the second of fifteen early missions to the Hopi [23, 13, 14]. In December of 2002 I discovered an uncatalogued and unidentified "Indian Vocabulary" in the LDS Church Archives, and I was able to identify it as English-to-Hopi. I have argued [8] that it was written by Marion J. Shelton during this mission, and it appears to be the oldest written evidence of the Hopi language.

The entire vocabulary has now been typed into an XML format, with fields added for modern English and Hopi orthography, modern dictionary definitions, and comments and references of various kinds. The XML file is downtranslated using a Perl-language script, with the helpful Perl XML::Twig package[55], to produce LaTeX source code with Deseret Alphabet output, using the desalph package and font, and equivalent phonemic IPA output, using the TIPA package. The use of XML, the desalph font, TIPA and LaTeX allows me and my co-author Dirk Elzinga to reproduce this extraordinary document for study and publication. Creating and maintaining the original data in an XML format gives us all the advantages of XML validation and abstraction; and the flexibility of downtranslation to LaTeX allows us to format the output in different ways suitable for proofreading or for final publication.

The English-Hopi Vocabulary (see Figure 30) is written entirely in the Deseret Alphabet and includes 486 entries like the following

$$\text{𐐿𐐷𐐮𐐻𐐲𐑌}\qquad\text{𐐸𐐬𐐶𐐮}$$

with an English word on the left and a Hopi word in Third Mesa (Orayvi) dialect on the right. Encoded as XML, and with auxiliary information added, this entry appears as shown in Figure 31. The XML file is validated using a Relax NG schema. Downtranslation of the XML entry currently yields the LaTeX output in Figure 32, which is a line in a table. When typeset, the entry appears as shown in Table 4. This open tabular format is ideal for proofreading, and for the final paper all that will be required is a modified Perl script to downtranslate the same XML file into other LaTeX codes that waste less space.

---

[53] Glossary of Isaac Bullock, University of Utah Library, Special Collections.

[54] Brigham Young to Jacob Hamblin, 18 September 1859, Brigham Young Outgoing Correspondence, LDS Church Archives.

[55] http://www.xmltwig.com/xmltwig/

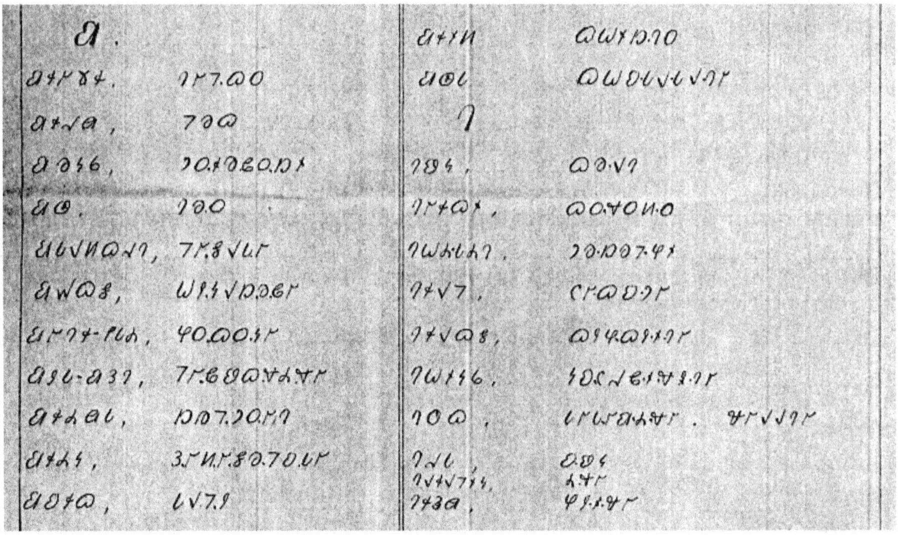

Fig. 30. A selection from the English-to-Hopi vocabulary showing parts of the entries for words starting with /b/ and /t/ in English. The entry for *bread*, /brɛd/=/pik/ (ɑ+Ↄ=ꞁɑꞠ), is the second from the top on the left; the Hopi word is now written *piiki*. The entry for *boy*, /bɔʲ/=/ti.o/ (ɑꞠ=ꞁɑ.Ꞡ), is the fourth from the top; the word is now written *tiyo*. LDS Church Archives.

```
<entry>
  <left>r\ae{}bIt-stIk</left>
  <eng>rabbit stick</eng>
  <right>pe\tS{}.ko.ho</right>
  <hd pages="449">puts$|$koho 'rabbit stick, a flat
boomerang-like stick used for hunting; used for throwing
and hitting it on the run'</hd>
  <mk></mk>
</entry>
```

Fig. 31. An XML entry for the Hopi vocabulary.

```
340 & \raggedright \index{rabbit stick, 340} rabbit stick \\
 \textda{r\ae{}bIt-stIk} \\
 \ipa{r\ae{}bIt-stIk} & \raggedright \ipa{pe\tS{}.ko.ho} \\
 \textda{pe\tS{}.ko.ho} & HD p.\@ 449: puts$|$koho
'rabbit stick, a flat boomerang-like stick
used for hunting; used for throwing and hitting
it on the run'\\
```

Fig. 32. LᴬTᴇX output from downloading an XML entry.

Table 4. Entry of the English-Hopi vocabulary typeset for proofreading.

340	rabbit stick	petʃ.ko.ho	HD p. 449: puts|koho 'rabbit stick, a flat boomerang-like stick used for hunting; used for throwing and hitting it on the run'

I have also transcribed the journal of Thales H. Haskell, kept in the Deseret Alphabet from October through December of 1859, and will include it in a general history of the second mission to the Hopi [7]. Here, for reading practice, is an extract from his journal in the original Deseret Alphabet and in equivalent phonemic IPA. Haskell idiosyncratically uses the 𐐦 glyph for the /ɔʲ/ diphthong instead of the 𐐯 glyph used by most other writers in 1859.

𐑜𐐯𐑌𐐻 𐐼𐐫𐑌 𐐻𐐭 𐑋𐐪 𐐶𐐳𐑊𐑁 𐐻𐑉𐐰𐐹 𐐺𐐲𐐻 𐑌𐐬 𐐶𐐳𐑊𐑝𐑆 𐐸𐐰𐐼 𐐺𐐯𐑌 𐐻𐐭 𐐮𐐻 𐐿𐐯𐑋 𐐸𐐬𐑋 𐐰𐑌𐐼 𐑁𐐪𐑌 𐐺𐑉 𐑇𐐯𐑊𐐻𐑌 𐐹𐑉𐐮𐐹𐐰𐑉𐐮𐑍 𐐯 𐐿𐑉𐐮𐑅𐐻𐑋𐐪𐑅 𐑁𐐮𐑅𐐻 𐑀𐐫𐐻 𐐮𐐻 𐑉𐐯𐐼𐐮 𐐰𐑌𐐼 𐐮𐑌𐑝𐐪𐐻𐐮𐐼 .3. 𐐬𐑝 𐑄 𐐸𐐯𐐼 𐑋𐐯𐑌 𐐬𐑝 𐑄 𐑝𐐮𐑊𐐮𐐾 𐐻𐐭 𐐮𐐻 𐐶𐐮𐑄 𐐰𐑅 𐐸𐐰𐐼 𐐺𐐫𐑊𐐼 𐑋𐐲𐐻𐑌 𐑅𐐻𐐷𐐭𐐼 𐐹𐐮𐐻𐑁𐐮𐑆 𐑅𐐷𐐳𐑉𐐻 𐐼𐐲𐑋𐐹𐑊𐐮𐑌𐑆 𐑁𐑉𐐪𐐷𐐼𐐿𐐯𐐿𐑅 𐐹𐐰𐑌𐐿𐐯𐐿𐑅 𐐰𐑌𐐼 𐐹𐐮𐐿 𐐰𐑁𐐻𐑉 𐐼𐐮𐑌𐑉 𐐶𐐮 𐑅𐑋𐐬𐐿𐐻 𐑅𐐪𐑍 𐐯 𐐸𐐮𐑋 𐐰𐑌𐐼 𐐸𐐰𐐼 𐑅𐐰𐑋 𐐿𐐲𐑌𐑝𐑉𐑅𐐯𐑁𐐲𐑌 𐐶𐐮𐑄 𐐪𐑉 𐐮𐑌𐐼𐐮𐐲𐑌 𐑁𐑉𐐯𐑌𐐼𐑆 𐑄 𐐩𐐹𐐮𐑉𐐼 𐐻𐐭 𐐯𐑌𐐾𐐫 𐑄𐐯𐑋𐑅𐐯𐑊𐑝𐑆 𐑝𐐯𐑉𐐮 𐑋𐐲𐐻𐑇

wɛnt daʷn tu maʲ wʊlf træp bʌt no wʊlvz hæd bɛn tʊ ɪt kɛm hom ænd faʷn br ʃɛltn pripærɪŋ e krɪstmʌs fɪst gɒt ɪt rɛdɪ ænd ɪnvaʲtɪd .3. ɔv ð hɛd mɛn ɔv ð vɪlɪʤ tu ɪt wɪð ʌs hæd bɔʲld mʌtn stʲud pɪtʃɪz sʲuɪt dʌmplɪnz fraʲdkɛks pænkɛks ænd pik æftr dɪnr wi smokt sʌŋ e hɪm ænd hæd sʌm kɒnvrsɛʃʌn wɪð aʷr ɪndɪʌn frɛndz ðe æpɪrd tu ɛnʤɔʲ ðɛmsɛlvz vɛrɪ mʌtʃ.

6.3   Other Possible Deseret Alphabet Typesetting Projects

Around 1985 the original Deseret Alphabet *Book of Mormon* was scanned and OCRed under the direction of Prof. John Robertson of the Brigham Young University Linguistics department, and the text was proofread by Kristen McKendry[56]. The surviving files from this project are not well organized, and may not be complete, but it appears that the Deseret Alphabet *Book of Mormon* could now be reproduced without too much difficulty. As the original *Book of Mormon* had a print run of only 500 copies, and as a copy today can fetch upwards of $7000 or $8000, there has always been some interest in retypesetting it.

The Deseret First Book and *The Deseret Second Book* had print runs of 10,000 copies each, are therefore much more plentiful, and copies today go for around $200. *The Deseret First Book* has even been reprinted photographically for sale to tourists as a Utah curiosity [26], and the text has been keyed in by John Jenkins, and proofread by Michael Everson and by myself. Such projects are of interest to linguists who want to search the texts electronically.

In 1967, LDS Church archivists found a bundle of forgotten Deseret Alphabet manuscripts, some of them ready for the typesetter but never printed [32]. These

---

[56] This project, circa 1985–86, used a Kurzweil scanner, which was trained to recognize Deseret text. However, McKendry reports (personal communication) that the raw output of the OCR was so poor and the proofreading so onerous that it might have been easier just to type in the text manually.

include *The Doctrine and Covenants*, with the *Lectures on Faith*; the *Catechism* of John Jaques; and the entire text of the *Bible*. The LDS Church Archives also hold the *History of Brigham Young*, a number of letters, an unfinished *Deseret Phonetic Speller*, journals, letters and probably a number of other documents still to be found.

7 Conclusion

Although the Deseret Alphabet was never intended for secrecy [6], few people then or now can be persuaded to learn it, and a number of interesting documents have been ignored and unstudied for over 140 years. The letters and journals are of interest to historians, and the phonemically written texts are also of interest to linguists. With the help of XML, LATEX, TIPA and new digital fonts for the Deseret Alphabet, these neglected documents are coming to light again.

References

1. Douglas D. Alder, Paula J. Goodfellow, and Ronald G. Watt. Creating a new alphabet for Zion: The origin of the Deseret Alphabet. *Utah Historical Quarterly*, pages 275–286, 1984.

2. Alfred Baker. *The Life of Sir Isaac Pitman: Inventor of Phonography*. Isaac Pitman and Sons, New York, 1908.

3. Edward Bateman. A brief history of the Deseret Alphabet. *Emigre*, (52):72–77, 1999. Fall.

4. Kenneth R. Beesley. The Deseret Alphabet: Can orthographical reform for English succeed? 1975.

5. Kenneth R. Beesley. Dialect determinants in the Deseret Alphabet journal of Thales H. Haskell. *Deseret Language and Linguistic Society Bulletin*, (3):2–35, 1977.

6. Kenneth R. Beesley. The Deseret Alphabet in Unicode. In *Proceedings of the 22nd International Unicode Conference*, volume 2, San Jose, California, September 11–13 2002. Unicode Consortium. Paper C10.

7. Kenneth R. Beesley. The second Mormon mission to the Hopi: 1859–60. Forthcoming, 2004.

8. Kenneth R. Beesley and Dirk Elzinga. An 1860 English-to-Hopi vocabulary written in the Deseret Alphabet. Forthcoming, 2004.

9. Juanita Brooks. Journal of Thales H. Haskell. *Utah Historical Quarterly*, pages 69–98, 1944.

10. Bernard Desgraupes. *METAFONT: Guide pratique*. Vuibert, Paris, 1999.

11. Leah R. Frisby and Hector Lee. The Deseret readers. *Utah Humanities Review*, 1:240–244, 1947.

12. IPA. *Handbook of the International Phonetic Association: A Guide to the Use of the International Phonetic Alphabet*. Cambridge University Press, Cambridge, 1999.

13. Harry C. James. *The Hopi Indians: Their history and their culture*. Caxton, Caldwell, ID, 1956.

14. Harry C. James. *Pages from Hopi History*. The University of Arizona Press, Tucson, AZ, 1974.

15. J. Kelly. The 1847 Alphabet: An episode of phonotypy. In R. E. Asher and Eugénie J. A. Henderson, editors, *Towards a History of Phonetics*, pages 248–264. Edinburgh University Press, Edinburgh, 1981.

16. Donald E. Knuth. *The METAFONTbook*. Addison-Wesley, New York, 1986.

17. Peter Ladefoged. *A Course in Phonetics*. Harcourt College Publishers, Orlando, FL, fourth edition, 2001.

18. P. A. D. MacCarthy. The Bernard Shaw alphabet. In Werner Haas, editor, *Alphabets for English*, pages 105–117. Manchester University Press, Manchester, 1969.

19. Samuel C. Monson. The Deseret Alphabet. Master's thesis, Columbia University, 1947.

20. Samuel C. Monson. The Deseret Alphabet. In *Utah Academy of Sciences, Arts & Letters*, volume 30, pages 1952–53, 1953.

21. William V. Nash. The Deseret Alphabet. Master's thesis, University of Illinois Library School, Urbana, Illinois, May 1957.

22. Douglas Allen New. *History of the Deseret Alphabet and other attempts to reform English Orthography*. PhD thesis, Utah State University, 1985.

23. Charles S. Peterson. The Hopis and the Mormons: 1858-1873. *Utah Historical Quarterly*, 39(2):179–194, Spring 1971.

24. Benn Pitman. *Sir Isaac Pitman: His Life and Labors*. C. J. Krehbiel, Cincinnati, 1902.

25. Thomas Allen Reed. *A Biography of Isaac Pitman: Inventor of Phonography*. Griffith, Farran, Okeden and Welsh, London, 1890.

26. Regents of the Deseret University. *Deseret Alphabet: The Deseret First Book*. Buffalo River Press, Salt Lake City, historical reprint edition, 1996.

27. Jules Rémy and Julius Brenchley. *A Journey to Great-Salt-Lake City*. W. Jeffs, London, 1861.

28. Bernard Shaw. *Androcles and the Lion*. Penguin, Harmondsworth, Middlesex, Shaw Alphabet edition, 1962.

29. Albert E. Smith. Thales Hastings Haskell: Pioneer, scout, explorer, Indian missionary. Typescript, Brigham Young University Library, 1964.

30. Hosea Stout. *Journal of Hosea Stout*. University of Utah Press, Salt Lake City, 1964.

31. Roby Wentz. *Thirty-Eight Mormon Characters: A Forgotten Chapter in Western Typographic History: For the Zamorano Club Jubilee*. Zamorano Club, Los Angeles, 1978.

32. Albert L. Zobell. Deseret Alphabet manuscripts found. *Improvement Era*, pages 10–11, July 1967.

FEATPOST and a Review
of 3D METAPOST Packages

Luis Nobre Gonçalves

CFMC-UL, Av. Prof. Gama Pinto 2
1649-003 Lisboa
Portugal
nobre@lince.cii.fc.ul.pt
http://matagalatlante.org

Abstract. METAPOST is able to produce figures that look almost like ray-traced raster images but that remain vector-based. A small review of three-dimensional perspective implementations with METAPOST is presented. Special emphasis is given to the abilities of the author's implementation: FEATPOST.

1   Introduction

There are at least four METAPOST packages related to three-dimensional diagrams:

- GNU 3DLDF:
  http://www.gnu.org/directory/graphics/3D/3DLDF.html
- 3d/3dgeom:
  http://tug.org/tex-archive/graphics/metapost/macros/3d/
- m3D:
  http://www-math.univ-poitiers.fr/~phan/m3Dplain.html
- FEATPOST:
  http://matagalatlante.org/nobre/featpost/doc/featexamples.html

All of these packages are individual and independent works "under construction". There has been neither collaboration nor competition among the authors. Each produces different kinds of diagrams and each uses a different graphic pipeline. The following sections of this document describe these packages, in a mainly independent way.

2   GNU 3DLDF

3DLDF is not a pure METAPOST package, as it is written in C++ using CWEB. Diagrams are also coded in C++ and are compiled together with the package. Nevertheless, this is, of all four, the package with the greatest promise for a future three-dimensional-capable METAPOST.

A. Syropoulos et al. (Eds.): TUG 2004, LNCS 3130, pp. 112–124, 2004.

1. It outputs METAPOST.
2. Its syntax is similar to METAPOST.
3. It overcomes the arithmetic limitations inherent in METAPOST.
4. Both the affine transformations and the graphics pipeline are implemented through 4×4 matrices.
5. Its author, Laurence D. Finston, is actively improving and maintaining the package. His plan includes, among many other ideas, the development of an input routine (to allow interactive use) and the implementation of three-dimensional paths via NURBS.

Given the possible computational efficiency of this approach, one can foresee a system that merges the METAPOST language with the capabilities of standard ray-tracing software.

3   3d/3dgeom

This was the first documented extension of METAPOST into the third dimension – and also into the fourth dimension (time). Denis B. Roegel created, back in 1997, the 3d package to produce animations of polyhedra. In 2003 he added the 3dgeom "module" which is focused on space geometry. It remains the least computationally intensive package of those presented here.

1. Each component of a point or a vector is stored in a different numeric array. This eases control of a stack of points. Points are used to define planar polygons (faces of polyhedra) and the polygons are used to define *convex* polyhedra.
2. When defining a polygon, a sequence of points must be provided such that advancing on the sequence is the same as rotating clockwise on the polygon, when the polygon is visible. This means that, when a polyhedron is to be drawn, the selection of polygons to be drawn is very easy: only those whose points rotate clockwise (the visible ones). Hidden line removal is thus achieved without sorting the polygons.
3. Points can also be used to define other points according to rules that are common in the geometry of polyhedra or according to operations involving straight lines and/or planes and/or angles.
4. The author plans to release an updated version with the ability to graph parametric lines and surfaces.

4   m3D

Anthony Phan developed this very interesting package but has not yet written its documentation. Certainly, this is, of all four, the package that can produce the most complex and beautiful diagrams. It achieves this using, almost exclusively, four-sided polygons.

Fig. 1. A diagram produced by m3D showing a single object, composed of spheres and cylindrical connections, under a spherical perspective.

Fig. 2. A diagram produced by m3D showing a revolution surface under a central perspective.

1. Complex objects can be defined and composed (see Figure 1). For example, one of its many predefined objects is the fractal known as the "Menger Sponge".
2. It can render revolution surfaces defined from a standard METAPOST path (see Figure 2).
3. Objects or groups of polygons can be sorted and drawn as if reflecting light from a punctual source and/or disappearing in a foggy environment.

5   FEATPOST

Geared towards the production of physics diagrams, FEATPOST sacrifices programming style and computational efficiency for a large feature set.

1. Besides the usual parallel and central perspectives it can make a sort of "spherical distortion" as if a diagram is observed through a fish-eye lens[1]. This kind of perspective is advantageous for animations as it allows the point of view to be inside or among the diagram objects. When using the central

---

[1] Also possible with m3D.

perspective, points that are as distant from the projection plane as the point of view get projected at infinity, and METAPOST overflows and crashes. The spherical projection is always finite.

2. It can mark and measure angles in space.
3. It can produce shadows of some objects (see Figure 9). Shadows are calculated in much the same way as perspectives. The perspective projection, from 3D into 2D, is a calculation of the intersection of a straight line and a plane. A shadow is also a projection from 3D into 2D, only the line and the plane are different. The shadow must be projected onto the paper page before the object that creates the shadow. Shadows are drawn after two projections, objects are drawn after one projection and after their shadows.
4. It can correctly draw intersecting polygons (see Figure 12).
5. It knows how to perform hidden line removal on some curved surface objects. Imagine a solid cylinder. Now consider the part of the cylinder's base that is the farthest away. You only see a part of its edge. In order to draw that part, it is necessary to know the two points at which the edge becomes hidden. FEATPOST calculates this. Note that the edge is a circle, a curved line. FEATPOST does not use polygons to hide lines on some curved surface objects.
6. Supported objects include: dots, vectors, angles, ropes, circles, ellipses, cones, cylinders, globes, other curved surface objects, polygons, cuboids, polyhedra, functional and parametric surface plots, direction fields, field lines and trajectories in conservative force fields.

Many of the drawable objects are not made of polygons, but rather of two-dimensional paths. FEATPOST does not attempt to draw surfaces of these objects, only their edges. This is partly because of the use of intrinsic METAPOST functions and partly because it eases the production of diagrams that combine space and planar (on paper) objects.

One of the intrinsic METAPOST functions that became fundamental for FEATPOST is the composition `makepath makepen`. As this converts a `path` into its convex form, it very much simplifies the determination of some edges.

Another important aspect of the problem is hidden line removal. Hidden line removal of a group of polygons can, in some cases, be performed by drawing the polygons by decreasing order of distance to the point of view. FEATPOST generally uses the Shell sorting method, although when the polygons are just the faces of one cuboid FEATPOST has a small specific trick. There is also a specific method for hidden line removal on cylinders and another for other curved surface objects.

5.1 Examples

Some of the FEATPOST macros are presented here. Detailed information is available at

- http://matagalatlante.org/nobre/featpost/doc/macroMan.html
- CTAN:/graphics/metapost/macros/featpost/

Each perspective depends on the point of view. FEATPOST uses the global variable f, of type color, to store the (X, Y, Z) coordinates of the point of view. Also important is the aim of view (global variable viewcenter). Both together define the line of view.

The perspective consists of a projection from space coordinates into planar (u, v) coordinates on the projection plane. FEATPOST uses a projection plane that is perpendicular to the line of view and contains the viewcenter. Furthermore, one of the projection plane axes is horizontal and the other is on the intersection of a vertical plane with the projection plane. "Horizontal" means parallel to the XY plane.

One consequence of this setup is that f and viewcenter must not be on the same vertical line (as long as the author avoids solving this problem, at least!). The three kinds of projection known to FEATPOST are schematized in Figures 3, 4 and 5. The macro that actually does the projection is, in all cases, rp.

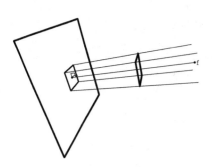
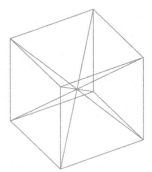

Fig. 3. Parallel projection.

Physics problems often require defining angles, and diagrams are needed to visualize their meanings. The angline and squareangline macros (see Figure 6 and the code below) support this.

```
f := (5,3.5,1);
beginfig(2);
  cartaxes(1,1,1);
  color va, vb, vc, vd;
  va = (0.29,0.7,1.0);
  vb = (X(va),Y(va),0);
  vc = N((-Y(va),X(va),0));
  vd = (0,Y(vc),0);
  drawarrow rp(black)--rp(va);
  draw rp(black)--rp(vb)--
                  rp(va) dashed evenly;
  draw rp(vc)--rp(vd) dashed evenly;
  drawarrow rp(black)--rp(vc);
```

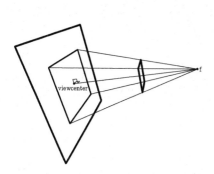

Fig. 4. Central projection.

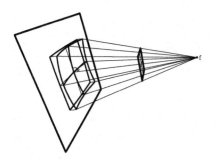

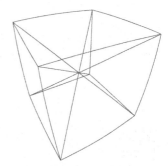

Fig. 5. Spherical projection. The spherical projection is the composition of two operations: (i) there is a projection onto a sphere and (ii) the sphere is placed onto the projection plane.

```
    squareangline( va, vc, black, 0.15 );
    angline(va,red,black,0.75,
            decimal getangle(va,red),lft);
endfig;
```

Visualizing parametric lines is another need of physicists. When two lines cross, one should be able to see which line is in front of the other. The macro emptyline can help here (see Figure 7 and the code below).

```
f := (2,4,1.8);
def theline( expr TheVal ) =
  begingroup
    numeric cred, cgre, cblu, param;
    param = TheVal*(6*360);
    cred = -0.3*cosd( param );
    cblu = 0.3*sind( param );
    cgre = param/850;
    ( (cred,cgre,cblu) )
```

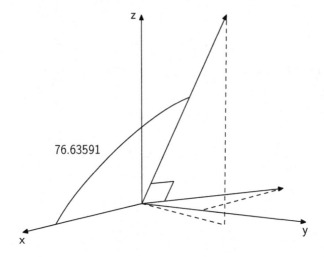

Fig. 6. FEATPOST diagram using `angline`.

```
    endgroup
  enddef;
  beginfig(1);
    numeric axsize, zaxpos, zaxlen;
    color xbeg, xend, ybeg,
                       yend, zbeg, zend;
    axsize = 0.85;
    zaxpos = 0.55;
    zaxlen = 2.1;
    pickup pencircle scaled 1.5pt;
    xbeg = (axsize,0,0);
    xend = (-axsize,0,0);
    ybeg = (0,0,-axsize);
    yend = (0,0,axsize);
    zbeg = (zaxpos,-zaxpos,0);
    zend = (zaxpos,zaxlen,0);
    drawarrow rp( xbeg )--rp( xend );
    drawarrow rp( ybeg )--rp( yend );
    defaultscale := 1.95;
    label.rt( "A", rp( xend ) );
    label.lft( "B", rp( yend ) );
    emptyline(false,1,black,
        0.5black,1000,0.82,2,theline);
    drawarrow rp( zbeg )--rp( zend );
    label.bot( "C", rp( zend ) );
  endfig;
```

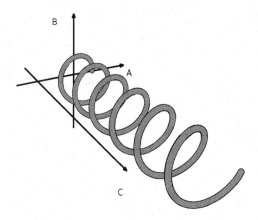

Fig. 7. FEATPOST diagram using `emptyline`.

Cuboids and labels are always needed. The `kindofcube` and `labelinspace` macros fulfill this need (see Figure 8 and the code below). The `labelinspace` macro does not project labels from 3D into 2D. It only `Transforms` the label in the same way as its bounding box, that is, the same way as two perpendicular sides of its bounding box. This is only exact for parallel perspectives.

```
f := (2,1,0.5);
ParallelProj := true;
verbatimtex
\documentclass{article}
\usepackage{beton,concmath,ccfonts}
\begin{document}
etex
beginfig(1);
  kindofcube(false,true,(0,-0.5,0),
             90,0,0,1.2,0.1,0.4);
  kindofcube(false,true,(0,0,0),
             0,0,0,0.5,0.1,0.8);
  labelinspace(false,(0.45,0.1,0.65),
             (-0.4,0,0),(0,0,0.1),
          btex
            \framebox{\textsc{Label}}
          etex);
endfig;
verbatimtex \end{document} etex
```

Some curved surface solid objects can be drawn with FEATPOST. Among them are cones (`verygoodcone`), cylinders (`rigorousdisc`) and globes (`trop-icalglobe`). These can also cast their shadows on a horizontal plane (see Figure 9 and the code below). The production of shadows involves the global variables `LightSource`, `ShadowOn` and `HoriZon`.

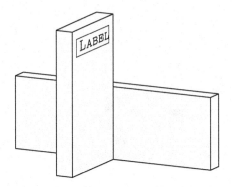

Fig. 8. FEATPOST diagram using the macros `kindofcube` and `labelinspace`.

```
f := (13,6,4.5);    ShadowOn := true;
LightSource := 10*(4,-3,6);
beginfig(3);
  numeric reflen, frac, coordg;
  numeric fws, NumLines;
  path ella, ellb;
  color axe, cubevertex, conecenter,
     conevertex, allellaxe, ellaaxe,
                         pca, pcb;
  frac := 0.5;           wang := 60;
  axe := (0,cosd(90-wang),
          sind(90-wang));
  fws := 4;       reflen := 0.35*fws;
  coordg := frac*fws;
  NumLines := 45;
  HoriZon := -0.5*fws;
  setthestage(0.5*NumLines,3.3*fws);
  cubevertex = (0.3*fws,-0.5*fws,0);
  tropicalglobe( 7, cubevertex,
                    0.5*fws, axe );
  allellaxe:=reflen*(0.707,0.707,0);
  ellaaxe:= reflen*( 0.5, -0.5, 0 );
  pcb := ( -coordg, coordg, 0 );
  rigorousdisc( 0, true, pcb,
              0.5*fws, -ellaaxe );
  conecenter =
      ( coordg, coordg, -0.5*fws );
  conevertex = conecenter +
                ( 0, 0, 0.9*fws );
  verygoodcone(false,conecenter,
           blue,reflen,conevertex);
endfig;
```

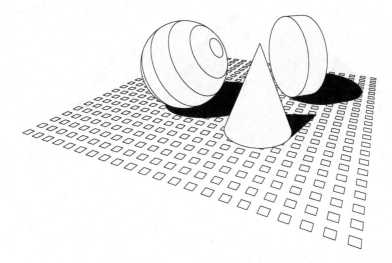

Fig. 9. FEATPOST diagram using the macros `rigorousdisc`, `verygoodcone`, `tropicalglobe` and `setthestage`.

Another very common need is the plotting of functions, usually satisfied by software such as Gnuplot (`http://www.gnuplot.info/`). Nevertheless, there are always new plots to draw. One kind of FEATPOST plot that just became possible is the "triangular grid triangular domain surface" (see Figure 10 and this code):

```
f  := 16*(4,1,1);
LightSource := 10*(4,-3,4);
def zsu( expr xc, yc ) =
  cosd(xc*57)*cosd(yc*57)+
    4*mexp(-(xc**2+yc**2)*6.4) enddef;
beginfig(1);
  hexagonaltrimesh(false,52,15,zsu);
endfig;
```

One feature that merges 2D and 3D involves what might be called "fat sticks". A fat stick resembles the Teflon magnets used to mix chemicals. They have volume but can be drawn like a small straight line segment stroked with a `pencircle`. Fat sticks may be used to represent direction fields (unitary vector fields without arrows). See Figure 11 (the source code follows).

```
f  := 2*(5,3,2);
Spread := 70;
NF := 0;
beginfig(1);
  numeric hstep, hmax, hsdev;
  numeric basestep, basemax, basesdev;
  numeric i, j, k, angsdev, cylength;
```

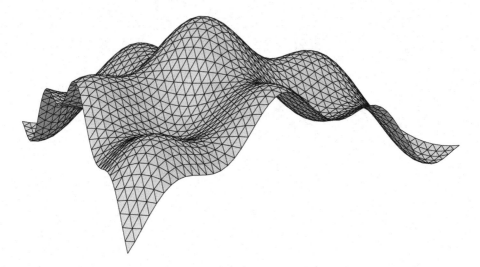

Fig. 10. FEATPOST surface plot using the macro **hexagonaltrimesh**.

```
numeric cyradius, basen, hn;
numeric vcx, vcy, vcz, hcurr, xcurr;
numeric ycurr, hbase, aone;
numeric atwo, zcurr, counter;
color lenvec, currpos;
cylength   := 0.45;
cyradius   := 0.1;
basen      := 11;
hn         := 3;
basestep   := cyradius*2.4;
hstep      := cylength*2.1;
basesdev   := cyradius*0.3;
hsdev      := hstep*0.04;
hbase      := -0.8;
angsdev    := 7;
basemax    := basen*basestep;
hmax       := hn*hstep;
hcurr      := hbase;
counter    := 0;
for k=1 upto hn:
  hcurr    := hcurr + hstep;
  for i=1 upto basen:
    for j=1 upto basen:
      zcurr:=hcurr+hsdev*normaldeviate;
      xcurr:= (i-1)*basestep
           +uniformdeviate( basestep );
      ycurr:= (j-1)*basestep
```

```
                  +uniformdeviate( basestep );
           aone:= uniformdeviate( 360 );
           atwo:= angsdev*normaldeviate;
           vcz := cosd( atwo );
           vcy := sind( atwo )*sind( aone );
           vcx := sind( atwo )*cosd( aone );
           currpos:=( xcurr, ycurr, zcurr );
           lenvec:=cylength*(vcx,vcy,vcz);
           counter := incr( counter );
           generatedirline( counter, aone,
                   90-atwo, cylength, currpos );
        endfor;
     endfor;
  endfor;
  NL := counter;
  director_invisible( true, 5, false );
endfig;
```

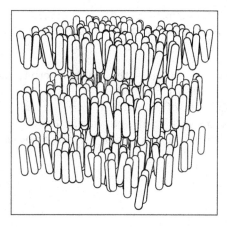

Fig. 11. FEATPOST direction field macro `director_invisible` was used to produce this representation of the molecular structure of a Smectic A liquid crystal.

Finally, it is important to remember that some capabilities of FEATPOST, although usable, may be considered "buggy" or only partially implemented. These include the calculation of intersections among polygons, as in Figure 12, and the drawing of toruses, as in Figure 13. These two figures show "usable" situations but their code is skipped.

FEATPOST has many macros: some are specifically for physics diagrams, others may be useful for general purposes, some do not fit in this article and, sadly, some are not anywhere documented. For instance, the tools for producing animations are not yet documented. (These tools are completely external to TEX:

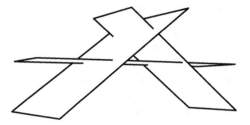

Fig. 12. Intersecting polygons drawn with the macro `sharpraytrace`.

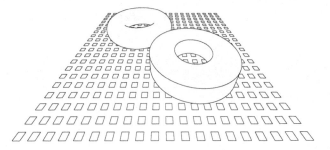

Fig. 13. Final FEATPOST example containing a `smoothtorus` and a `rigorousdisc` with a hole. These macros may fail for some view points.

the control of an animation is done with a Python script, and Ghostscript and `netpbm` are used to produce MPEG videos.)

In summary, the collection of three-dimensional METAPOST software, such as the four reviewed packages, is large and growing in many independent directions. It constitutes an excellent resource for those desiring to produce good diagrams.

Acknowledgements

Many people have contributed to make FEATPOST what it is today. Perhaps it would have never come into being without the early intervention of Jorge Bárrios, providing access to his father's computer. Another fundamental moment happened when José Esteves first spoke about METAPOST.

More recently, the very accurate criticism of Cristian Barbarosie has significantly contributed to the improvement of these macros. Jens Schwaiger contributed new macros. Pedro Sebastião, João Dinis and Gonçalo Morais proposed challenging new features. The authors of the other packages graciously reviewed the paper, and Karl Berry actually entered new text into this document. They all have my deep thanks.

Interactive Editing of MathML Markup Using TeX Syntax[*]

Luca Padovani

Department of Computer Science
University of Bologna
Mura Anteo Zamboni, 7
I-40127 Bologna, Italy
lpadovan@cs.unibo.it
http://www.cs.unibo.it/~lpadovan/

Abstract. We describe the architecture of a syntax-directed editor for authoring structured mathematical documents that can be used for the generation of MathML markup [4]. The author interacts with the editor by typing TeX markup as in a normal text editor, with the difference that the typed markup is parsed and displayed on-the-fly. We discuss issues regarding both the parsing and presentation phases and we propose implementations for them. In contrast with existing similar tools, the architecture we propose offers better compatibility with TeX syntax, a pervasive use of standard technologies and a clearer separation of content and presentation aspects of the information.

1 Introduction

MathML [4] is an XML [2] application for the representation of mathematical expressions. Like most XML applications, MathML is unsuitable to be written directly because of its verbosity except in the simplest cases. Hence the editing of MathML documents needs the assistance of dedicated tools. As of today, such tools can be classified into two main categories:

1. WYSIWYG (What You See Is What You Get) editors that allow the author to see the formatted document on the screen while it is being composed. The editor usually provides some "export mechanism" that creates XML with embedded MathML from the internal representation of the document;
2. Conversion tools that generate MathML markup from different sources, typically other markup languages for scientific documents, such as TeX [5].

Tools in the first category are appealing, but they suffer from at least two limitations: a) Editing is typically *presentation oriented* – the author is primarily concerned about the "look" of the document and tends to forget about its content. b) They may slow down the editing process because they often involve

---

[*] This work has been supported by the European Project IST-2001-33562 MoWGLI.

A. Syropoulos et al. (Eds.): TUG 2004, LNCS 3130, pp. 125–138, 2004.
© Springer-Verlag Berlin Heidelberg 2004

the use of menus, palettes of symbols, and, in general, the pointing device for completing most operations.

In this paper we describe the architecture of a tool that tries to synthesize the "best of both worlds". The basic idea is to create a WYSIWYG editor in that editing is achieved by typing concrete markup as the author would do in an actual plain text editor. The markup is then tokenized and parsed on-the-fly, a corresponding presentation is created by means of suitable transformations, and finally displayed. The editor is meant not only as an authoring tool, but more generally as an interface for math applications.

Although in the paper we assume that the concrete markup typed by the user is TEX (more precisely the subset of TEX concerned about mathematics) and that presentation markup is MathML, the system we are presenting is by no means tied to these languages and can be targeted to other contexts as well. One question that could arise is: "why TEX syntax?" We can see at least three motivations: first of all because of TEX popularity in many communities. Second, because macros, which are a fundamental concept in TEX, are also the key to editing at a more content-oriented level, which is a primary requirement for many applications handling mathematics. Finally, because, as we will see, TEX markup has good *locality* properties which make it suitable in the interactive environment of our concern.

The body of the paper is structured into four main sections: in Section 2 we overview the architecture of the tool while in Sections 3, 4, 5 we describe in more detail the main phases of the editing process (lexing, parsing, and transformation). Familiarity with TEX syntax and XML-related technologies is assumed.

2   Architecture

Several tools for the conversion of TEX markup suffer from two major drawbacks that we are not willing to tolerate in our design: (1) they rely on the TEX system itself for parsing the markup. While guaranteeing perfect compatibility with TEX, this implies the installation of the whole system. Moreover, the original TEX parser does not meet the incremental requirements that we need; (2) the lack of flexibility in the generation of the target document representation, which is either fixed by the conversion tool or is only slightly customizable by the user.

To cope with problem (1) we need to write our own parser for TEX markup. This is well known to be a non-trivial task, because of some fancy aspects regarding the very nature of TEX syntax and the lack of a proper "TEX grammar". We will commit ourselves with a subset of TEX syntax which appears to be just what an average author needs when writing a document. As we will see, the loss in the range of syntactic expression is compensated by a cleaner and more general transformation phase. As for the lack of a TEX grammar, we perceive this as a feature rather than a weakness: after all TEX is built around the fact that authors are free to define their own macros. Macros are the fundamental entities giving structure to the document.

Let us now turn our attention to problem (2): recall that the general form of a TEX macro definition (see *The TEXbook*, [5]) is

$$\text{\textbackslash def}\,\langle\text{control sequence}\rangle\langle\text{parameter text}\rangle$$
$$\{\langle\text{replacement text}\rangle\}$$

where the ⟨parameter text⟩ gives the syntax for invoking the macro and its parameters whereas the ⟨replacement text⟩ defines somehow the "semantics" of the macro (typically a presentational semantics). Thus the ultimate semantic load of a macro is invariably associated with the configuration of the macro at the point of definition.

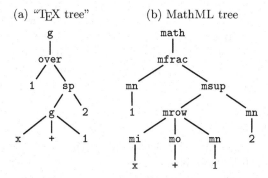

Fig. 1. Tree representation for {1\over{x+1}^2} and corresponding MathML markup.

We solve problem (2) by splitting up macro definitions so that structure and semantics can be treated independently. A well-formed TEX document can be represented as a tree whose leaves are either literals (strings of characters) or macros with no parameters, and each internal node represents a macro and the node's children are the macro's parameters. Entities like delimiters, square brackets surrounding optional parameters or literals occurring in the ⟨parameter text⟩ of macro definitions are purely syntactic and need not be represented in the tree if our main concern is capturing the structure of the document. Fig. 1(a) shows the tree structure of a simple mathematical formula.

Once the document is represented as a tree, the process of macro expansion – that is, *interpretation* – can be defined as a recursive transformation on the nodes of the tree. As we will represent trees using XML, transformations can be very naturally implemented by means of XSLT stylesheets [3]. Fig. 1(b) shows the MathML tree corresponding to the TEX tree on the left hand side. The two trees are basically isomorphic except for the name of the nodes and the presence of explicit token nodes for literals in the MathML tree. This is to say that the MathML tree can be generated from the TEX tree by simple transformations. However, once the interpretation phase is independent of parsing (which does not happen in TEX) it is natural to define much more general transformations that are not just node-by-node rewritings.

The following are the main components of an interactive, syntax-based editor for structured documents:

INPUT BUFFER: the sequence of concrete characters typed by the author;

LEXICAL ANALYZER: responsible for the tokenization of the characters in the input buffer;

DICTIONARY: a map from ⟨control sequence⟩ to ⟨parameter text⟩ which is used to know the syntax of macros;

PARSER: for the creation of the internal tree structure representing the document;

TRANSFORMATION ENGINE: to map the internal tree into the desired format.

No doubt these entities are common to all tools converting TEX markup into a different format, but the degree of mutual interdependence and the way they are implemented may differ considerably, especially when interactivity is a main concern. The added value of our approach is that it allows the author to independently customize both the dictionary and the transformation engine, and the advanced user of the editor the possibility of adapting the lexical analyzer to languages other than TEX (we will spend a few more words on this topic in the conclusions).

Notation. We will use the following conventions regarding lists. Lists are uniformly typed, that is elements of a list are all of the same type. We use α^* to denote the type of a list whose elements have type α. $[]$ is the empty list; $n :: x$ is the list with head element n and tail x; $x@y$ is the concatenation of two lists x and y; $[n_1; \ldots; n_k]$ is a short form for $n_1 :: \cdots :: n_k :: []$.

3   Lexical Analysis

The purpose of this phase is to tokenize the input buffer. As we are talking about an interactive tool, the presence of an input buffer may look surprising. Implementations for the input buffer range from *virtual* buffers (there is no buffer at all, characters are collected by the lexical analyzer which outputs tokens as they are completed) to *flat* buffers (just a string of characters as in a text editor) to *structured* buffers. For efficiency, we do not investigate in detail all the possibilities in this paper, but early experiments have shown that working with virtual buffers can be extremely difficult. As long as insert operations are performed at the right end of the buffer the restructuring operations on the parse tree are fairly easy, but when it comes to deletion or to modifications in arbitrary positions, the complexity of restructuring operations rises rapidly to an unmanageable level. Hence, from now on we will assume that a flat input buffer is available. Whether the buffer should be visible or not is a subjective matter, and may also depend on the kind of visual feedback given by the editor on incomplete and/or incorrect typed markup.

The outcome of the lexer is a stream (list) of tokens. Each token may have one of three forms: a *literal*, that is a single character to be treated "as is", a *space*, that is a sequence of one or more space-like characters, or a *control sequence*, that is the name of a macro.

Since the token stream is the only interface between the lexer and the parser, the lexer has the freedom to perform arbitrary mappings from the characters in the input buffer to tokens in the stream. In particular, some TEX commands like \alpha or \rightarrow are just placeholders for Unicode characters. There is no point in communicating these entities as control sequences as the internal tree representation (XML) is able to accommodate Unicode characters naturally; also, treating them as literals simplifies the subsequent transformation phase.

On the other hand, there are characters, such as curly braces { and } or scripting operators _ and ^, that have a special meaning. Logically these are just short names for macros that obey their own rules regarding parameters. What we propose is a general classification of parameter types which, in addition to parameters in normal TEX definitions, allows us

- to deal with optional parameters as LATEX [6] does;
- to treat { as just an abbreviation for \bgroup and make \bgroup a macro with one parameter delimited by \egroup, which we treat as the expansion for }. In order for this "trick" to work we have to design the parser carefully, as we will see in Sect. 4;
- to treat scripting operators _ and ^ as the two macros \sb and \sp both accepting a so-called pre-parameter (a parameter that occurs *before* the macro in the input buffer) and a so-called post-parameter (a parameter that occurs *after* the macro in the input buffer);
- to deal with macros that have "open" parameters. For instance \rm affects the markup following it until the first delimiter coming from an outermost macro is met. We treat \rm as a macro with an open post-parameter that extends as far as possible to the right. Similarly, \over can be seen as a macro with open pre- and post-parameters.

In order to describe parameter types we need to define the concept of *term*. A *term* is either a literal or a macro along with all its parameters (equivalently, a term is a subtree in the parsing tree). A *simple* parameter consists of one sole term. A *compound* parameter consists of one or more terms extending as far as possible to the left or to the right of the macro depending on whether the parameter is "pre-" or "post-". A *delimited* parameter consists of one or more terms extending as far as possible to the right up to but not including a given token t. An *optional* parameter is either empty or it consists of one or more terms enclosed within a pair or square brackets [and]. The absence of the opening bracket means that the optional parameter is not given. A *token* parameter is a given token t representing pure syntactic sugar. It does not properly qualify as a parameter and does not appear in the parsing tree.

Formally tokens and parameter types are defined as follows:

$$token ::= \mathsf{literal}(v) \mid \mathsf{space} \mid \mathsf{control}_{\langle p_1, p_2 \rangle}(v)$$
$$type ::= \mathsf{simple} \mid \mathsf{compound} \mid \mathsf{delimited}(t)$$
$$\mid \mathsf{optional} \mid \mathsf{token}(t)$$

Table 1. Examples of TEX and LATEX macros along with their signature.

Macro	Parameters	
	pre	post
overline		[simple]
sqrt		[simple] (TEX)
		[optional; simple] (LATEX)
root		[delimited(control(of)); simple]
over, choose	[compound]	[compound]
frac		[simple; simple]
rm, bf, tt, it		[compound]
left		[simple; delimited(control(right)); simple]
sb, sp	[simple]	[simple]
bgroup		[delimited(control(egroup)))]
begin		[simple; optional; delimited(control(end)); simple]
proclaim		[token(space); delimited(literal(.)); token(space); delimited(control(par)))]

where $t \in token$, $v \in string$ is an arbitrary string of Unicode characters, $p_1 \in \{simple, compound\}^*$ and $p_2 \in type^*$ are lists of parameter types for the pre- and post-parameters respectively. Note that pre-parameters can be of type simple or compound only.

The dictionary is a total map

$$dictionary : string \mapsto token$$

such that for each unknown control sequence v, $dictionary(v) = \text{control}_{\langle [], [] \rangle}(v)$. Table 1 shows part of a possible dictionary for some TEX and LATEX commands (mostly for mathematics). Note how it is possible to encode the signature for the \begin control sequence, although it is not possible to enforce the constraint that the first and the last parameters must have equal value in order for the construct to be balanced.

4   Parsing

We now come to the problem of building the TEX parse tree starting the stream of tokens produced by the lexical analyzer. As we have already pointed out there is no fixed grammar that we can use to generate the parser automatically: authors are free to introduce new macros and hence new ways of structuring the parse tree. Thus we will build the parser "by hand". More reasons for writing an ad-hoc parser, namely error recovery and incrementality, will be discussed later in this section.

The following grammar captures formally the structure of a TeX parsing tree, which is the outcome of the parser:

$$node ::= \text{empty}$$
$$|\quad \text{literal}(v) \qquad v \in string$$
$$|\quad \text{macro}(v, x) \qquad v \in string, x \in param^*$$
$$param ::= \{a\} \qquad a \in node^*$$

Note that a parameter is made of a list of nodes and that literals are strings instead of single characters. The empty node is used to denote a missing term when one was expected; its role will be clarified later in this section.

The appendix contains the Document Type Definition for the XML representation of TeX parsing trees. It is simpler than the TeXML DTD [7] and we are providing it as mere reference.

4.1   Parsing Functions

Table 2 gives the operational semantics of the parser. In this table only, for each $a \in node^*$ we define $a! = [\text{empty}]$ if $a = []$ and $a! = a$ otherwise. There are four parsing functions: $\mathcal{T}$ for terms, $\mathcal{A}$ for pre-parameters, $\mathcal{B}$ for post-parameters, and $\mathcal{C}$ for delimited sequences of terms. Each parsing function is defined by induction on the structure of its arguments. Axioms (rules with no horizontal line) denote base cases, while inference rules define the value of a parsing function (the conclusion, below the line) in terms of the value of one or more recursive calls to other functions (the premises, above the line). Right arrows denote the action of parsing. Arrows are decorated with a label that identifies the parser along with its parameters, if any. The $\mathcal{T}$, $\mathcal{B}$, and $\mathcal{C}$ parsers have a parameter representing the list of delimiters in the order they are expected, with the head of the list being the first expected delimiter. The $\mathcal{C}$ parser also has a Boolean parameter indicating whether the parser should or should not "eat" the delimiter when it is eventually met.

The root parsing function is $\mathcal{T}$. Given a delimiter $t \in token$ and a token stream $l \in token^*$ we have

$$[], l \xrightarrow{\mathcal{T}([t])} [n], l'$$

where $n \in node$ is the parsed term and $l' \in token^*$ is the part of the token stream that has not been consumed. Spaces are ignored when parsing terms and pre-parameters (rule $\mathcal{T}.4$), but not when parsing post-parameters (rule $\mathcal{B}.4$). The $\mathcal{A}$ function differs from the other parsing functions because by the time a macro with pre-parameters is encountered, pre-parameters have already been parsed. The lists $a \in node^*$ in the $\mathcal{T}$, $\mathcal{A}$, and $\mathcal{C}$ parsers represent the terms accumulated before the term being parsed. Note that pre-parameters are inserted at the end of the parameter list (rules $\mathcal{A}.2$ to $\mathcal{A}.4$) and that post-parameters are inserted at the beginning of the parameter list (rules $\mathcal{B}.5$ to $\mathcal{B}.10$). This way parameter nodes appear in the parse tree in the same order as in the original token stream (rule $\mathcal{T}.5$).

Table 2. Parsing functions for the simplified TEX markup.

$$\forall d \in token^* \quad \xrightarrow{\mathcal{T}(d)} \quad : node^* \times token^* \to node^* \times token^*$$

$$\xrightarrow{\mathcal{A}} \quad : node^* \times type^* \to node^* \times param^*$$

$$\forall d \in token^* \quad \xrightarrow{\mathcal{B}(d)} \quad : type^* \times token^* \to param^* \times token^*$$

$$\forall d \in token^*, \forall b \in bool \quad \xrightarrow{\mathcal{C}(d,b)} \quad : node^* \times token^* \to node^* \times token^*$$

$$(T.1)\ a, [] \xrightarrow{\mathcal{T}(d)} a, [] \qquad (T.2)\ a, t :: l \xrightarrow{\mathcal{T}(d)} a, t :: l \quad (t \text{ occurs in } d)$$

$$(T.3)\ a, \mathsf{literal}(v) :: l \xrightarrow{\mathcal{T}(d)} a@[\mathsf{literal}(v)], l \qquad (T.4)\ \frac{a, l \xrightarrow{\mathcal{T}(d)} a', l'}{a, \mathsf{space} :: l \xrightarrow{\mathcal{T}(d)} a', l'}$$

$$(T.5)\ \frac{a, p_1 \xrightarrow{\mathcal{A}} a', x \qquad p_2, l \xrightarrow{\mathcal{B}(d)} y, l'}{a, \mathsf{control}_{\langle p_1, p_2 \rangle}(v) :: l \xrightarrow{\mathcal{T}(d)} a'@[\mathsf{macro}(v, x@y)], l'}$$

$$(A.1)\ a, [] \xrightarrow{\mathcal{A}} a, [] \qquad (A.2)\ \frac{[], p \xrightarrow{\mathcal{A}} a, x}{[], s :: p \xrightarrow{\mathcal{A}} a, x@[\{[\mathsf{empty}]\}]}$$

$$(A.3)\ \frac{a, p \xrightarrow{\mathcal{A}} a', x}{a@[n], \mathsf{simple} :: p \xrightarrow{\mathcal{A}} a', x@[\{[n]\}]} \qquad (A.4)\ \frac{[], p \xrightarrow{\mathcal{A}} a', x}{a, \mathsf{compound} :: p \xrightarrow{\mathcal{A}} a', x@[\{a\}]}$$

$$(B.1)\ [], l \xrightarrow{\mathcal{B}(d)} [], l \qquad (B.2)\ \frac{p, t' :: l \xrightarrow{\mathcal{B}(d)} x, a}{\mathsf{token}(t) :: p, t' :: l \xrightarrow{\mathcal{B}(d)} x, a} \dagger \quad (t \neq t')$$

$$(B.3)\ \frac{p, [] \xrightarrow{\mathcal{B}(d)} x, l}{\mathsf{token}(t) :: p, [] \xrightarrow{\mathcal{B}(d)} x, l} \dagger \qquad (B.4)\ \frac{p, l \xrightarrow{\mathcal{B}(d)} x, l'}{\mathsf{token}(t) :: p, t :: l \xrightarrow{\mathcal{B}(d)} x, l'}$$

$$(B.5)\ \frac{[], l \xrightarrow{\mathcal{T}(d)} a, l' \qquad p, l' \xrightarrow{\mathcal{B}(d)} x, l''}{\mathsf{simple} :: p, l \xrightarrow{\mathcal{B}(d)} \{a!\} :: x, l''} \qquad (B.6)\ \frac{[], l \xrightarrow{\mathcal{C}(d,\mathsf{false})} a, l' \qquad p, l' \xrightarrow{\mathcal{B}(d)} x, l''}{\mathsf{compound} :: p, l \xrightarrow{\mathcal{B}(d)} \{a!\} :: x, l''}$$

$$(B.7)\ \frac{p, [] \xrightarrow{\mathcal{B}(d)} x, l}{\mathsf{optional} :: p, [] \xrightarrow{\mathcal{B}(d)} \{[]\} :: x, l} \qquad (B.8)\ \frac{[], l \xrightarrow{\mathcal{C}(\mathsf{literal}([])::d,\mathsf{true})} a, l' \qquad p, l' \xrightarrow{\mathcal{B}(d)} x, l''}{\mathsf{optional} :: p, \mathsf{literal}([) :: l \xrightarrow{\mathcal{B}(d)} \{a\} :: x, l''}$$

$$(B.9)\ \frac{p, t :: l \xrightarrow{\mathcal{B}(d)} x, l'}{\mathsf{optional} :: p, t :: l \xrightarrow{\mathcal{B}(d)} \{[]\} :: x, l'} \quad (t \neq \mathsf{literal}([))$$

$$(B.10)\ \frac{[], l \xrightarrow{\mathcal{C}(t::d,\mathsf{true})} a, l' \qquad p, l' \xrightarrow{\mathcal{B}(d)} x, l''}{\mathsf{delimited}(t) :: p, l \xrightarrow{\mathcal{B}(d)} \{a!\} :: x, l''}$$

$$(C.1)\ a, [] \xrightarrow{\mathcal{C}(d,b)} a, []$$

$$(C.2)\ a, t :: l \xrightarrow{\mathcal{C}(t::d,\mathsf{true})} a, l \qquad (C.3)\ a, t :: l \xrightarrow{\mathcal{C}(d,b)} a, t :: l \quad (t \text{ occurs in } d)$$

$$(C.4)\ \frac{a, t :: l \xrightarrow{\mathcal{T}(d)} a', l' \qquad a', l' \xrightarrow{\mathcal{C}(d,b)} a'', l''}{a, t :: l \xrightarrow{\mathcal{C}(d,b)} a'', l''} \quad (t \notin d)$$

Example. Given that the input buffer contains the TeX source shown in Fig. 1, the lexical analyzer would produce the following stream of tokens:

$$l_0 \overset{\text{def}}{=} [\text{control}_{\langle[],[\text{delimited}(\text{control}(\text{egroup}))]\rangle}(\textbf{bgroup});$$
$$\text{literal}(1); \text{control}_{\langle[\text{compound}],[\text{compound}]\rangle}(\textsf{over});$$
$$\text{control}_{\langle[],[\text{delimited}(\text{control}(\text{egroup}))]\rangle}(\textbf{bgroup});$$
$$\text{literal}(x); \text{literal}(+); \text{literal}(1);$$
$$\text{control}(\text{egroup}); \text{control}_{\langle[\text{simple}],[\text{simple}]\rangle}(\textsf{sp});$$
$$\text{literal}(2); \text{control}(\text{egroup})]$$

By the application of the parsing rules given in Table 2 it can be shown that

$$[], l_0 @[\text{control}(\text{eoi})] \overset{\mathcal{T}([\text{control}(\text{eoi})])}{\longrightarrow} [n], [\text{control}(\text{eoi})]$$

where $n \in node$ is the same tree shown in Fig. 1 except that the **g** nodes are labeled with **bgroup**.

4.2 Error Recovery

Parsing functions are all total functions, they always produce a result, even when the input token stream is malformed. Unlike parsers of batch TeX converters or the TeX parser itself, there will often be moments during the editing process when the input buffer contains incorrect or incomplete markup, for example because not all the required parameters of a macro have been entered yet. The parser must recover from such situations in a tolerant and hopefully sensible way. We distinguish three kinds of situations: *missing parameters*, *pattern mismatch*, and *ambiguity*, which we examine in the rest of this section.

Missing Parameters. Consider an input token stream representing the sole \over macro with no arguments provided:

$$l_1 \overset{\text{def}}{=} [\text{control}_{\langle[\text{compound}],[\text{compound}]\rangle}(\textsf{over});$$
$$\text{control}(\text{eoi})]$$

It is easy to check that

$$[], l_1 \overset{\mathcal{T}([\text{control}(\text{eoi})])}{\longrightarrow} [\text{macro}(\text{over}, [\text{empty}; \text{empty}])],$$
$$[\text{control}(\text{eoi})]$$

More generally the parser inserts empty nodes in the parsing tree wherever an expected parameter is not found in the token stream. This behavior can be seen in rule *A.2* and also in rules *B.5*, *B.6*, and *B.10* where the ! operator is used. For optional parameters an empty node list is admitted (rules *B.7* and *B.8*).

The presence of empty nodes guarantees that the generated tree is structurally well-formed, which is crucial for the subsequent transformation phase. It also allows the application to give the user feedback indicating the absence of required parameters. In the example above, for instance, the application may display something like $\frac{\square}{\square}$ suggesting that a fraction was entered, but neither the numerator nor the denominator have been.

Pattern Mismatch. Rules $B.2$ and $B.3$ have been marked with a † to indicate that the parser expects a token which is not found in the token stream. In both cases the parser will typically notify the user with a warning message.

Ambiguities. In TEX one cannot pass a macro with parameters as the parameter of another macro, unless the parameter is enclosed within a group. For example, it is an error to write \sqrt\sqrt{x}, the correct form is \sqrt{\sqrt{x}}. Because we treat the left curly brace like any other macro, grouping would not help our parser in resolving ambiguities. However, the parser knows how many parameters a macro needs, because the token representing the control sequence has been annotated with such information by the lexer. When processing a macro with arguments the parser behaves "recursively", it does not let an incomplete macro to be "captured" if it was passed as parameter of an outer macro. A consequence of this extension is that any well-formed fragment of TEX markup is accepted by our parser resulting in the same structure, but there are some strings accepted by our parser that cause the TEX parser to fail.

4.3   Incremental Parsing

Parsing must be efficient because it is performed in real-time, in principle at every modification of the input buffer, no matter how simple the modification is. Fortunately TEX markup exhibits good *locality*, that is small modifications in the document cause small modifications in the parsing tree. Consequently we can avoid re-parsing the whole source document, we just need to re-parse a small interval of the input buffer around the point where the modification has occurred, and adjust the parsing tree accordingly. Let us consider again the example of Fig. 1 and suppose that a change is made in the markup

$$\{1\backslash\text{over}\{\underline{1+x}\}^2\} \quad \Rightarrow \quad \{1\backslash\text{over}\{\underline{1+x+y}\}^2\}$$

(a +y is added to the denominator of the fraction). To be conservative we can re-parse the smallest term within braces that includes the modified part (the underlined fragments). Once the term has been re-parsed it has to be substituted in place of the old term in the parsing tree.

In order to compute the interval of the input buffer to be re-parsed we annotate the nodes of the parsing tree with information about the first and the last characters of the buffer which were scanned while building the node and all of its children. A simple visit of the tree can locate the smaller interval affected by the modification.

Curly braces occur frequently enough in the markup to give good granularity for re-parsing. At the same time limiting re-parsing to braced terms helps control the costs related to the visit to the parsing tree and to the implementation of the incremental parsing and transformation machinery.

5   Transformation

The transformation phase recognizes structured patterns in the parsing tree and generates corresponding fragments of the result document. We have already

```
<xsl:template                          <xsl:template
 match="macro[@name='over']">           match="macro[@name='sb']
 <m:mfrac>                                      [p[1]/*[1][self::macro[@name='sp']]]">
  <xsl:if test="@id">                   <m:msubsup>
   <xsl:attribute name="xref">           <xsl:if test="@id">
    <xsl:value-of select="@id"/>          <xsl:attribute name="xref">
   </xsl:attribute>                        <xsl:value-of select="@id"/>
  </xsl:if>                               </xsl:attribute>
  <xsl:apply-templates select="p[1]"/>  </xsl:if>
  <xsl:apply-templates select="p[2]"/>  <xsl:apply-templates select="p[1]/*/p[1]"/>
 </m:mfrac>                              <xsl:apply-templates select="p[2]"/>
</xsl:template>                          <xsl:apply-templates select="p[1]/*/p[2]"/>
                                        </m:msubsup>
                                       </xsl:template>
```

(a)   (b)

Fig. 2. Example of XSLT templates for the transformation of the internal parsing tree into a MathML tree. MathML elements can be distinguished because of the m: prefix.

anticipated that XSLT is a very natural choice for the implementation of this phase. Besides, XSLT stylesheets can be extended very easily, by providing new *templates* that recognize and properly handle new macros that an author has introduced.

We can see in Fig. 2 two sample templates taken from an XSLT stylesheet for converting the internal parsing tree into a MathML tree. Both templates have a preamble made of an `xsl:if` construct which we will discuss later in this section. Since the TEX tree and the MathML tree are almost isomorphic (Fig. 1) the transformation is generally very simple and in many cases it amounts at just renaming the node labels. Template (a) is one such case: it matches any node in the parsing tree with label `macro` and having the `name` attribute set to `over`. The node for the \over macro corresponds naturally to the `mfrac` element in MathML. The two parameters of \over are transformed recursively by applying the stylesheet templates to the first and second child nodes (`p[1]` means "the first p child of this node", similarly `p[2]` refers to the second p child).

Template (b) is slightly more complicated and shows one case where there is some change in the structure. For combined sub/super scripts TEX accepts a sequence of _ and ^ no matter in what order they occur, but MathML has a specific element for such expressions, namely `msubsup`. The template matches an `sb` node whose first parameter contains an `sp` node, thus detecting a ... ^ ... _ ... fragment of markup, then the corresponding `msubsup` element is created and its three children accessed in the proper position of the parsing tree. A symmetric template will handle the case where the subscript occurs before the superscript.

5.1   Incremental Transformation

As we have done for parsing, for transformations we also need to account for their cost. In a batch, one-shot conversion from TEX this is not generally an issue, but in an interactive authoring tool a transformation is required at every modification of the parsing tree in order to update the view of the document.

Intuitively, we can reason that if only a fragment of the parsing tree has changed, we need re-transform only that fragment and substitute the result in the final document. This technique makes two assumptions: (1) that transformations are context-free; that is, the transformation of a fragment in the parsing tree is not affected by the context in which the fragment occurs; (2) that we are able to relate corresponding fragments between the parsing and the result trees.

Template (b) in Fig. 2 shows one case where the transformation is not context free: the deeper `sp` node is not processed as if it would occur alone, but it is "merged" together with its parent. More generally we can imagine that transformations can make almost arbitrary re-arrangements of the structure. This problem cannot be solved unless we make some assumptions, and the one we have already committed to in Sect. 4 is that braces define "black-box" fragments which can be transformed in isolation, without context dependencies.

As for the matter of relating corresponding fragments of the two documents, we use identifiers and references. Each node in the parsing tree is annotated with a unique identifier (in our sample templates we are assuming that the identifier is a string in the `id` attribute). Templates create corresponding `xref` attributes in the result document "pointing" to the fragment with the same identifier in the parsing tree. This way, whenever a fragment of the parsing tree is re-transformed, it replaces the fragment in the result document with the same identifier.

More generally, back-pointers provide a mechanism for relating the view of the document with the source markup. This way it is possible to perform operations like selection or cut-and-paste that, while having a visual effect in the view, act indirectly at the content/markup level.

6   Conclusion

We have presented architectural and implementation issues of an interactive editor based on TeX syntax which allows flexible customization and content-oriented authoring. TeXmacs[1] is probably the existing application that most closely adopts such architecture, with the difference that TeXmacs does not stick to TeX syntax as closely as we do and that, apart from being a complete (and cumbersome) editing tool and not just an interface, it uses encoding and transformation technologies not based on standard languages (XML [2] and XSLT [3]).

Among batch conversion tools we observe a tendency to move towards the processing of content. The TeX to MathML converter by Igor Rodionov and Stephen Watt at the University of Western Ontario [8, 9] is one such tool, and the recent Hermes converter by Romeo Anghelache [10] is another. These represent significant steps forwards when compared to converters such as LaTeX2HTML[2].

A prototype tool called EdiTeX, based on the architecture described in this paper, has been developed and is freely available along with its source code[3]. No

---

[1] http://www.texmacs.org/

[2] http://www.latex2html.org/

[3] http://helm.cs.unibo.it/software/editex/

mention of MathML is made in the name of the tool to remark the fact that the architecture is very general and can be adapted to other kinds of markup. The prototype is currently being used as interface for a proof-assistant application where editing of complex mathematical formulas and proofs is required. In this respect we should remark that TEX syntax is natural for "real" mathematics, but it quickly becomes clumsy when used for writing terms of programming languages or λ-calculus. This is mainly due to the conventions regarding spaces (for instance, spaces in the λ-calculus denote function application) and identifiers (the rule "one character is one identifier" is fine for mathematics, but not for many other languages). Note however that, since the lexical analyzer is completely separate from the rest of the architecture, the token stream being its interface, it can be easily targeted to a language with different conventions than those of TEX.

The idea of using some sort of restricted TEX syntax for representing mathematical expressions is not new. For example, John Forkosh's MimeTEX[4] generates bitmap images of expressions to be embedded in Web pages. However, to the best of our knowledge the formal specification of the parser for simplified TEX markup presented in Sect. 4 is unique of its kind. A straightforward implementation based directly on the rules given in Table 2 amounts at only just 70 lines of functional code (in an ML dialect), which can be considered something of an achievement given that parsing TEX is normally regarded as a hard task. By comparison, the parsing code in MimeTEX amounts to nearly 350 lines of C code after stripping away the comments.

One may argue that the simplified TEX markup is too restrictive, but in our view this is just the sensible fragment of TEX syntax that the average user should be concerned about. In fact the remaining syntactic expressiveness provided by TEX is mainly required for the implementation of complex macros and of system internals, which should never surface at the document level. By separating the transformation phase we shift the mechanics of macro expansion to a different level which can approached with different (more appropriate) languages. Since this mode of operation makes the system more flexible we believe that our design is a valuable contribution which may provide an architecture for other implementers to adopt.

References

1. The Unicode Consortium: The Unicode Standard, Version 4.0, Boston, MA, Addison-Wesley (2003). http://www.unicode.org/
2. Tim Bray, Jean Paoli, C.M. Sperberg-McQueen, Eve Maler (editors): Extensible Markup Language (XML) 1.0 (2nd Edition), W3C Recommendation (2000). http://www.w3.org/TR/2000/REC-xml-20001006
3. James Clark (editor): XML Transformations (XSLT) Version 1.0, W3C Recommendation (1999). http://www.w3.org/TR/1999/REC-xslt-19991116

---

[4] http://www.ctan.org/tex-archive/support/mimetex/

4. Ron Ausbrooks, Stephen Buswell, Stéphane Dalmas, Stan Devitt, Angel Diaz, et al.: Mathematical Markup Language (MathML) Version 2.0 (2nd Edition) W3C Recommendation, (2003). http://www.w3.org/TR/2003/REC-MathML2-20031021/

5. Donald E. Knuth: The TeXbook, Addison-Wesley, Reading, MA, USA (1994).

6. Leslie Lamport: A Document Preparation System: LaTeX, Addison-Wesley, Reading, MA, USA (1986).

7. Douglas Lovell: TeXML: Typesetting XML with TeX, TUGBoat, 20(3), pp. 176–183 (September 1999).

8. Sandy Huerter, Igor Rodionov, Stephen M. Watt: Content-Faithful Transformations for MathML, Proc. International Conference on MathML and Math on the Web (MathML 2002), Chicago, USA (2002). http://www.mathmlconference.org/2002/presentations/huerter/

9. Stephen M. Watt: Conserving implicit mathematical semantics in conversion between TeX and MathML, TUGBoat, 23(1), pp. 108–108 (2002).

10. Romeo Anghelache: LaTeX-based authoring tool, Deliverable D4.d, MoWGLI Project (2003). http://relativity.livingreviews.org/Info/AboutLR/mowgli/index.html

Appendix: The TML DTD

```
<!ENTITY % TML.node "
  empty|space|literal|macro">
<!ENTITY % TML.common.attrib "
  id        CDATA #IMPLIED
  xref      CDATA #IMPLIED
  start     NMTOKEN #IMPLIED
  end       NMTOKEN #IMPLIED">
<!ELEMENT empty EMPTY>
<!ATTLIST empty %TML.common.attrib;>
<!ELEMENT space EMPTY>
<!ATTLIST space
  %TML.common.attrib
  name    NMTOKEN #IMPLIED
  literal CDATA #IMPLIED>
<!ELEMENT literal #PCDATA>
<!ATTLIST literal
  %TML.common.attrib;
  name    NMTOKEN #IMPLIED>
<!ELEMENT macro (p)*>
<!ATTLIST macro
  %TML.common.attrib;
  name    NMTOKEN #REQUIRED
  literal CDATA #IMPLIED>
<!ELEMENT p (%TML.node;)*>
<!ATTLIST p %TML.common.attrib;>
```

Typesetting CJK Languages with Ω

Jin-Hwan Cho[1] and Haruhiko Okumura[2]

[1] Korean TeX Users Group
chofchof@ktug.or.kr
[2] Mie University
Faculty of Education
514-8507
Japan
okumura@acm.org

Abstract. This paper describes how to typeset Chinese, Japanese, and Korean (CJK) languages with Omega, a 16-bit extension of Donald Knuth's TeX. In principle, Omega has no difficulty in typesetting those East Asian languages because of its internal representation using 16-bit Unicode. However, it has not been widely used in practice because of the difficulties in adapting it to CJK typesetting rules and fonts, which we will discuss in the paper.

1 Introduction

Chinese, Japanese, and Korean (CJK) languages are characterized by multibyte characters covering more than 60% of Unicode. The huge number of characters prevented the original 8-bit TeX from working smoothly with CJK languages. There have been three methods for supporting CJK languages in the TeX world up to now.

The first method, called the *subfont scheme*, splits CJK characters into sets of 256 characters or fewer, the number of characters that a TeX font metric file can accommodate. Its main advantage lies in using 8-bit TeX systems directly. However, one document may contain dozens of subfonts for each CJK font, and it is quite hard to insert glue and kerns between characters of different subfonts, even those from the same CJK font. Moreover, without the help of a DVI driver (e.g., DVIPDFM*x* [2]) supporting the subfont scheme, it is not possible to generate PDF documents containing CJK characters that can be extracted or searched. Many packages are based on this method; for instance, CJK-LaTeX[1] by Werner Lemberg, HLaTeX[2] by Koaunghi Un, and the Chinese module in ConTeXt[3] by Hans Hagen.

On the other hand, in Japan, the most widely used TeX-based system is pTeX [1] (formerly known as ASCII Nihongo TeX), a 16-bit extension of TeX

---

[1] Avaliable on the as `language/chinese/CJK/`
[2] Available on the "Comprehensive TeX Archive Network" (CTAN) as `language/korean/HLaTeX/`
[3] Available on CTAN as `macros/context/`

A. Syropoulos et al. (Eds.): TUG 2004, LNCS 3130, pp. 139–148, 2004.

localized to the Japanese language. It is designed for high-quality Japanese book publishing (the "p" of pTeX stands for publishing; the name jTeX was used by another system). pTeX can handle multibyte characters natively (i.e., without resorting to subfonts), and it can typeset both horizontally and vertically within a document. It is upward compatible[4] with TeX, so it can be used to typeset both Japanese and Latin languages, but it cannot handle Chinese and Korean languages straightforwardly. pTeX supports three widely-used Japanese encodings, JIS (ISO-2022-JP), Shift JIS, and EUC-JP, but not Unicode-based encodings such as UTF-8.

The third route, Omega [3, 4], is also a 16-bit extension of TeX, having 16-bit Unicode as its internal representation. In principle, Omega is free from the limitations mentioned above, but thus far there is no thorough treatment of how it can be used for professional CJK typesetting and how to adapt it to popular CJK font formats such as TrueType and OpenType. We set out to fill in this blank.

2   CJK Typesetting Characteristics

Each European language has its own hyphenation rules, but their typesetting characteristics are overall fairly similar. CJK languages differ from European languages in that there are no hyphenation rules. All CJK languages allow line breaking almost anywhere, without a hyphen. This characteristic is usually implemented by inserting appropriate glues between CJK characters.

One fine point is the treatment of blank spaces and end-of-line (EOL) characters. Korean uses blank spaces to separate words, but Chinese and Japanese rarely use blank spaces. An EOL character is converted in TeX to a blank space and then to a skip, which is unnecessary for Chinese and Japanese typesetting. To overcome this problem, pTeX ignores an EOL when it follows a CJK character.

Moreover, whereas Korean uses Latin punctuation marks (periods, commas, etc.), Chinese and Japanese use their own punctuation symbols. These CJK punctuation symbols need to be treated somewhat differently from ordinary characters. The appropriate rules are described in this paper.

3   CJK Omega Translation Process

We introduce here the CJK Omega Translation Process (CJK-OTP)[5] developed by the authors to implement the CJK typesetting characteristics mentioned above.

An Omega Translation Process (OTP) is a powerful preprocessor, which allows text to be passed through any number of finite state automata, which can achieve many different effects. Usually it is quite hard or impossible to do the same work with other TeX-based systems.

---

[4] Although pTeX doesn't actually pass the `trip` test, it is thought to be upward compatible with TeX in virtually all practical situations.

[5] Available at `http://project.ktug.or.kr/omega-cjk/`

For each CJK language, the CJK-OTP is divided into two parts. The first OTP (boundCJK.otp) is common to all CJK languages, and controls the boundaries of blocks consisting of CJK characters and blank spaces. The second OTP (one of interCHN.otp, interJPN.otp, and interKOR.otp) is specific to each language, and controls typesetting rules for consecutive CJK characters.

4 Common Typesetting Characteristics

The first task of boundCJK.otp is to split the input stream into CJK blocks and non-CJK blocks, and insert glue (\boundCJKglue) in between to allow line breaking.

However, combinations involving some Latin and CJK symbols (quotation marks, commas, periods, etc.), do not allow line breaking. In this case, \bound-CJKglue is not inserted so that the original line breaking rule is applied. This corresponds to pTeX's primitives \xspcode and \inhibitxspcode.

boundCJK.otp defines seven character sets; the role of each set is as follows.

1. {CJK} is the set of all CJK characters; its complement is denoted by ^{CJK}.
2. {XSPCODE1} (e.g., ([{') is the subset of ^{CJK} such that \boundCJKglue is inserted only between {CJK} and {XSPCODE1} in this order.
3. {XSPCODE2} (e.g.,)]}';,.) is the subset of ^{CJK} such that \boundCJK-glue is inserted only between {XSPCODE2} and {CJK} in this order.
4. {XSPCODE3} (e.g., 0-9 A-Z a-z) is the subset of ^{CJK} such that \bound-CJKglue is inserted between {CJK} and {XSPCODE3}, irrespective of the order.
5. {INHIBITXSPCODE0} (e.g., ——‿⋯￥) is the subset of {CJK} *not* allowing \boundCJKglue between {INHIBITXSPCODE0} and ^{CJK}, irrespective of the order.
6. {INHIBITXSPCODE1} (e.g., 、 。 ） 》 」 』 】], CJK right parentheses and periods) is the subset of {CJK} *not* allowing \boundCJKglue between ^{CJK} and {INHIBITXSPCODE1} in this order.
7. {INHIBITXSPCODE2} (e.g.,（ 《 「 『 【 〔 〖 〘, CJK left parentheses) is the subset of {CJK} *not* allowing \boundCJKglue in between {INHIBITXSPCODE2} and ^{CJK} in this order.

The second task of boundCJK.otp is to enclose each CJK block in a group '{\selectCJKfont␣ ... }', and convert all blank spaces inside the block to the command \CJKspace.

The command \selectCJKfont switches to the appropriate CJK font, and \CJKspace is defined to be either a \space (for Korean) or \relax (for Chinese and Japanese) according to the selected language.

Note that if the input stream starts with blank spaces followed by a CJK block or ends with a CJK block followed by blank spaces, then these spaces must be preserved regardless of the language, because of math mode:

{{CJK} {SPACE} $...$ {SPACE} CJK}}

and restricted horizontal mode:

```
\hbox{{SPACE} {CJK} {SPACE}}
```

5 Language-Dependent Characteristics

The line breaking mechanism is common to all of the language-dependent OTPs (interCHN.otp, interJPN.otp, and interKOR.otp). The glue \interCJKglue is inserted between consecutive CJK characters, and its role is similar to the glue \boundCJKglue at the boundary of a CJK block.

Some combinations of CJK characters do not allow line breaking. This is implemented by simply inserting a \penalty 10000 before the relevant \inter-CJKglue. In the case of boundCJK.otp, however, no \boundCJKglue is inserted where line breaking is inhibited.

The CJK characters not allowing line breaking are defined by the following two classes in interKOR.otp for Korean typesetting.

1. {CJK_FORBIDDEN_AFTER} does not allow line breaking between CJK_FORBID-DEN_AFTER and {CJK} in this order.
2. {CJK_FORBIDDEN_BEFORE} does not allow line breaking in between {CJK} and {CJK_FORBIDDEN_BEFORE} in this order.

On the other hand, interJPN.otp defines six classes for Japanese typesetting, as discussed in the next section.

6 Japanese Typesetting Characteristics

Most Japanese characters are designed on a square 'canvas'. pTEX introduced a new length unit, zw (for *zenkaku* width, or full-width), denoting the width of this canvas. The CJK-OTP defines \zw to denote the same quantity.

For horizontal (left-to-right) typesetting mode, the baseline of a Japanese character typically divides the square canvas by 0.88 : 0.12. If Japanese and Latin fonts are typeset with the same size, Japanese fonts appear larger. In the sample shown in Figure 1, Japanese characters are typeset 92.469 percent the size of Latin characters, so that 10 pt (1 in = 72.27 pt) Latin characters are mixed with 3.25 mm (= 13 Q; 4 Q = 1 mm) Japanese characters. Also, Japanese and Latin words are traditionally separated by about 0.25 zw, though this space is getting smaller nowadays.

Some characters (such as punctuation marks and parentheses) are designed on a half-width canvas: its width is 0.5 zw. For ease of implementation, actual glyphs may be designed on square canvases. We can use the virtual font mechanism to map the logical shape and the actual implementation.

interJPN.otp divides Japanese characters into six classes:

1. Left parentheses: ' " (〔 [{ 〈 《 「 『 【
Half width, may be designed on square canvases flush right. In that case we

Fig. 1. The width of an ordinary Japanese character, 1 zw, is set to 92.469% the design size of the Latin font, and a gap of 0.25 zw is inserted. The baseline is set to 0.12 zw above the bottom of the enclosing squares.

ignore the left half and pretend they are half-width, e.g., \hbox to 0.5zw {\hss}. If a class-1 character is followed by a class-3 character, then an \hskip 0.25zw minus 0.25zw is inserted in between.

2. Right parentheses: 、，' ") 〕] 〉 》 」 』 】
   Half width, may be designed flush left on square canvases. If a class-2 character is followed by a class-0, -1, or -5 character, then an \hskip 0.5zw minus 0.5zw is inserted in between. If a class-2 character is followed by a class-3 character, then a \hskip 0.25zw minus 0.25zw is inserted in between.

3. Centered points: ・ ： ；
   Half width, may be designed centered on square canvases. If a class-3 character is followed by a class-0, -1, -2, -4, or -5 character, then an \hskip 0.25zw minus 0.25zw is inserted in between. If a class-3 character is followed by a class-3 character, then an \hskip 0.5zw minus 0.25zw is inserted in between.

4. Periods: 。 ．
   Half width, may be designed flush left on square canvases. If a class-4 character is followed by a class-0, -1, or -5 character, then an \hskip 0.5zw is inserted in between. If a class-4 character is followed by a class-3 character, then an \hskip 0.75zw minus 0.25zw is inserted in between.

5. Leaders: ＿……．
   Full width. If a class-5 character is followed by a class-1 character, then an \hskip 0.5zw minus 0.5zw is inserted in between. If a class-5 character is followed by a class-3 character, then an \hskip 0.25zw minus 0.25zw is inserted in between. If a class-5 character is followed by a class-5 character, then a \kern 0zw is inserted in between.

0. Class-0: everything else.
   Full width. If a class-0 character is followed by a class-1 character, then an \hskip 0.5zw minus 0.5zw is inserted in between. If a class-0 character is followed by a class-3 character, then an \hskip 0.25zw minus 0.25zw is inserted in between.

Chinese texts can be typeset mostly with the same rules. An exception is the comma and the period of Traditional Chinese. These two letters are designed at the center of the square canvas, so they should be treated as Class-3 characters.

7 Example: Japanese and Korean

Let us discuss how to use CJK-OTP in a practical situation. Figure 2 shows sample output containing both Japanese and Korean characters, which is typeset by Omega with the CJK-OTP and then processed by DVIPDFMx.

TeX はスタンフォード大学のクヌース教授によって開発された組版システムであり、組版の美しさと強力なマクロ機能を特徴としている。

TeX은 스탠포드 大學의 크누스 教授에 의해 開發된 組版 시스템으로, 組版의 美와 强力한 매크로 機能이 特徵이다.

Fig. 2. Sample CJK-OTP output.

The source of the sample above was prepared with the text editor Vim as shown in Figure 3. Here, the UTF-8 encoding was used to see Japanese and Korean characters at the same time. Note that the backslash character (\) is replaced with the yen currency symbol in Japanese fonts.

```
¥input omega-cjk-sample

¥hsize=75mm ¥parindent=¥zw

{¥japanese
¥TeXはスタンフォード大学のクヌース教授によって
開発された組版システムであり、組版の美しさと強
力なマクロ機能を特徴としている。
}
¥par¥vskip 10pt
{¥korean
¥TeX은 스탠포드 大學의 크누스 教授에 의해 開發
된 組版 시스템으로, 組版의 美와 强力한 매크로
機能이 特徵이다.
}

¥bye
```

Fig. 3. Sample CJK-OTP source.

The first line in Figure 3 calls another TeX file omega-cjk-sample.tex which starts with the following code, which loads[6] the CJK-OTP.

[6] Omega requires the binary form of OTP files compiled by the utility otp2ocp included in the Omega distribution.

```
\ocp\OCPindefault=inutf8
\ocp\OCPboundCJK=boundCJK
\ocp\OCPinterJPN=interJPN
\ocp\OCPinterKOR=interKOR
```

Note that   inutf8.otp has to be loaded first to convert the input stream encoded with UTF-8 to UCS-2, the 16-bit Unicode.

```
\ocplist\CJKOCP=
  \addafterocplist 1 \OCPboundCJK
  \addafterocplist 1 \OCPindefault
  \nullocplist
\ocplist\JapaneseOCP=
  \addbeforeocplist 2 \OCPinterJPN \CJKOCP
\ocplist\KoreanOCP=
  \addbeforeocplist 2 \OCPinterKOR \CJKOCP
```

The glues \boundCJKglue and \interCJKglue for CJK line breaking mechanism are defined by new skip registers to be changed later according to the language selected.

```
\newskip\boundCJKskip % defined later
\def\boundCJKglue{\hskip\boundCJKskip}
\newskip\interCJKskip % defined later
\def\interCJKglue{\hskip\interCJKskip}
```

Japanese typesetting requires more definitions to support the six classes defined in interJPN.otp.

```
\newdimen\zw \zw=0.92469em
\def\halfCJKmidbox#1{\leavevmode%
  \hbox to .5\zw{\hss #1\hss}}
\def\halfCJKleftbox#1{\leavevmode%
  \hbox to .5\zw{#1\hss}}
\def\halfCJKrightbox#1{\leavevmode%
  \hbox to .5\zw{\hss #1}}
```

Finally, we need the commands \japanese and \korean to select the given language. These commands have to include actual manipulation of fonts, glues, and spaces.

```
\font\defaultJPNfont=omrml
\def\japanese{%
  \clearocplists\pushocplist\JapaneseOCP
  \let\selectCJKfont\defaultJPNfont
  \let\CJKspace\relax % remove spaces
  \boundCJKskip=.25em plus .15em minus .06em
```

```
   \interCJKskip=0em plus .1em minus .01em
}
\font\defaultKORfont=omhysm
\def\korean{%
   \clearocplists\pushocplist\KoreanOCP
   \let\selectCJKfont\defaultKORfont
   \let\CJKspace\space % preserve spaces
   \boundCJKskip=0em plus .02em minus .01em
   \interCJKskip=0em plus .02em minus .01em
}
```

It is straightforward to extend these macros to create a LATEX (Λ) class file.

8   CJK Font Manipulation

At first glance, the best font for Omega seems to be the one containing all characters defined in 16-bit Unicode. In fact, such a font cannot be constructed.

There are several varieties of Chinese letters: Traditional letters are used in Taiwan and Korea, while simplified letters are now used in mainland China. Japan has its own somewhat simplified set. The glyphs are significantly different from country to country.

Unicode unifies these four varieties of Chinese letters into one, if they look similar. They are *not* identical, however. For example, the letter 'bone' has the Unicode point 9AA8, but the top part of the Chinese Simplified letter and the Japanese letter are almost mirror images of each other, as shown in Figure 4. Less significant differences are also distracting to native Asian readers. The only way to overcome this problem is to use different CJK fonts according to the language selected.

(a) Chinese Simplified   (b) Japanese

Fig. 4. Two letters with the same Unicode point.

OpenType (including TrueType) is the most popular font format for CJK fonts. However, it is neither easy nor simple, even for TEX experts, to generate OFM and OVF files from OpenType fonts.

The situation looks simple for Japanese and Chinese fonts, having fixed width, because one (virtual) OFM is sufficient which can be constructed by hand. However, Korean fonts have proportional width. Since most of the popular Korean fonts are in OpenType format, a utility that extracts font metrics from OpenType fonts is required.

There are two patches of the ttf2tfm and ttf2pk utilities[7] using the freetype library. The first[8], written by one of the authors, Jin-Hwan Cho, generates OFM and OVF files from TrueType fonts (not OpenType fonts). The other[9], written by Won-Kyu Park, lets ttf2tfm and ttf2pk run with OpenType (including TrueType) fonts with the help of the freetype2 library. Moreover, two patches can be used together.

Unfortunately, ovp2ovf 2.0 included in recent TEX distributions (e.g., teTEX 2.x) does not seem to work correctly, so the previous version 1.x must be used.

9   Asian Font Packs and **DVIPDFM**x

A solution avoiding the problems mentioned above is to use the CJK fonts included in the Asian font packs of Adobe (Acrobat) Reader as non-embedded fonts when making PDF output.

It is well known that Adobe Reader can display and print several common fonts even if they are not embedded in the document. These are fourteen base Latin fonts, such as Times, Helvetica, and Courier – and several CJK fonts, if Asian font packs[10] are installed. These packs have been available free of charge since the era of Adobe Acrobat Reader 4. Four are available: Chinese Simplified, Chinese Traditional, Japanese, and Korean. Moreover, Adobe Reader 6 downloads the appropriate font packs on demand when a document containing non-embedded CJK characters is opened. Note that these fonts are licensed solely for use with Adobe Readers.

Professional CJK typesetting requires at least two font families: serif and sans serif. As of Adobe Acrobat Reader 4, Asian font packs, except for Chinese Simplified, included both families, but newer packs include only a serif family. However, newer versions of Adobe Reader can automatically substitute a missing CJK font by another CJK font installed in the operating system, so displaying both families is possible on most platforms.

If the CJK fonts included in Asian font packs are to be used, there is no need to embed the fonts when making PDF output. The PDF file should contain the font names and code points only. Some 'generic' font names are given in Table 1, which can be handled by Acrobat Reader 4 and later. However, these names depend on the PDF viewers[11]. Note that the names are not necessarily true

---

[7] Available from the FreeType project, http://www.freetype.org.

[8] Available from the Korean TEX Users group, http://ftp.ktug.or.kr/pub/ktug/freetype/contrib/ttf2pk-1.5-20020430.patch.

[9] Available as http://chem.skku.ac.kr/~wkpark/project/ktug/ttf2pk-freetype2_20030314.tgz.

[10] Asian font packs for Adobe Acrobat Reader 5.x and Adobe Reader 6.0, Windows and Unix versions, can be downloaded from http://www.adobe.com/products/acrobat/acrrasianfontpack.html. For MacOS, an optional component is provided at the time of download.

[11] For example, these names are hard coded in the executable file of Adobe (Acrobat) Reader, and each version has different names.

font names. For example, Ryumin-Light and GothicBBB-Medium are the names of commercial (rather expensive) Japanese fonts. They are installed in every genuine (expensive) Japanese PostScript printer. PDF readers and PostScript-compatible low-cost printers accept these names but use compatible typefaces instead.

Table 1. Generic CJK font names.

	Serif	Sans Serif
Chinese Simplified	STSong-Light	STHeiti-Regular
Chinese Traditional	MSung-Light	MHei-Medium
Japanese	Ryumin-Light	GothicBBB-Medium
Korean	HYSMyeongJo-Medium	HYGoThic-Medium

While TeX generates DVI output only, pdfTeX generates both DVI and PDF output. But Omega and pTeX do not have counterparts generating PDF output yet. One solution is DVIPDFM*x* [2], an extension of dvipdfm[12], developed by Shunsaku Hirata and one of the authors, Jin-Hwan Cho.

10 Conclusion

We have shown how Omega, with CJK-OTP, can be used for the production of quality PDF documents using the CJK languages.

CJK-OTP, as it stands, is poorly tested and documented. Especially needed are examples of Chinese typesetting, in which the present authors are barely qualified. In due course, we hope to upload CJK-OTP to CTAN.

References

1. ASCII Corporation. ASCII Nihongo TeX (Publishing TeX).
   http://www.ascii.co.jp/pb/ptex/.
2. Jin-Hwan Cho and Shunsaku Hirata. The DVIPDFM*x* Project.
   http://project.ktug.or.kr/dvipdfmx/.
3. John Plaice and Yannis Haralambous. The Omega Typesetting and Document Processing System. http://omega.enstb.org.
4. Apostolos Syropoulos, Antonis Tsolomitis, and Nick Sofroniou. *Digital Typography Using LaTeX*. Springer-Verlag, New York, NY, USA, 2003.

---

[12] The utility dvipdfm is a DVI to PDF translator developed by Mark A. Wicks. The latest version, 0.13.2c, was released in 2001. Available from http://gaspra. kettering.edu/dvipdfm/.

Dynamic Arabic Mathematical Fonts

Mostafa Banouni[1], Mohamed Elyaakoubi[2], and Azzeddine Lazrek[2]

[1] Physics Department, University Ibn Zohr, Faculty of Sciences
Agadir, Morrocco
mbanouni@voila.fr
[2] Department of Computer Sciences, Faculty of Sciences, University Cadi Ayyad
P.O. Box 2390, Marrakech, Morocco
{m.elyaakoubi,lazrek}@ucam.ac.ma
http://www.ucam.ac.ma/fssm/RyDArab

Abstract. This paper describes a font family designed to meet the requirements of typesetting mathematical documents in an *Arabic presentation*. Thus, not only is the text written in an Arabic alphabet-based script, but specific symbols are used and mathematical expressions also spread out from right to left. Actually, this font family consists of two components: an Arabic mathematical font and a dynamic font. The construction of this font family is a first step of a project aiming at providing a complete and homogeneous Arabic font family, in the OpenType format, respecting Arabic calligraphy rules.

Keywords: Mathematical font, Dynamic font, Variable-sized symbols, Arabic mathematical writing, Multilingual documents, Unicode, POST-SCRIPT, and OpenType.

1 Overview

The Arabic language is native for roughly three hundred million people living in the Middle East and North Africa. Moreover, the Arabic script is used, in various slightly extended versions, to write many major languages such as Urdu (Pakistan), Persian and Farsi (Iran, India), or other languages such as Berber (North Africa), Sindhi (India), Uyghur, Kirgiz (Central Asia), Pashtun (Afghanistan), Kurdish, Jawi, Baluchi, and several African languages. A great many Arabic mathematical documents are still written by hand. Millions of learners are concerned in their daily learning by the availability of systems for typesetting and structuring mathematics.

Creating an Arabic font that follows calligraphic rules is a complex artistic and technical task, due in no small part to the necessity of complex contextual analysis. Arabic letters vary their form according to their position in the word and according to the neighboring letters. Vowels and diacritics take their place over or under the character, and that is also context dependent. Moreover, the *kashida*, a small flowing curve placed between Arabic characters, is to be produced and combined with characters and symbols. The *kashida* is also used for the text justification. The techniques for managing the *kashida* are similar to

A. Syropoulos et al. (Eds.): TUG 2004, LNCS 3130, pp. 149–157, 2004.

those that can be used for drawing curvilinear extensible mathematical symbols, such as *sum*, *product* or *limit*.

There are several Arabic font styles. Of course, it is not easy to make available all existing styles. The font style *Naskh* was the first font style adopted for computerization and standardization of Arabic typography. So far, only Naskh, Koufi, Ruqaa, and to a limited extent Farsi have really been adapted to the computer environment. Styles like Diwani or Thuluth, for example, don't allow enough simplification, they have a great variation in characters shapes, the characters don't share the same baseline, and so on. Considering all that, we have decided to use the Naskh style for our mathematical font.

The RyDArab [10] system was developed for the purpose of typesetting Arabic mathematical expressions, written from right to left, using specific symbols. RyDArab is an extension of the TEX system. It runs with K. Lagally's Arabic system ArabTEX [8] or with Y. Haralambous and J. Plaice's multilingual Ω [6] system. The RyDArab system uses characters belonging to the ArabTEX font xnsh or to the omsea font of Ω, respectively. Further Arabic alphabetic symbols in different shapes can be brought from the font NasX that has been developed, for this special purpose, using METAFONT. The RyDArab system also uses symbols from Knuth's Computer Modern family, obtained through adaptation to the right-to-left direction of Arabic.

Since different fonts are in use, it is natural that some heterogeneity will appear in mathematical expressions typeset with RyDArab [9]. Symbol sizes, shapes, levels of boldness, positions on the baseline will not quite be in harmony. So, we undertook building a new font in OpenType format with two main design goals: on the one hand, all the symbols will be drawn with harmonious dimensions, proportions, boldness, etc., and on the other hand, the font should contain the majority of the symbols in use in the scientific and technical writing based on an Arabic script.

Both Arabic texts and mathematical expressions need some additional variable-sized symbols. We used the CurExt [11] system to generate such symbols. This application was designed to automatically generate curvilinear extensible symbols for TEX with the font generator METAFONT. The new extension of CurExt does the same with the font generator POSTSCRIPT.

While METAFONT generates bitmap fonts and thus remains inside the TEX environment, OpenType [14] gives outline and multi-platform fonts. Moreover, since Adobe and Microsoft have developed it jointly, OpenType has become a standard combining the two technologies TrueType and POSTSCRIPT. In addition, it offers some additional typographic layout possibilities thanks to its multi-table feature.

2   A Mathematical Font

The design and the implementation of a *mathematical font* are not easy [5]. It becomes harder when it is oriented to Arabic presentation. Nevertheless, independent attempts to build an Arabic mathematical font have been undertaken.

In fact, F. Alhargan [1] has sent us proofs of some Arabic mathematical symbols in TrueType format.

Now we will describe the way we constructed the OpenType Arabic mathematical font `RamzArab`. The construction of the font started by drawing the whole family of characters by hand. This task was performed by a calligrapher. Then the proofs were scanned to transform them into vectors. The scanning tools alone don't produce a satisfying result, so once the design is finalized, the characters are processed and analyzed using special software to generate the file defining the font.

In Arabic calligraphy, the feather's quill (*kalam*) is a flat rectangle. The writer holds it so that the largest side makes an angle of approximately 70° with the baseline. Except for some variations, this orientation is kept all along the process of drawing the character. Furthermore, as Arabic writing goes from right to left, some boldness is produced around segments from top left toward the bottom right and conversely, segments from top right to the bottom left will rather be slim as in Figure 1.

The `RamzArab` font in Figure 4 contains only symbols specific to Arabic mathematics presentation plus some usual symbols found even in text mode. It is mainly composed of the following symbols:

- alphabetic symbols: Arabic letters in various forms, such as characters in isolated standard form, isolated double-struck, initial standard, initial with tail, initial stretched and with loop (ٮ ٮ ٮـ ٮـ ٮـ ٮـ respectively);
- punctuation marks (e.g., ، ؛ : ! ؟);
- digits as used in the Maghreb Arab (North Africa), and as they are in the Machreq Arab (Middle East);
- accents to be combined with alphabetic symbols (e.g., ◌̂ ◌̃ ◌̈);
- ordinary mathematical symbols such as delimiters, arithmetic operators, etc.
- mirror image of some symbols such as sum, integral, etc.

In Arabic mathematics, the order of the alphabetic symbols differs from the Arabic alphabetic order. Some problems can appear with the alphabetic symbols in their multi-form.

Generally, in Arabic mathematical expressions, alphabetic symbols are written without dots (e.g., ◌̇ ◌̈ ◌ۛ) or diacritics. This helps to avoid confusions with accents. The dots can be added whenever they are needed, however. Thus, few symbols are left.

Moreover, some deviation from the general rules will be necessary: in a mathematical expression, the isolated form of the letter ALEF can be confused with the Machreq Arab digit ONE. The isolated form of the letter HEH can also present confusion with the Machreq Arab digit FIVE. The choice of the glyphs أ and هـ to denote respectively these two characters will help to avoid such confusions. Even though these glyphs are not in conformity with the homogeneity of the font style and calligraphic rules, they are widely used in mathematics. In the same way, the isolated form of the letter KAF ك , resulting from the combination of two other basic elements, will be replaced by the KAF glyph in Ruqaa style, ﻛ.

For the four letters ALEF, DAL, REH and WAW, the initial and the isolated forms are the same, and these letters will be withdrawn from the list of letters in initial form. On the other hand, instead of a unique cursive element, the stretched form of each of the previous letters will result from the combination of two elements. It follows that these letters will not be present in the list of the letters in the stretched form.

The stretched form of a letter is obtained by the addition of a MADDA-FATHA or ALEF in its final form ﺍ to the initial form of the letter to be stretched (e.g., ﺩ + ﺍ ⟶ ﺩﺍ). The glyph of LAM-ALEF ﻻ has a particular ligature that will be added to the list. The stretched form of a character is used if there is no confusion with any usual function abbreviation (e.g., ﺣﺎ or ﺟﺎ for the sine function).

The form with tail is obtained starting from the initial form of the letter followed by an alternative of the final form of the letter HEH ﺱ (e.g., ﺩ + ﺱ ⟶ ﺳ). These two forms are not integrated into the font because they can be obtained through a simple composition.

The form with loop is another form of letters with a tail. It is obtained through the combination of the final form with a particular curl that differs from one letter to another (e.g., ﻊ ﺹ). This form will be integrated into the font because it cannot be obtained through a simple composition.

The following particular glyphs are also in use:

ﺀ ﺀ ﻫ ﺭ ﺯ ﺩ ﻙ ﻣ ﻥ ﻉ ﻻ.

The elements that are used in the composition of the operator sum, product, limit and factorial in a conventional presentation (ﻣ ﺩ ﻟ ﺩ) are also added. These symbols are extensible. They are stretched according to the covered expression, as we will see in the next section.

Reversed glyphs, with respect to the vertical – and sometimes also to the horizontal – axis, as in Figure 1, are taken from the Computer Modern font family. For example, there are:

ٱ ٲ Ⅴ ٲ ∞ ١ E ʃ ⌐ ⅃ Ɜ.

Other symbols with mirror image forms already in use[1] are not added to this font. Of course, Latin and Greek alphabetic symbols can be used in Arabic mathematical expressions. In this first phase of the project, we aren't integrating these symbols into the font. They can be brought in from other existing fonts.

---

[1] The Bidi Mirrored property of characters used in Unicode.

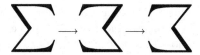

Fig. 1. Sum symbol with vertical then horizontal mirror image.

3   A Dynamic Font

The composition of variable-sized letters and curvilinear symbols is one of the hardest problems in digital typography. In high-quality printed Arabic works, justification of the line is performed through using the kashida, a curvilinear variable lengthening of letters along the baseline. The composition of curvilinear extensible mathematical symbols is another aspect of dynamic fonts. Here, the distinction between fixed size symbols and those with variable width, length, or with bidimensional variability, according to the mathematical expression covered by the symbol, is of great importance.

Certain systems [11] solve the problem of vertical or horizontal curvilinear extensibility through the a priori production of the curvilinear glyphs for certain sizes. New compositions are therefore necessary beyond these already available sizes. This option doesn't allow a full consideration of the curvilinearity of letters or composed symbols at large sizes. A better approach to get curvilinear letters or extensible mathematical symbols consists of parameterizing the composition procedure of these symbols. The parameters then give the system the required information about the size or the level of extensibility of the symbol to extend. As an example, we will deal with the particular case of the opening and closing parenthesis as *vertically* extensible curvilinear symbol and with the kashida as a *horizontally* extensible curvilinear symbol. This can be generalized to any other extensible symbol.

The CurExt system was developed to build extensible mathematical symbols in a curvilinear way. The previous version of this system was able to produce automatically certain dynamic characters, such as parentheses, using META-FONT. In this adaptation, we propose to use the Adobe POSTSCRIPT Type 3 format [13].

The POSTSCRIPT language defines several types of font, 0, 1, 2, 3, 9, 10, 11, 14, 32, 42. Each one of these types has its own conventions to represent and to organize the font information. The most widely used POSTSCRIPT font format is Type 1. However, a dynamic font needs to be of Type 3 [3].

Although the use of Type 3 loses certain advantages of Type 1, such as the possibility of producing hints for when the output device is of low resolution, and in the case of small glyphs, a purely geometrical treatment can't prevent the heterogeneity of characters. Another lost advantage is the possibility of using Adobe Type Manager (ATM) software. These two disadvantages won't arise in our case, since the symbols are generally without descenders or serifs and the font is intended to be used with a composition system such as TEX, not directly in Windows.

The POSTSCRIPT language [7] produces a drawing by building a path. Here, a path is a set of segments (`lineto`) and third degree Bézier curves (`curveto`). The path can be open or closed on its origin (`closepath`). A path can contain several control points (`moveto`). Once a path is defined, it can be drawn as a line (`stroke`) or filled with a color (`fill`). From the graphical point of view, a glyph is a procedure defined by the standard operators of POSTSCRIPT.

To parameterize the procedure, the form of the glyph has to be examined to determine the different parts of the procedure. This analysis allows determining exactly what should be parameterized. In the case of an opening or closing parenthesis, all the parts of the drawing depend on the size: the width, the length, the boldness and the end of the parenthesis completely depend on the size. Figure 2 shows the variation of the different parameters of the open parenthesis according to the height. We have chosen a horizontally-edged cap with a boldness equal to half of the boldness of the parenthesis. The same process is applied to the kashida.

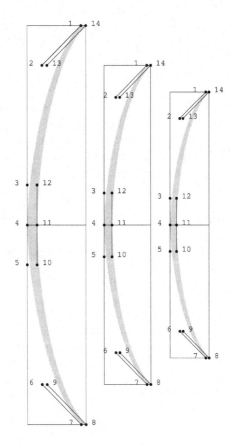

Fig. 2. Parametrization of dynamic parenthesis.

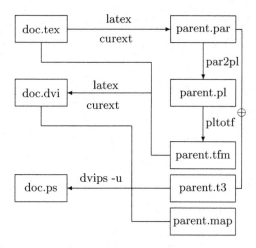

Fig. 3. Generation of dynamic parentheses.

Producing a dynamic parenthesis such as that in Figure 3 follows these steps:

– collecting the various needed sizes in a parameter file `par`;
– generating a file `pl` with the local tool **par2pl** starting from the `par` file;
– converting the file `pl` into a metric file `tfm` with the application `pltotf`;
– compiling the document to generate a `dvi` file;
– converting the file from `dvi` to `ps` format.

This process should be repeated as many times as needed to resolve overlapping of extensible symbols.

The curvilinear parentheses are produced by CurExt as follows:

```
$\parentheses{
\matrix{1 & 2 & 3\cr
        4 & 5 & 6\cr
        7 & 8 & 9\cr
        0 & 1 & 2\cr}
}$
```

$$\begin{pmatrix} 1 & 2 & 3 \\ 4 & 5 & 6 \\ 7 & 8 & 9 \\ 0 & 1 & 2 \end{pmatrix}$$

instead of the straight parentheses given by the usual encoding in TEX:

```
$\left(
\matrix{1 & 2 & 3\cr
        4 & 5 & 6\cr
        7 & 8 & 9\cr
        0 & 1 & 2\cr}
\right)$
```

$$\begin{pmatrix} 1\,2\,3 \\ 4\,5\,6 \\ 7\,8\,9 \\ 0\,1\,2 \end{pmatrix}$$

	0	1	2	3	4	5	6	7	8	9
1x										
2x										
3x				!	#	$	%	&	'	(
4x	)	*	+	,	-	.	/	0	1	2
5x	3	4	5	6	7	8	9	:	;	،
6x	=	—	؟	@	.	..	..	.	..	٭
7x	‰	٪	٪.	.	١	٢	٣	٤	٥	٦
8x	٧	٨	٩	○	○	[	\	]	^	.
9x	۴	،	ٮ	ﺤ	ﺝ	ﺰ	ﺡ	٤	ﻻ	ﻝ
10x	ﻊ	ﻌﺮ	٣	ﺪ	؟	٥	ﻭ	ﺢ	ﻛ	ﺮ
11x	ٯ	ﻉ	ﻻ	–	—	~	..	١	ﺏ	ﺡ
12x	ﺩ	ﻩ	ﻭ	ﺭ	ﻁ	ﻯ	ﻙ	ﻝ	ﻡ	ﻥ
13x	ﺱ	ﻉ	ﻑ	ﺹ	ﻕ	ﺩ	ﺯ	ﻩ	ﻁ	ﻙ
14x	ﺍ	ﺥ	ﺵ	ﻉ	ﺫ	ﺽ	ﺡ	ﺏ	ﺝ	ﺥ
15x	ﻪ	ﻭ	ﻥ	ﻁ	ﻕﺱ	ﻙ	ﺩ	ﻡ	ﻅ	ﺱ
16x	ﻉ	ﻮﺏ	ﻮﺻ	ﻗﺢ	١	ﺏ	ﺡ	ﺩ	ﻅ	ﺯ
17x	ﺭ	ﻁ	ﻯ	ﻙ	ﻝ	ﻡ	ﺩ	ﺱ	ﻉ	ﻑ
18x	ﺹ	ﻕ	ﻝ	–	ﻝ	^	.	١	ﻝ	ﻝ
19x	ﻝ	ﻝ	∨	∨	∤	∞	١	E	ς	⊏
20x	ﻝ	ﻝ								

Fig. 4. RamzArab Arabic mathematical font.

In the same way, we get the curvilinear kashida with CurExt:

```
\amarabmath
${\csum_{b=T-1}^{s}}$
```

instead of the straight lengthened one obtained by RyDArab:

```
\amarabmath
${\lsum_{b=T-1}^{s}}$
```

We can stretch Arabic letters in a curvilinear way through the kashida by CurExt:

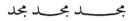

4 Conclusion

The main constraints observed in this work were:

- a close observation of the Arabic calligraphy rules, in the Naskh style, toward their formalization. It will be noticed, though, that we are still far from meeting all the requirements of Arabic calligraphy;
- the heavy use of some digital typography tools, rules and techniques.

RamzArab, the Arabic mathematical font in Naskh style, is currently available as an OpenType font. It meets the requirements of:

- homogeneity: symbols are designed with the same nib. Thus, their shapes, sizes, boldness and other attributes are homogeneous;
- completeness: it contains most of the usual specific Arabic symbols in use.

These symbols are about to be submitted for inclusion in the Unicode standard. This font is under test for Arabic mathematical e-documents [12] after having been structured for Unicode [2, 4].

The dynamic component of the font also works in PostScript under CurExt for some symbols such as the open and close parenthesis and the kashida. That will be easily generalized to other variable-sized symbols. The same adaptation can be performed within the OpenType format.

References

1. http://www.linux.org.sa
2. Jacque André, Caractères numériques : introduction, *Cahiers GUTenberg*, vol. 26, 1997.
3. Daniel M. Berry, Stretching Letter and Slanted-baseline Formatting for Arabic, Hebrew and Persian with `ditroff/ffortid` and Dynamic PostScript Fonts, *Software–Practice & Experience*, no. 29:15, 1999, pp. 1417–1457.
4. Charles Bigelow et Kris Holmes, Création d'une police Unicode, *Cahiers GUTenberg*, vol. 20, 1995.
5. Yannis Haralambous, Une police mathématique pour la Société Mathématique de France : le SMF Baskerville, *Cahiers GUTenberg*, vol. 32, 1999, pp. 5–19.
6. Yannis Haralambous and John Plaice, Multilingual Typesetting with Ω, a Case Study: Arabic, *Proceedings of the International Symposium on Multilingual Information Processing (Tsukuba)*, 1997, pp. 137–154.
7. Adobe Systems Incorporated, *PostScript Language Reference Manual*, Second ed., Addison-Wesley, 1992.
8. Klaus Lagally, *ArabTEX — Typesetting Arabic with Vowels and Ligatures*, EuroTEX'92 (Prague), 1992.
9. Azzeddine Lazrek, Aspects de la problématique de la confection d'une fonte pour les mathématiques arabes, *Cahiers GUTenberg*, vol. 39–40, Le document au XXIe siècle, 2001, pp. 51–62.
10. Azzeddine Lazrek, A package for typesetting arabic mathematical formulas, *Die TEXnische Komödie*, DANTE e.V., vol. 13. (2/2001), 2001, pp. 54–66.
11. Azzeddine Lazrek, CurExt, Typesetting variable-sized curved symbols, EuroTEX 2003 preprints, pp. 47–71 (to appear in TUGBoat).
12. Mustapha Eddahibi, Azzeddine Lazrek and Khalid Sami, *Arabic mathematical e-documents*, International Conference on TEX, XML and Digital Typography (TUG 2004, Xanthi, Greece), 2004.
13. Włodzimierz Bzyl, The Tao of Fonts, *TUGboat*, vol. 23, 2002, pp. 27–39.
14. Thomas W. Phinney, *TrueType, PostScript Type 1 & OpenType: What's the Difference?*, Version 2.00 (2001).

Arabic Mathematical e-Documents

Mustapha Eddahibi, Azzeddine Lazrek, and Khalid Sami

Department of Computer Sciences
Faculty of Sciences
University Cadi Ayyad
P.O. Box 2390,
Marrakech, Morocco
{m.eddahibi,lazrek,k_sami}@ucam.ac.ma
http://www.ucam.ac.ma/fssm/RyDArab

Abstract. What problems do e-documents with mathematical expressions in an Arabic presentation present? In addition to the known difficulties of handling mathematical expressions based on Latin script on the Web, Arabic mathematical expressions flow from *right to left* and use *specific symbols* with a *dynamic cursivity*. How might we extend the capabilities of tools such as MathML in order to structure Arabic mathematical e-documents? Those are the questions this paper will deal with. It gives a brief description of some steps toward an extension of MathML to mathematics in Arabic exposition. In order to evaluate it, this extension has been implemented in Mozilla.

Keywords: Mathematical expressions, Arabic mathematical presentation, Multilingual documents, e-documents, Unicode, MathML, Mozilla.

1 Overview

It is well known that HTML authoring capabilities are limited. For instance, mathematics is difficult to search and Web formatting is poor. For years, most mathematics on the Web consisted of texts with scientific notation rendered as images. Image-based equations are generally harder to see, read and comprehend than the surrounding text in the browser window. Moreover, the large size of this kind of e-document can represent a serious problem. These problems become worse when the document is printed. For instance, the resolution of the equations will be around 72 dots per inch, while the surrounding text will typically be 300 or more dots per inch. In addition to the display problems, there are encoding difficulties. Mathematical objects can neither be searched nor exchanged between software systems nor cut and pasted for use in different contexts nor verified as being mathematically correct. As mathematical e-documents may have to be converted to and from other mathematical formats, they need encoding with respect to both the mathematical notation and mathematical meaning.

The mathematical markup language MathML [14] offers good solutions to the previous problems. MathML is an XML application for describing mathematical notation and capturing both its structure, for high-quality visual display,

A. Syropoulos et al. (Eds.): TUG 2004, LNCS 3130, pp. 158–168, 2004.

and content, for more semantic applications like scientific software. XML stands for eXtensible Markup Language. It is designed as a simplified version of the meta-language SGML used, for example, to define the grammar and syntax of HTML. One of the goals of XML is to be suitable for use on the Web by separating the presentation from the content. At the same time, XML grammar and syntax rules carefully enforce document structure to facilitate automatic processing and maintenance of large document collections.

MathML enables mathematics to be served, received, and processed on the web, just as HTML has enabled this functionality for text. MathML elements can be included in XHTML documents with namespaces and links can be associated to any mathematical expression through XLink. Of course, there are complementary tools. For instance, the project OpenMath [12] also aims at encoding the semantics of mathematics without being in competition with MathML.

Now, what about some of the MathML internationalization aspects – say, for instance, its ability to structure and produce e-documents based on non-Latin alphabets, such as mathematical documents in Arabic?

2   Arabic Mathematical Presentation

Arabic script is cursive. Small curves and ligatures join adjacent letters in a word. The shapes of most of the letters are context-dependent; that is, they change according to their position in the word. Certain letters have up to four different shapes.

Although some mathematical documents using Arabic-based writing display mathematics in Latin characters, in general, not only the text is encoded with the Arabic script but mathematical objects and expressions are also encoded with special symbols flowing from right to left according to the Arabic writing. Moreover, some of these symbols are extensible.

Mathematical expressions are for the most part handwritten and introduced as images. A highly-evolved system of calligraphic rules governs Arabic handwriting. Though Arabic mathematical documents written by hand are sometimes of fair quality, the mere presentation of scientific documents is no longer enough, since there is a need for searchability, using them in software and so on.

The RyDArab [8] system makes it possible to compose Arabic mathematical expressions of high typographical quality. RyDArab complements TeX for typesetting Arabic mathematical documents. RyDArab uses the Computer Modern fonts and those of Ω [4] or ArabTeX [7]. The output is DVI, PS, PDF or HTML with mathematical expressions as images. The RyDArab [2] system does not replace or modify the functionality of the TeX engine, so it does not restrict in any way the set of macros used for authoring. Automatic translation from and to Latin-based expressions is provided beginning with the latest RyDArab version. Will this be enough to structure and typeset e-documents with mathematics even when they are based on an alternative script? Starting from this material with TeX and Ω, will MathML be able to handle Arabic mathematics?

3   MathML and Arabic Mathematics

Of course, semantically speaking, an Arabic mathematical expression is the same as a Latin-based one. Thus, only display problems need be taken into account. In any way, encoding semantics are beyond the scope of this paper.

In order to know if there really is a need to construct a new tool or only to improve an already available one, what are the possibilities offered by the known MathML renderers? As much of the work is built around TEX, an *open source community effort*, it is hard to be precise about the current status of all TEX/MathML related projects. Most of these projects belong to one of three basic categories:

- Conversions from TEX to MathML. Of particular note here, are Ω [5,6] and `TeX4ht` [13], a highly specialized editor/DVI driver. Both of these systems are capable of writing presentation MathML from TEX documents. There are other converters such as `LaTeX2HTML` and `tralics` [1].
- Conversions from MathML to TEX. The conversion from MathML to TEX can be done for instance, through reading MathML into Mathematica or other similar tools and then saving the result back out as TEX, or using Scientific WorkPlace for suitable LATEX sources. The ConTEXt system is another example.
- Direct typesetting of MathML using TEX.

Currently, MathML is supported by many applications. This fact shows not only that it is the format of choice for publishing equations on the web but also that it is a universal interchange format for mathematics. More than twenty implementations are listed on the MathML official website, showing that all categories of mathematical software can handle MathML. Actually,

- most mathematical software, such as Scientific WorkPlace, Maple, MathCad and Mathematica, can export and import MathML;
- all common browsers can display MathML equations either natively or using plug-ins;
- editors such as MathType, Amaya, TEXmacs, and WebEQ support MathML.

Once non-free or non-open-source tools are omitted, two Web browsers remain: the well-known Mozilla system [11] and Amaya. The W3C's Amaya editor/browser allows authors to include mathematical expressions in Web pages, following the MathML specification. Mathematical expressions are handled as structured components, in the same way and in the same environment as HTML elements. All editing commands provided by Amaya for handling text are also available for mathematics, and there are some additional controls to enter and edit mathematical constructs. Amaya shows how other W3C specifications can be used in conjunction with MathML.

In the end, we chose to adapt Mozilla to the needs of the situation, mainly because of its popularity and widespread adoption as well as the existence of an Arabic version. The layout of mathematical expressions in Latin writing, and consequently that of the mathematical documents in Mozilla is more elegant and of good typographical quality compared to other systems.

For this implementation, we used the Mozilla 1.5 C++ source under Linux. Until now, there was no Mozilla version with support for bidirectionality or cursivity in a mathematical environment. In math mode, only left-to-right arrangement is supported. Thus, the first step is to find out how to get bidirectionality and cursivity inside a MathML passage.

In fact, adding the property of bidirectionality to MathML elements is a delicate task. It requires a careful study of the various possible conflicts. The bidirectionality algorithm for mathematical expressions is probably different from that originally in use for text.

Now, let us have a look at what would happen if the bidirectionality algorithm for HTML were used for MathML elements.

The MathML expression

```
<mn>1</mn>
<mo>+</mo>
<mi>ب</mi>
<mo>-</mo>
<mn>2</mn>
```

will be rendered as $1 + 2 - \text{ب}$ instead of the expected equation: $1 + \text{ب} - 2$.

Since XML supports Unicode, we might expect that the introduction of Arabic text into MathML encoding would go without any problem. In other words, the Arabic text would be rendered from right to left, and letters would be connected just as they should be in their cursive writing. Will the use of the element <mtext> (similar to the use of the TEX command \hbox) be enough to get a satisfactory rendering of Arabic?

The following Arabic text is a sample of what is obtained with <mtext> in Mozilla:

```
<mtext>
ييضايد صرن |نص رياضي
</mtext>
```

The following Arabic abbreviation of the cosine function is an example of what we get if we introduce it with <mi>:

```
<mi>جتا</mi>| اجت
```

In order to allow the arrangement of sub-expressions from right to left in a given mother expression, a new element denoted <rl> is introduced[1].

---

[1] The name **rl** reminds us of the initials of right-to-left. Furthermore, because of the expected heavy use of this element, its name should be as short as possible.

```
<mrow>
 <rl>
  <mi>ب</mi>
  <mo>+</mo>
  <mi>س</mi>
 </rl>
</mrow>
```

ب ＋ س

The use of the element `<rl>` also allows solving the previous problem of introducing Arabic text in a mathematical expression.

```
<mtext>
 <rl>نص رياضي</rl>
</mtext>
```

نص رياضي

```
<mi><rl>جتا</rl></mi>
```

جتا

The element `<rl>` can be used to transform some mathematical objects, such as left/right or open/close parentheses, into their mirror image.

```
<rl>
 <mo><rl>[</rl></mo>
 <mi>ب</mi>
 <mo>,</mo>
 <mn>3</mn>
 <mo><rl>)</rl></mo>
</rl>
```

(3 , ب]

We can remark here that the symbol "," has not changed to its mirror image "٬". The result is the same even when the comma is governed by `<rl>` (i.e., `<rl>,</rl>`). This symbol is not yet mentioned in the Bidi Mirroring list in the Unicode Character Database.

Particular arrangement of the arguments is made necessary by the MathML renderer for any presentation elements requiring more than one argument. On the other hand, elements of vertical arrangement such as `<mfrac>` do not need special handling.

```
<mfrac>
 <rl>
  <mi>ب</mi>
  <mo>+</mo>
  <mi>س</mi>
 </rl>
 <mn>3</mn>
</mfrac>
```

$$\frac{\text{ب} + \text{س}}{3}$$

Although the addition of `<rl>` helps to get Arabic text rendered as expected and to solve arrangement of sub-expressions within an expression, for certain elements, it does not work.

Using the element `<rl>` to get a superscript element `<msup>` or a subscript element `<msub>`, in the suitable right to left positions, generates a syntax error because `<msup>` requires two arguments, whereas there is only one argument, as can be seen in the following example:

```
<msup>
 <rl>
  <mi>س</mi>
  <mi>ب</mi>     invalid-markup
 </rl>
</msup>
```

In this case, we introduce a new markup element `<amsup>`[2]. It changes the direction of rendering expressions while keeping the size of superscripts as it is with `<msup>`.

```
<amsup>
 <mi>س</mi>     ٮس
 <mi>ب</mi>
</amsup>
```

The same principle is applied to other elements like `<msub>`. The notation of the arrangement in the Arabic combination analysis is different from its Latin equivalent.

```
<amarrange>
 <mi>ل</mi>     ل²
 <mn>5</mn>     5
 <mn>2</mn>
</amarrange>
```

The next step is related to the shape of some symbols. In Arabic mathematical presentation, certain symbols, such as the square root symbol or the sum, in some Arabic areas, are built through a symmetric reflection of the corresponding Latin ones. These symbols require first the introduction of a new font family such as the one offered in the Arabic Computer Modern fonts. This family corresponds to the Computer Modern fonts with a mirror effect on some glyphs. In the same way that the Computer Modern fonts are used in the Latin mathematical environment with `<math>` the new element `<amath>` will allow the use of the Arabic Computer Modern fonts in the Arabic mathematical environment. The

---

[2] The following new elements defined in this system are prefixed with the initial of Arabic "a".

element `<amath>` would not be necessary if the Arabic mathematical symbols were already added in the Unicode tables. In fact, we use the same entity name and code for some symbols and their mirror images used in the Arabic presentation. For example, the Unicode name `N-ARY SUMMATION` coded by `U+02211` is associated simultaneously to the Latin sum[3] symbol $\sum$ and to its Arabic equivalent mirror $\mathcal{Z}$. Thus, to specify which glyph, and consequently which font, is called, the introduction of a new element `<amath>` is necessary. This element would not be necessary if the symbols were denoted with two different entity names and consequently two different codes.

```
<amath>
 <rl>
  <mstyle displaystyle="true">
   <munderover>
    <mo>&sum;</mo>
    <mrow>
     <rl>
      <mi>س</mi>
      <mo>=</mo>
      <mn>1</mn>
     </rl>
    </mrow>
    <mi>ف</mi>
   </munderover>
  </mstyle>
  <mi>س</mi>
 </rl>
</amath>
```

In order to distinguish alphabetical symbols, in different shapes, from letters used in Arabic texts, and to avoid the heterogeneity resulting from the use of several fonts, there is a need for a complete Arabic mathematical font. That's exactly what we are trying to do in another project discussed elsewhere in this volume [10]. While waiting for their adoption by Unicode, the symbols in use in this font will be located in the Private Use Area E000-F8FF in the Basic Multilingual Plane.

```
<mi>&#xE004;</mi>
```

The use of the Arabic Computer Modern fonts is not enough for composed symbols. For example, the square root symbol is composed of the square root glyph supplemented by an over bar. This over bar is added by the renderer, which, thanks to a calculation of the width of the base, gives the length of this over bar.

---

[3] Introduced as ∑ or ∑.

In this case, neither the inversion of the glyph nor the use of the right-to-left element `<rl>` changes the direction of the visual rendering of the square root. For this reason we have introduced a new element (`<amsqrt>`), which uses the square root glyph from the Arabic Computer Modern font that shows the over bar to its left.

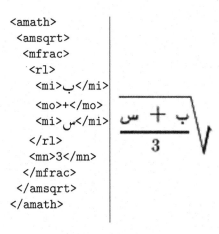

```
<amath>
 <amsqrt>
  <mfrac>
   <rl>
     <mi>ب</mi>
     <mo>+</mo>
     <mi>س</mi>
   </rl>
   <mn>3</mn>
  </mfrac>
 </amsqrt>
</amath>
```

The root element `<amroot>` requires a treatment similar to that of the square root combined with the positioning of the index on the right of the baseline.

```
<amath>
 <amroot>
   <mi>س</mi>
   <mn>3</mn>
 </amroot>
</amath>
```

For the elements `<munderover>`, `<munder>`, `<mover>`, and `<msubsup>`, italic correction needs to be done. In fact, mathematical symbols like the integral are slanted and the indices and exponents are shifted in the direction of the symbol's slant. This fact appears clearly in the following example representing two integrals, while using `<amsubsup>` in the first:

```
<amath>
 <rl>
  <mstyle displaystyle="true">
   <amsubsup>
    <mo>&int;</mo>
    <mn>0</mn>
    <mn>1</mn>
   </amsubsup>
  </mstyle>
  <amsup>
   <mi>س</mi>

   <mi>ب</mi>
  </amsup>
   <mi>ء</mi>

   <mi>س</mi>
 </rl>
</amath>
```

or <amunderover> in the second:

```
<amath>
 <rl>
  <mstyle displaystyle="true">
   <amunderover>
    <mo>&int;</mo>
    <mn>0</mn>
    <mn>1</mn>
   </amunderover>
  </mstyle>
  <amsup>
   <mi>س</mi>

   <mi>ب</mi>
  </amsup>
   <mi>ء</mi>

   <mi>س</mi>
 </rl>
</amath>
```

For the limit of an expression, manual lengthening of the limit symbol is performed. Of course, dynamic lengthening via automatic calculation of the width of the text under the limit sign would be better.

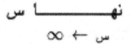

A lengthening of the straight line is not in conformity with the rules of Arabic typography. A curvilinear lengthening is required, which can be obtained by using CurExt [9], which makes it possible to stretch Arabic letters according to calligraphic rules.

The following mathematical expression is an example of the use of <mover>, with automatic lengthening of the over arrow.

$$\overleftarrow{\text{ب} + \text{س}}$$

In fact, the use of element <rl> doesn't represent a very practical solution as the encoding becomes heavier. The addition of this element must be transparent for the user; the same for all other new elements since they affect only the presentation and not the semantics of expression. An alternative solution consists of either building a new algorithm of bidirectionality for mathematics, or of adding attributes that will make it possible to choose the mathematical notation of the expression. We intend to use a new attribute **nota** for the root element <math>. It would indicate whether Arabic or Latin is used inside the mathematical expression. As the layout of a mathematical expression follows a precise logic, the direction of writing would be handled automatically without requiring the use of direction attributes for each child of the element <math>.

The FIGUE [3] system is an engine for the interactive rendering of structured objects. It allows the rendering of an Arabic text from right to left including some Latin mathematical expressions flowing from left to right thanks to a proposed bidirectional extension of MathML.

4 Conclusion

Our goal was to identify the difficulties and limitations that might obstruct the use of MathML for writing mathematics in Arabic. The main adaptation we made to MathML for Arabic mathematics was the addition of the element <rl> that allows:

- writing mathematical expressions from right-to-left;
- the use of specific symbols thanks to the modification of other elements;
- and handling the cursivity of writing.

Now, Arabic mathematical e-documents can be structured and published on the Web using this extended version of Mozilla. Such documents can thus benefit from all the advantages of using MathML. Our project for the development of communication and publication tools for scientific and technical e-documents in Arabic is still at its beginning. We hope that the proposals contained in this paper will help to find suitable recommendations for Arabic mathematics in Unicode and MathML.

References

1. http://www-sop.inria.fr/miaou/tralics/
2. Mustapha Eddahibi and Azzeddine Lazrek, *Arabic scientific document composition*, International Conference on Information Technology and Natural Sciences (ICITNS 2003, Amman, Jordan), 2003.
3. Hanane Naciri et Laurence Rideau, *Affichage et diffusion sur Internet d'expressions en langue arabe de preuves mathématiques*, CARI 2002 (Cameroun), 2002.
4. Yannis Haralambous and John Plaice, Multilingual Typesetting with Ω, a Case Study: Arabic, *Proceedings of the International Symposium on Multilingual Information Processing (Tsukuba)*, 1997, pp. 137–154.
5. Yannis Haralambous and John Plaice, Produire du MathML et autres *ML à partir d'Ω: Ω se généralise, *Cahiers GUTenberg*, vol. 33-34, 1999, pp. 173–182.
6. Yannis Haralambous and John Plaice, *XℲTEX, a DTD/Schema Which is Very Close to LATEX*, EuroTEX 2003: 14th European TEX Conference (ENST Bretagne, France), 2003 (to appear in TUGBoat).
7. Klaus Lagally, *ArabTEX — Typesetting Arabic with Vowels and Ligatures*, EuroTEX'92 (Prague), 1992.
8. Azzeddine Lazrek, A package for typesetting Arabic mathematical formulas, *Die TEXnische Komödie*, DANTE e.V., vol. 13. (2/2001), 2001, pp. 54–66.
9. Azzeddine Lazrek, *CurExt, Typesetting variable-sized curved symbols*, EuroTEX 2003 preprints: 14th European TEX Conference (Brest, France), 2003, pp. 47–71 (to appear in TUGBoat).
10. Mostafa Banouni, Mohamed Elyaakoubi and Azzeddine Lazrek, *Dynamic Arabic mathematical fonts*, International Conference on TEX, XML and Digital Typography (TUG 2004, Xanthi, Greece), 2004.
11. Mozilla, http://www.mozilla.org
12. OpenMath, http://www.openmath.org/
13. TEX4ht, http://www.cis.ohio-state.edu/~gurari/TeX4ht/mn.html
14. Presentation MathML and Content MathML, http://www.w3.org/TR/MathML2

Migrating to XML:
The Case of the GUST Bulletin Archive

Włodzimierz Bzyl[1] and Tomasz Przechlewski[2]

[1] Instytut Matematyki, Uniwersytet Gdański
80-952 Gdańsk
ul. Wita Stwosza 57
Poland
matwb@univ.gda.pl

[2] Wydział Zarzadzania, Uniwersytet Gdański
81-824 Sopot
ul. Armii Krajowej 119/121
Poland
tomasz@gnu.univ.gda.pl

Abstract. Ten years of experience with TeX publishing of the GUST bulletin shows that Knuth's dream of highly portable TeX files is apparently an illusion in practice. Over the last decade, articles in the GUST bulletin have used at least six major formats (LaTeX 2.09, transitional LaTeX+NFSS, LaTeX 2_ε, plain-based *TUGboat*, Eplain, and ConTeXt), numerous macro packages, fonts, and graphic formats. Many old articles are typeset differently nowadays, and some even cause TeX errors.

This situation motivates the following question: how do we avoid the same problem in the future? As the World Wide Web is quickly becoming the mainstream both of publishing and of information exchange we argue for migration to XML – a Web compatible data format.

In the paper we examine a possible strategy for storing GUST articles in a custom XML format and publishing them with both TeX and XSLT/FO. Finally, the problems of converting the TeX files to XML and possibility of using TeX4ht – an authoring system for producing hypertext – are discussed.

1 Introduction

The dominant role played by the Web in information exchange in modern times has motivated publishers to make printed documents widely available on the Internet. It is now common that many publications are available on the Web only, or before they are printed on paper. Articles published in the GUST bulletin are available on the Web in POSTSCRIPT and PDF. Unfortunately, these formats decrease document accessibility, searching and indexing by Web search engines. For broad accessibility to automated services, it is better to use XML as the format of such data. However, one issue with XML is that it is difficult to maintain the high quality presentation of TeX documents. This

A. Syropoulos et al. (Eds.): TUG 2004, LNCS 3130, pp. 169–178, 2004.

is caused by incompatibilities between browsers and incomplete or immature implementations of W3C Consortium standards.

We are optimistic that these issues will disappear in the near future, and believe that XML will become pervasive in the online environment. However, in our context, a key to the adoption of XML is the degree to which it can be integrated with existing TEXnologies.

In this paper we examine one strategy for storing GUST articles in a custom XML format and publishing them with *both* TEX and XSLT/FO. Also, the problems of converting the existing TEX files to XML and the possibility of using TEX4ht – an authoring system for producing hypertext – are discussed.

2   TEX/LATEX and Other Document Formats

When the authors started work with TEX (many years ago), there was only a choice between closed-source applications based on proprietary formats, or TEX, for publishing significant documents. Nowadays, the choice is much wider, as XML-based solutions are based on open standards and supported by a huge number of free applications. We do not need to write the tools ourselves. Thus the strategy of reusing what is publicly available is key in our migration plan.

On the other hand it would be unwise to switch to XML as the only acceptable submission format, because it would force many authors to abandon their powerful TEX-based editing environments to which they are accustomed, just to submit texts to our bulletin. Following this route, we would more likely end up with a shortage of submissions. Thus, we are preparing a mixed strategy with both TEX and XML as accepted formats. Papers submitted in LATEX will ultimately be converted to XML as an archival or retrieval format. Presentation formats will be XHTML, with corresponding PDF generated by a variety of tools. The work-flow of documents in this proposed framework is depicted on Fig. 1.

The XML implementation project described in the paper can be broadly divided into the following subtasks: DTD development, formatting development, and legacy information conversion [19]. We'll now describe these stages in detail.

3   DTD Development Considerations

There is no doubt (see for example [14, 19]) that the DTD development phase is of critical importance for the overall success of any SGML/XML project. Fortunately, thanks to the great interest in XML technology in recent years, there are several production-quality publicly available DTDs which could be adapted for our project. To make this choice, we preferred those which are widely used and for which formatting applications and tools are available. The following possible schemes were considered:

– DocBook [21], a complete publishing framework, i.e., schemes plus XSLT or DSSSL stylesheets for conversion to presentation formats; actively developed

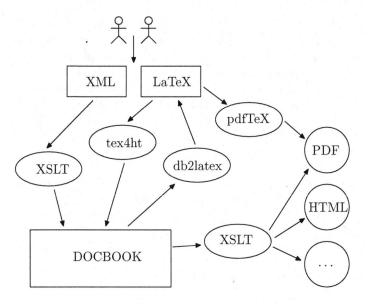

Fig. 1. Processing diagram for XML/LaTeX documents.

and maintained; the de facto standard of many Open Source projects; widely known and used.

- TEI [1], another complete, actively developed publishing framework. Not as popular as DocBook, used mainly in academia.
- The LaTeX-based DTD developed in [7] (further referred as LWC DTD). The similarity to the structure of LaTeX is an advantage of this DTD for our project.
- Others, such as DTD for GCA/Extreme conferences, X-DiMi from the Electronic Thesis and Dissertations Project, and the LaTeX-like PMLA developed by one of the authors [15].

Industry-standard DTDs tend to be too big, too complex, and too general for practical use in specific cases (cf. [14, p. 29]). In particular, the DocBook and TEI DTDs seem to be too complex for marking-up documents conforming to LaTeX format.

As a result, users frequently employ the technique of using different DTDs at different stages of the editorial process. Following Maler [14], we will call the DTD common to a group of users within an interest group as a *reference* DTD, while those used solely for editing purposes as an *authoring* DTD. Translation from one DTD to another may be easily performed with an XSLT stylesheet.

We decided to use a simplified LWC DTD as authoring DTD and DocBook as reference DTD. Providing a simple DTD should expand the group of prospective authors. For example, many GUST members are experts in typography or Web design but not necessarily TeX hackers.

The simplification consists of restricting the document hierarchy only to article-like documents, and removing back matter tags (`index`, `glossary`) and all presentation tags (`newline`, `hspace`, etc.). Also, the optional status of metadata, for example the `title`, `abstract`, `keywords` tags, was changed to required. The resulting DTD contains 45 elements compared to 64 in the original one.

For better maintainability, we rewrote our version of LWC DTD into RNC syntax. The RNC schema was introduced by Clark [6], and recently adopted as an ISO standard. It has many advantages over DTD or W3C Schema syntax, namely simplicity and an included documentation facility[1].

As the structure of our documents is not particularly complex, it may be feasible to develop several authoring DTDs targeted at different groups of authors, for example one for those preferring ConTEXt-like documents, another for those used to GCA conference markup, etc., and then map those documents to the reference DTD with XSLT.

4   Formatting with XSLT

For presentation, LWC documents are first transformed to DocBook with a simple XSLT stylesheet.

The DocBook XSL stylesheets [22] translate an XML document to XHTML or FO [18]. As they are written in a modular fashion, they can be easily customized and localized. To publish XHTML from XML documents, an XSLT engine is needed such as Kay's `saxon` [11] or Veillard's `xsltproc` [20].

For hard copy output, a two-step process is used. First, the XSLT engine produces formatting objects (FO) which then must be processed with a formatting object processor for PDF output[2]. The detailed transformation work-flow is depicted in Fig. 2.

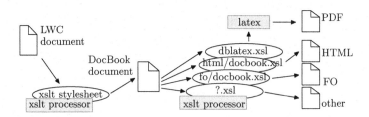

Fig. 2. Processing details of LWC documents with XSLT/FO.

---

[1] It is possible to convert between different schema languages for XML with the `trang` program [5]. There is also a nxml-mode for GNU Emacs for editing of XML which features highlighting, indentation, and on the fly validation against an RNC schema [4].

[2] Modern browsers have XSLT engines built-in. So, it suffices to attach to a document appropriate stylesheets to make the transformation on the fly.

With just a few customizations the translation from XML to XHTML presents no obstacles (except for math formulas). On the other hand, the quality of the PDF produced with the publicly available fop processor from the Apache project is poor compared to that obtained with TEX.

Instead of generating FO objects one can use XSLT to translate XML directly to high-level LaTeX. That is the method used in db2latex [3] (see also a clone project: dblatex/dbcontext [9]; the latter, of course, generates files processable by ConTeXt). The output can be customized at XSLT stylesheet level as well as by redefining appropriate LaTeX style files. MathML markup is translated with XSLT to LaTeX and supported natively[3].

The translation from DocBook to LaTeX implemented in these tools is incomplete. To get reasonable results, prior customization to local needs is required. The main advantage of this approach is that we use TEX – a robust and well known application.

5   The GUST Bulletin Archive

When considering the conversion of the GUST archive to XML we have two points in mind: first, we recognize the long-term benefits of an electronic archive of uniformly and generically marked-up documents; and second, to take the opportunity to test the whole framework using 'real' data.

During the last 10 years, 20 volumes of the GUST bulletin were published, containing more than 200 papers. From the very beginning GUST was tagged in a modified TUGBOAT style [2]. The total output is not particularly impressive, but the conversion of all articles to XML isn't a simple one-night job for a bored TEX hacker:

- they were produced over an entire decade and were written by over 100 different authors.
- they were processed with at least six major formats (LaTeX 2.09, transitional LaTeX+NFSS, LaTeX 2_ε, plain-based TUGBOAT, eplain, and finally ConTeXt), using numerous macro packages, fonts, and graphic formats[4].

As a group, the GUST authors are not amateurs, producing naïve TEX code. On the contrary they are TEX experts, writing on a diverse range of subjects using non-standard fonts, packages and macros. For example, Fig. 3 shows the detailed distribution of the TEX formats used in GUST.

In total, there were 134 plain TEX articles, compared to 87 for LaTeX. LaTeX authors used 74 different packages, while those preferring plain TEXnology used 139 different style files. The proportion of other formats (Eplain, ConTeXt, BLUE) was insignificant (only a few submissions). It can also be noted from

---

[3] One approach which we did not try is to format FO files with TEX. This method is implemented by S. Rahtz' Passive TEX [17].

[4] Needless to say, all of these packages have been evolving during the last 10 years, many of them becoming incompatible with each other.

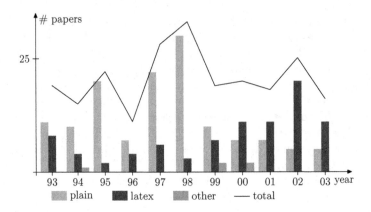

Fig. 3. Distribution of TeX formats used by GUST authors.

Fig. 3 that in recent years, the proportion of plain TeX submissions has decreased substantially in favor of LaTeX.

It is obviously very difficult to maintain a repository containing papers requiring such a diverse range of external resources (macros, fonts). As a result, many old papers can no longer be typeset due to changes in underlying macros or fonts.

6   Conversion from TeX to XML

It may be surprising that only few papers report successful conversion from TeX to XML: Grim [8] describes successful large-scale conversion in a large academic institution, while Rahtz [16] and Key [12] describe translation to SGML at Elsevier.

Basically when converting TeX to XML the following three approaches have been adopted [16]:

- Perl/Python hackery combined with manual retyping and/or manual XML marking-up.
- Parsing TeX source files not with `tex`, but with another program which generates SGML/XML. This is the approach used by `ltx2x` [23], `tralics` [8] and `latex2html`[5], which replace LaTeX commands in a document by user-defined strings.
- Processing files with TeX and post-processing the DVI files to produce XML. This is the way `tex4ht` works.

Although the conversion performed with `tralics` is impressive, we found the application very poorly documented. After evaluation of the available tools and consulting the literature [7], we decided to use TeX4ht – a TeX-based authoring system for producing hypertext [10].

---

[5] `latex2html` was not considered as its output is limited to HTML.

Because TeX formats contain many visually-oriented tags, we could not expect to automatically convert them to content-oriented XML markup[6].

For example, the TUGBOAT format requires only the metadata elements title and author name(s); author address(es) and webpage(s) of the author(s) are often absent and there is no obligation for abstracts and keywords. Therefore, most of the GUST articles lack these valuable elements. Moreover, bibliographies are inconsistently encoded[7].

Having said that, our plan is to markup as many elements as possible.

7   Translating TeX to XML with TeX4ht

Out of the box, the TeX4ht system is configured to translate from plain, LaTeX, TUGBOAT (ltugboat, ltugproc), and Lecture Notes in Computer Science (llncs) formats to HTML, XHTML, DocBook, or TEI. To translate from, say, TUGBOAT to our custom XML format the system needs to be manually configured. Because the configuration of TeX4ht from scratch is a non-trivial task, we consider other more efficient possibilities.

The TeX4ht system consists of three parts: (1) Style files which enhance existing macros with features for the output format (HTML, XHTML, etc.)[8]. (2) The `tex4ht` processor which extracts HTML or XHTML, or DocBook, or TEI files from DVI files produced by `tex`. (3) The `t4ht` processor which is responsible for translating DVI code fragments which need to be converted to pictures; for this task the processor uses tools available on the current platform.

As mentioned above, the conversion from a visual format to an information-oriented one cannot be done automatically. Let's illustrate this statement with the following example marked with plain TeX macros[9]:

```
\noindent {\bf exercise, left as an} {\it adj\/} {\ss Tech} Used
to complete a proof when one doesn't mind a {\bf handwave}, or
to avoid one entirely. The complete phrase is: {\it The proof
\rm(or \it the rest\/\rm) \it is left as an exercise for the
reader.\/} This comment has occasionally been attached to
unsolved research problems by authors possessed of either an
evil sense of humor or a vast faith in the capabilities of
their audiences.\hangindent=1em
```

---

[6] For example, see [16, 8]. Other examples, based on GUST articles, are presented below.

[7] Publicly available tools (see [13] for example) can automatically mark up manually keyed bibliographies.

[8] Altogether over 2.5M lines of TeX code. Compare this with 1M code of the LaTeX base macros.

[9] The text comes from "The Project Gutenberg Etext of The Jargon File", Version 4.0.0.

After translation of this fragment to XHTML by `tex4ht` we obtain:

```
<p class="noindent"><span class="cmbx-10">exercise, left as an
</span><span class="cmti-10">adj </span><span
class="cmss-10">Tech </span>Used to complete a proof when one
doesn&#x2019;t mind a <span class="cmbx-10">handwave</span>,
or to avoid one entirely. The complete phrase is: <span
class="cmti-10">The proof </span>(or <span class="cmti-10">the
rest</span>) <span class="cmti-10">is left as an exercise for
the reader. </span>This comment has occasionally been attached
to unsolved research problems by authors possessed of either
an evil sense of humor or a vast faith in the capabilities
of their audiences.</p>
```

and this could be rendered by a browser as:

> **exercise, left as an** *adj* Tech Used to complete a proof when one doesn't mind a handwave, or to avoid one entirely. The complete phrase is: *The proof* (or *the rest*) *is left as an exercise for the reader.* **This comment has occasionally been attached to unsolved research problems by authors possessed of either an evil sense of humor or a vast faith in the capabilities of their audiences.**

We can see that `tex4ht` uses 'span' elements to mark up font changes. These visual tags could be easily remapped to logical ones unless fragments of text with different meaning are marked with the same tag. Here the tag `cmti-10` was used to tag both the short form 'adj' and the example phrase (shown in the green italic font). To tag them differently we need different TEX macros specially configured for TEX4ht. Note that the \hangindent=1em was ignored by tex4ht. This command could not be fully simulated, because TEX's hanging indentation is not supported by browsers in full generality.

So, the markup produced by the `tex4ht` program is not logical markup. To get logical markup the GUST format should be reworked and reconfigured for TEX4ht.

Instead of configuring TEX4ht we could use an XSLT stylesheet to remap elements referencing XML format. This could be an easier route than configuring the system from scratch, while some TEX4ht configuration could also help. So, a combination of the two methods is envisaged to provide the best results.

8   Conclusion and Future Work

We have not completed the conversion yet. However, based on the experience gained so far we can estimate that almost 70% of the whole archive should be converted with little manual intervention. Semi-automatic conversion of another 15% (34 papers) is possible, with prior extensive changes in markup. Conversion of remaining 15% is impossible or useless, where 'impossible' means the paper is easier to retype than try to recompile and adjust `tex4ht` just for a particular single case, and 'useless' applies to papers demonstrating complicated graphical layouts, or advanced typesetting capabilities of TEX.

Although our system needs improvement – conversion of math is the most important remaining item to investigate – we are determined to start to use it in a production environment.

Finally, we note that many of our conclusions and methods are also applicable to TUGBOAT, because the format used for typesetting GUST bulletin differs only slightly from the one used for TUGBOAT.

References

1. Lou Burnard and C. M. Sperberg-McQueen. TEI lite: An introduction to text encoding for interchange. http://www.tei-c.org/Lite/, 2002.
2. Włodek Bzyl and Tomasz Przechlewski. An application of literate programming: creating a format for the Bulletin of the Polish TUG. *TUGboat*, 14(3):296–299, October 1993.
3. Ramon Casellas and James Devenish. DB2LaTeX XSL stylesheets. http://db2latex.sourceforge.net, 2004.
4. James Clark. NXML mode for the GNU Emacs editor. http://www.thaiopensource.com/download, 2003.
5. James Clark. Trang – multi-format schema converter based on RELAX NG. http://www.thaiopensource.com/relaxng/trang.html, 2003.
6. James Clark and Makoto Murata. Relax NG specification. http://www.relaxng.org/, 2001.
7. Michel Goossens and Sebastian Rahtz. *LaTeX Web Companion*. Addison-Wesley, 2001.
8. Jose Grim. Tralics. In *EuroTEX Preprints*, pages 38–49, 2003. http://www-sop.inria.fr/miaou/tralics. Final version to appear in TUGBOAT.
9. Benoît Guillon. DocBook to LaTeX/ConTEXt publishing. http://dblatex.sourceforge.net, 2004.
10. Eitan Gurari. tex4ht: LaTeX and TEX for hypertext. http://www.cis.ohio-state.edu/~gurari/TeX4ht/mn.html, 2004.
11. Michael Kay. SAXON – the XSLT and XQuery Processor. http://saxon.sourceforge.net, 2003.
12. Martin Key. Theory into practice: working with SGML, PDF and LaTeX. *Baskerville*, 5(2), 1995. ftp://tug.ctan.org/pub/tex/usergrps/uktug/baskervi/5_2/.
13. Language Technology Group. LT TTT version 1.0. http://www.ltg.ed.ac.uk/software/ttt, 1999.
14. Eve Maler and Jeanne El Andaloussi. *Developing SGML DTDs: From Text to Model to Markup*. Prentice Hall PTR, 1995.
15. Tomasz Przechlewski. Definicja dokumentu typu PMLA. http://gnu.univ.gda.pl/~tomasz/sgml/pmla/, 2002.
16. Sebastian Rahtz. Another look at LaTeX to SGML conversion. *TUGboat*, 16(3):315–324, September 1995. http://www.tug.org/TUGboat/Articles/tb16-3/tb48raht.pdf.
17. Sebastian Rahtz. PassiveTEX. http://www.tei-c.org.uk/Software/passivetex, 2003.

18. Robert Stayton. *Using the DocBook* XSL *Stylesheets.* Sagehill Enterprises, http://www.sagehill.net/docbookxsl/index.html, 2003.
19. Brian E. Travis and Dale C. Waldt. *The* SGML *Implementation Guide: A Blueprint for* SGML *Migration.* Springer-Verlag, 1996.
20. Daniel Veillard. LIBXSLT – the XSLT C library for Gnome. http://xmlsoft.org/XSLT, 2003.
21. Norman Walsh and Leonard Muelner. *DocBook: The Definitive Guide.* O'Reilly, 1999. http://www.docbook.org/tdg/en/html/docbook.html.
22. Wiki. DocBook XSL Stylesheets. http://docbook.org/wiki/moin.cgi/DocBookXslStylesheets, 2004.
23. Peter R. Wilson. LTX2X: A LaTeX to X Auto-tagger. http://www.ctan.org/tex-archive/support/ltx2x, 1999.

Animations in pdfTeX-Generated PDF
A New Method for Directly Embedding Animation into PDF

Jan Holeček and Petr Sojka

Faculty of Informatics, Masaryk University
Botanická 68a, 602 00 Brno, Czech Republic
{holecek,sojka}@fi.muni.cz

Abstract. This paper presents a new approach for creating animations in Portable Document Format (PDF). The method of animation authoring described uses free software (pdfTeX) only. The animations are viewable by any viewer that supports at least some features of Acrobat JavaScript, particularly Adobe (Acrobat) Reader, which is available at no cost for a wide variety of platforms. Furthermore, the capabilities of PDF make it possible to have a single file with animations both for interactive viewing and printing.

The paper explains the principles of PDF, Acrobat JavaScript and pdfTeX needed to create animations for Adobe Reader using no other software except pdfTeX. We present a step by step explanation of animation preparation, together with sample code, using a literate programming style. Finally, we discuss other possibilities of embedding animations into documents using open standards (SVG) and free tools, and conclude with their strengths and weaknesses with respect to the method presented.

1 Introduction

Extensive use of electronic documents leads to new demands being made on their content. Developing specific document versions for different output devices is time consuming and costly. A very natural demand, especially when preparing educational materials, is embedding animations into a document.

A widely used open format for electronic documents is the Adobe PDF [2] format, which combines good typographic support with many interactive features. Even though it contains no programming language constructs such as those found in PostScript, the format allows for the inclusion of *Document Level JavaScript* (DLJS) [1]. Widely available PDF viewers such as Adobe Reader (formerly Acrobat Reader) benefit from this possibility, allowing interactive documents to be created.

One of the first applications showing the power of using JavaScript with PDF was Hans Hagen's calculator [5]. Further, the AcroTeX bundle [9] uses several LaTeX packages and the full version of the Adobe Acrobat software for preparing PDF files with DLJS [10]; macro support for animations is rudimentary and

A. Syropoulos et al. (Eds.): TUG 2004, LNCS 3130, pp. 179–191, 2004.

it is stressed in the documentation that it works only with the full commercial version of Acrobat.

Our motivation is a need for PDF animations in a textbook [3] published both on paper and on CD. We have published it using Acrobat [7, 8], and eventually discovered a method to create animations using pdfTEX [11] only.

pdfTEX facilitates the PDF creation process in several ways. We can directly write the PDF code which is actually required to insert an animation. We can also utilise the TEX macro expansion power to produce PDF code. And finally, we can write only the essential parts directly, leaving the rest to pdfTEX. pdfTEX introduces new primitives to take advantage of PDF features. The ones we are going to use will be described briefly as they appear.

In this paper, we present this new 'pdfTEX only' way of embedding animations. We require no previous knowledge either of the PDF language or of pdfTEX extensions to TEX. However, the basics of TEX macro definitions and JavaScript are assumed.

The structure of the paper is as follows. In the next section we start with the description of the PDF internal document structure with respect to animations. The core of the paper consists of commented code for the pdfTEX that generates a simple all-in-one animation. The examples are written in plain TEX [6], so that others can use it in elaborate macro packages, in a literate programming style. In the second example the animation is taken from an external file, allowing the modification of the animation without modifying the primary document. Finally, we compare this approach with the possibilities of other formats, including the new standard for Scalable Vector Graphics (SVG) [12] from the W3C.

2   The PDF Document Structure

A PDF file typically consists of a header, a body, a cross-reference table and a trailer. The body is the main part of the PDF document. The other parts provide meta-information and will not be discussed here. A PDF document is actually a graph of interconnected objects, each being of a certain type. There are basic data types (boolean, numeric, string) and some special and compound types which require some explanation.

A *name* object has the form /MYNAME. There is a set of names with predefined meanings when used as a dictionary key or value. Other names can be defined by the user as human readable references to indirect objects (dictionaries and indirect objects are treated below). An *array* object is a one-dimensional list, enclosed by square brackets, of objects not necessarily of the same type. A *dictionary* object is a hash, i.e., a set of key-value pairs where the keys are name objects and the values are arbitrary objects. A dictionary is enclosed by the << and >> delimiters. *Stream* objects are used to insert binary data into a PDF document. There is also a special *null* object used as an "undefined" value.

The body of a PDF file consists of a sequence of labelled objects called *indirect objects*. An object of any other type which is given a unique *object identifier* can form an indirect object. When an object is required in some place (an array element, a value of a key in a dictionary), it can be given explicitly (a direct reference) or as an object identifier to an indirect object (an *indirect reference*). In this way objects are interconnected to form a graph. An indirect reference consists of two numbers. The first number is a unique object number. The second is an object version number and is always 0 in indirect objects newly created by pdfTEX – the first one therefore suffices to restore an indirect reference.

Various document elements are typically represented by dictionary objects. Each element has a given set of required and optional keys for its dictionary. For example, the document itself is represented by a Catalog dictionary, the root node of the graph. Its key-value pairs define the overall properties of the document. A brief description of concrete objects will be given when encountered for the first time. See [2] for more detailed information.

3   Insertion of the Animation Frames

We are not interested in constructing the animation frames themselves – any graphics program such as METAPOST will do. Let us hence assume we have a PDF file, each page of which forms a single animation frame and the frames are in the order of appearance.

Every image is inserted into PDF as a so-called *form XObject* which is actually an indirect stream object. There are three primitives that deal with images in pdfTEX. The \pdfximage creates an indirect object for a given image. The image can be specified as a page of another PDF file. However, the indirect object is actually inserted only if referred to by the \pdfrefximage primitive or preceded by \immediate. \pdfrefximage takes an object number (the first number of indirect reference) as its argument and adds the image to the TEX list being currently built. The object number of the image most recently inserted by \pdfximage is stored in the \pdflastximage register.

A general PDF indirect object can be created similarly by \pdfobj, \pdf-refobj and \pdflastobj. \pdfobj takes the object content as its argument. TEX macro expansion can be used for generating PDF code in an ordinary manner.

In our example, we first define four macros for efficiency. The \ximage macro creates a form XObject for a given animation frame (as an image) and saves its object number under a given key. The \insertobj macro creates a general PDF object and saves its object number under a given key. The \oref macro expands to an indirect reference of an object given by the argument. The last "R" is an operator that creates the actual indirect reference from two numbers. We are not going to use \pdfref* primitives, so \immediate must be present. References will be put directly into the PDF code by the \oref macro. The \image macro actually places an image given by its key onto the page.

```
1    % an image for further use
2    \def\ximage#1#2{%
3      \immediate\pdfximage
4        page #2 {frames-in.pdf}%
5      \expandafter\edef
6        \csname pdf:#1\endcsname
7        {\the\pdflastximage}}
8
9    % a general object for further use
10   \def\insertobj#1#2{%
11     \immediate\pdfobj{#2}%
12     \expandafter\edef
13       \csname pdf:#1\endcsname
14       {\the\pdflastobj}}
15
16   % expands to an indirect ref. for a key
17   \def\oref#1{%
18     \csname pdf:#1\endcsname\space 0 R}
19
20   % actually places an image
21   \def\image#1{%
22     \expandafter\pdfrefximage
23       \csname pdf:#1\endcsname}
```

Another new primitive introduced by pdfTeX is \pdfcatalog. Its argument is added to the document's Catalog dictionary every time it is expanded. The one below makes the document open at the first page and the viewer fit the page into the window. One more key will be described below.

```
24   % set up the document
25   \pdfcatalog{/OpenAction [ 0 /Fit ]}
```

Now we are going to insert animation frames into the document. We will use the \ximage macro defined above. Its first argument is the name to be bound with the resulting form XObject. The second one is the number of the frame (actually a page number in the PDF file with frames). One needs to be careful here because pdfTeX has one-based page numbering while PDF uses zero-based page numbering internally.

```
26   % all animation frames are inserted
27   \ximage{fr0}{1}  \ximage{fr1}{2}
28   \ximage{fr2}{3}  \ximage{fr3}{4}
29   \ximage{fr4}{5}  \ximage{fr5}{6}
30   \ximage{fr6}{7}  \ximage{fr7}{8}
31   \ximage{fr8}{9}
```

4   Setting Up an **AcroForm** Dictionary

The interactive features are realized by annotation elements in PDF. These form a separate layer in addition to the regular document content. Each one denotes an area on the page to be interactive and binds some actions to various events that can happen for that area. Annotations are represented by Annot dictionaries. The way pdfTEX inserts annotations into PDF is discussed in the section "Animation Dynamics" below.

Annotations are transparent by default, i.e., the page appearance is left unchanged when adding an annotation. It is up to the regular content to provide the user with the information that some areas are interactive.

We will be interested in a subtype of annotations called *interactive form fields*. They are represented by a Widget subtype of the Annot dictionary. Widgets can be rendered on top of the regular content. However, some resources have to be set. The document's Catalog refers to an AcroForm dictionary in which this can be accomplished.

The next part of the example first defines the name Helv to represent the Helvetica base-font (built in font). This is not necessary but it allows us to have a smooth control button. Next we insert the AcroForm dictionary. The DR stands for "resource dictionary". We only define the Font resource with one font. The DA stands for "default appearance" string. The /Helv sets the font, the 7 Tf sets the font size scale factor to 7 and the 0 g sets the color to be 0 % white (i.e., black). The most important entry in the AcroForm dictionary is NeedAppearances. Setting it to true (line 43) makes the Widget annotations visible. Finally, we add the AcroForm dictionary to the document's Catalog.

```
32   % the Helvetica basefont object
33   \insertobj{Helv}{
34   << /Type /Font   /Subtype /Type1
35      /Name /Helv
36      /BaseFont /Helvetica  >> }
37
38   % the AcroForm dictionary
39   \insertobj{AcroForm}{
40   << /DR << /Font <<
41       /Helv \oref{Helv} >> >>
42      /DA (/Helv 7 Tf 0 g )
43      /NeedAppearances true >> }
44
45   % add a reference to the Catalog
46   \pdfcatalog{/AcroForm \oref{AcroForm}}
```

To make a form XObject with an animation frame accessible to JavaScript, it has to be assigned a name. There are several namespaces in PDF in which this can be accomplished. The one searched for is determined from context. We are only interested in an AP namespace that maps names to annotation appearance streams. pdfTEX provides the \pdfnames primitive that behaves similarly to \pdfcatalog. Each time it is expanded it adds its argument to the Names dictionary referred from document's Catalog. The Names dictionary contains the name definitions for various namespaces. In our example we put definitions into a separate object AppearanceNames.

The name definitions may form a tree to make the lookup faster. Each node has to have Limits set to the lexically least and greatest names in its subtree. There is no extensive set of names in our example, so one node suffices. The names are defined in the array of pairs containing the name string and the indirect reference.

```
47    % defining names for frames
48    \insertobj{AppearanceNames}{
49    << /Names
50       [ (fr0) \oref{fr0}   (fr1) \oref{fr1}
51         (fr2) \oref{fr2}   (fr3) \oref{fr3}
52         (fr4) \oref{fr4}   (fr5) \oref{fr5}
53         (fr6) \oref{fr6}   (fr7) \oref{fr7}
54         (fr8) \oref{fr8} ]
55       /Limits [ (fr0) (fr8) ] >> }
56
57    % edit the Names dictionary
58    \pdfnames{/AP \oref{AppearanceNames}}
```

5   Animation Dynamics

We have created all the data structures needed for the animation in the previous section. Here we introduce the code to play the animation. It uses Acrobat JavaScript [1], an essential element of interactive forms. Acrobat JavaScript is an extension of Netscape JavaScript targeted to PDF and Adobe Acrobat. Most of its features are supported by Adobe Reader. They can, however, be supported by any other viewer. Nevertheless, the Reader is the only one known to us that supports interactive forms and JavaScript.

The animation is based on interchanging frames in a single widget. Here we define the number of frames and the interchange timespan in milliseconds to demonstrate macro expansion in JavaScript.

```
59    % animation properties
60    \def\frames{8}
61    \def\timespan{550}
```

Every document has its own instance of a JavaScript interpreter in the Reader. Every JavaScript action is interpreted within this interpreter. This means that one action can set a variable to be used by another action triggered later. Document-level JavaScript code, e.g., function definitions and global variable declarations, can be placed into a JavaScript namespace. This code should be executed when opening the document.

Unfortunately, there is a bug in the Linux port of the Reader that renders this generally unusable. The document level JavaScript is not executed if the

Reader is not running yet and the document is opened from a command line (e.g., 'acroread file.pdf'). Neither the first page's nor the document's open action are executed, which means they cannot be used as a workaround. Binding a JavaScript code to another page's open action works well enough to suffice in most cases.

We redeclare everything each time an action is triggered so as to make the code as robust as possible. First we define the Next function, which takes a frame index from a global variable, increases it modulo the number of frames and shows the frame with the resulting index. The global variable is modified.

The animation actually starts at line 78 where the frame index is initialized. The frames are displayed on an interactive form's widget that we name "animation" – see "Placing the Animation" below. A reference to this widget's object is obtained at line 79. Finally, line 80 says that from now on, the Next function should be called every \timespan milliseconds.

```
62   % play the animation
63   \insertobj{actionPlay}{
64   << /S /JavaScript /JS (
65   function Next() {
66     g.delay = true;
67     if (cntr == \frames) {
68       cntr = 0;
69       try { app.clearInterval(arun); }
70         catch(except) {}
71     } else {  cntr++; }
72     g.buttonSetIcon(
73         this.getIcon("fr" + cntr));
74     g.delay=false;
75   }
76   try { app.clearInterval(arun); }
77       catch(except) {}
78   var cntr = 0 ;
79   var g = this.getField("animation");
80   var arun = app.setInterval("Next()",
81                             \timespan);
82   ) >> }
```

Now, let us describe the Next function in more detail. Line 66 suspends widget's redrawing until line 74. Then the global variable containing the current frame index is tested. If the index reaches the number of frames, it is set back to zero and the periodic calling of the function is interrupted. The function would be aborted on error, but because we catch exceptions this is avoided. The getIcon function takes a name as its argument and returns the reference to the appearance stream object according to the AP names dictionary. This explains our approach of binding the names to animation frames – here we use the names for retrieving them. The buttonSetIcon method sets the object's appearance to the given icon.

Line 76 uses the same construct as line 69 to handle situations in which the action is relaunched even if the animation is not finished yet. It aborts the previous action. It would have been an error had the animation not been running, hence we must use the exception catching approach.

6   Placing the Animation

The animation is placed on an interactive form field – a special type of annotation. There are two primitives in pdfTEX, \pdfstartlink and \pdfendlink, to produce annotations. They are intended to insert hyperlink annotations but can be used for creating other annotations as well. The corresponding \pdfstartlink and \pdfendlink must reside at the same box nesting level. The resulting annotation is given the dimensions of the box that is enclosed by the primitives. We first create a box to contain the annotation. Note that both box and annotation size are determined by the frame itself – see line 91 where the basic frame is placed into the regular page content.

We will turn now to the respective entries in the annotation dictionary. The annotation is to be an interactive form field (/Subtype /Widget). There are many field types (FT). The only one that can take any appearance and change it is the *pushbutton*. It is a special kind of *button* field type (/FT /Btn). The type of button is given in an array of field bit flags Ff. The pushbutton has to have bit flag 17 set (/Ff 65536). To be able to address the field from JavaScript it has to be assigned a name. We have assigned the name animation to it as mentioned above (/T (animation)). Finally, we define the appearance characteristics dictionary MK. The only entry /TP 1 sets the button's appearance to consist only of an icon and no caption.

```
83    % an animation widget
84    \centerline{\hbox{%
85       \pdfstartlink user{
86       /Subtype /Widget   /FT /Btn
87       /Ff 65536          /T (animation)
88       /BS << /W 0 >>
89       /MK << /TP 1 >> }%
90       \image{fr0}%
91       \pdfendlink}}
```

For the sake of brevity and clarity we are going to introduce only one control button in our example. However, we have defined a macro for creating control buttons to show a very simple way of including multiple control buttons. The \controlbutton macro takes one argument: the caption of the button it is to produce. The macro creates a pushbutton and binds it to an action defined like actionPlay.

We have chosen control buttons to be pushbuttons again. They are little different from the animation widget – they are supposed to look like buttons. The BS dictionary (i.e., border style) sets the border width to 1 point and style to 3D button look. The MK dictionary (appearance characteristics dictionary) sets the background color to 60% white and the caption (line 98). The /H /P entry tells the button to push down when clicked on. Finally, an action is bound to the button by setting the value of the A key.

```
92    % control button for a given action
93    \def\controlbutton#1{%
94      \hbox to 1cm{\pdfstartlink user{
95      /Subtype /Widget    /FT /Btn
96      /Ff 65536           /T (Button#1)
97      /BS << /W 1 /S /B >>
98      /MK << /BG [0.6] /CA (#1) >>
99      /H /P  /A \oref{action#1}
100     }\hfil\strut\pdfendlink}}
```

And finally, we add a control button that plays the animation just below the animation widget.

```
101   % control button
102   \centerline{\hfil
103     \controlbutton{Play}\hfil}
104
105   \bye
```

7 External Animation

Let us modify the example a little so that the animation frames will be taken from an external file. This has several consequences which will be discussed at the relevant points in the code.

We are going to completely detach the animation frames from the document. As a result, we will need only the \insertobj and \oref macros from lines 1–23 from the previous example. Lines 26–31 are no longer required.

A problem arises here: the basic frame should be displayed in the animation widget when the document is opened for the first time. This can be accomplished by modifying the OpenAction dictionary at line 25 as follows.

```
\pdfcatalog{ /OpenAction <<
  /S /JavaScript /JS (
    var g = this.getField("animation");
    g.buttonImportIcon(
        "frames-ex.pdf",0);
    this.pageNum = 0;
    this.zoomType = zoomtype.fitP;
  ) >> }
```

This solution suffers from the bug mentioned in the "Animation Dynamics" section. The animation widget will be empty until a user performs an action every time the bug comes into play.

We still do need an AcroForm dictionary, so lines 32–46 are left without a change. Lines 47–58 must be omitted on the other hand, as we have nothing to name. We are going to use the same animation as in the previous example, so lines 59–61 are left untouched. There is one modification of the JavaScript code to be done. The buttonSetIcon function call is to be replaced by

```
g.buttonImportIcon(
    "frames-ex.pdf", cntr);
```

We have used the basic frame to determine a size of the widget in the previous example. This is impossible now because it has to be done at compile time. The replacement for lines 83–91 is as follows

```
% an animation widget
\centerline{\hbox to 6cm{%
  \vrule height 6cm depth 0pt width 0pt
  \pdfstartlink user{
    /Subtype /Widget   /FT /Btn
    /Ff 65536          /T (animation)
    /BS << /W 0 >>
    /MK << /TP 1
           /IF << /SW /A    /S /P
                  /A [0.5 0.5] >> >> }%
  \hfil\pdfendlink}}
```

Dimensions of the widget are specified explicitly and an IF (icon fit) dictionary is added to attributes of the pushbutton so that the frames would be always (/SW /A) proportionally (/S /P) scaled to fit the widget. Moreover, frames are to be centered in the widget (/A [0.5 0.5]) which would be the default behavior anyway. The basic frame is not placed into the document – there is only glue instead.

Lines 92–105 need not be modified.

8   Two Notes on Animation Frames

The examples with full TeX source files can be found at http://www.fi.muni.cz/~xholecek/animations/. As one can see in these examples, the all-in-one approach allows all frames to share a single background which is formed by the frame actually inserted into the page. However, it is possible to overlay pushbuttons. Elaborate constructions, the simplest of which is to use a common background frame in the example with external animations, can be achieved in conjunction with transparency.

One must ensure the proper size of all frames when fitting them into the widget. We have encountered situations (the given example being one of them) where the bounding box of a METAPOST generated graphics with a TeX label was not set properly using \convertMPtoPDF and a white line had to be drawn around the frames to force the proper bounding box as a workaround.

9   Animations in Other Formats

It is fair to list and compare other possible ways of creating animations. In this section we give a brief overview of a dozen other formats and technologies capable of handling animations.

9.1   GIF

One of the versions of the GIF format is the GIF89A format, which allows multi-image support, with bitmap only animations to be encoded within a single GIF file. GIF format supports transparency, interlacing and plain text blocks. It is widely supported in Internet browsers. However, there are licensing problems due to the compression methods used, and the format is not supported in freely available TEXware.

9.2   SWF

The SWF format by Macromedia allows storing frame-based animations, created e.g., by Macromedia's Flash authoring tool. The SWF authoring tools have to compute all the animation frames at export time. As proprietary Flash plug-ins for a wide range of Internet browsers are available, animations in SWF are relatively portable. The power of SWF can be enriched with scripting by Action-Script. At the time of writing, we are not aware of any TEXware supporting SWF.

9.3   Java

One can certainly program animations in a general programming language like Sun's Java. The drawback is that there are high demands on one's programming capabilities in Java when creating portable animations. With NTS (a TEX reimplementation in Java), one can possibly combine TEX documents with fully featured animations, at the expense of studying numerous available classes, interfaces and methods.

9.4   DOM

It is possible to reference every element in an HTML or XML document by means of the W3C's Document Object Model (DOM), a standard API for document structure.

DOM offers programmers the possibility of implementing animations with industry-standard languages such as Java, or scripting languages as ECMA-Script, JavaScript or JScript.

9.5 SVG

The most promising language for powerful vector graphic animation description seems to be Scalable Vector Graphics (SVG), a W3C recommendation [12]. It is being developed for XML graphical applications, and since SVG version 1.1 there is rich support for animations. The reader is invited to look at the freely available book chapter [13] about SVG animations on the publisher's Web site, or reading [4] about the first steps of SVG integration into TeX world. There are freely available SVG viewers from Adobe (browser plug-in), Corel, and the Apache Foundation (Squiggle).

SVG offers even smaller file sizes than SWF or our method. The description of animations is time-based, using another W3C standard, SMIL, Synchronised Multimedia Integration Language. The author can change only one object or its attribute in the scene at a time, allowing detailed control of animated objects through the declarative XML manner. Compared to our approach, this means a much wider range of possibilities for creators of animations.

The SVG format is starting to be supported in TeXware. There are SVG backends in VTEX and BaKoMaTeX, and a program Dvi2Svg by Adrian Frischauf, available at http://www.activemath.org/~adrianf/dvi2svg/. Another implementation of a DVI to SVG converter in C is currently being developed by Rudolf Sabo at the Faculty of Informatics, Masaryk University in Brno.

10 Conclusions

We have shown a method of preparing both space-efficient and high-quality vector frame-based animations in PDF format using only freely available, TeX-integrated tools.

Acknowledgments

Authors thank Oleg Alexandrov and Karl Berry for comments on an early draft of the paper.

The work has been supported by VZ MSM 143300003.

References

1. Adobe Systems Incorporated. Acrobat JavaScript Object Specification, Version 5.1, Technical Note #5186. Technical report, Adobe, 2003. http://partners.adobe.com/asn/developer/pdfs/tn/5186AcroJS.pdf.
2. Adobe Systems Incorporated. *PDF Reference: Adobe Portable Document Format Version 1.5*. Addison-Wesley, Reading, MA, USA, fourth edition, August 2003.
3. Zuzana Došlá, Roman Plch, and Petr Sojka. Mathematical Analysis with Maple: 2. Infinite Series. CD-ROM, http://www.math.muni.cz/~plch/nkpm/, December 2002.

4. Michel Goossens and Vesa Sivunen. LATEX, SVG, Fonts. *TUGboat*, 22(4):269–280, October 2001.

5. Hans Hagen. The Calculator Demo, Integrating TEX, METAPOST, JavaScript and PDF. *TUGboat*, 19(3):304–310, September 1998.

6. Petr Olšák. *TEXbook naruby (in Czech)*. Konvoj, Brno, 1997.

7. Petr Sojka. Animations in PDF. In *Proceedings of the 8th Annual Conference on Innovation and Technology in Computer Science Education, ITiCSE 2003*, page 263, Thessaloniki, 2003. Association of Computing Machinery.

8. Petr Sojka. Interactive Teaching Materials in PDF using JavaScript. In *Proceedings of the 8th Annual Conference on Innovation and Technology in Computer Science Education, ITiCSE 2003*, page 275, Thessaloniki, 2003. Association of Computing Machinery.

9. Donald P. Story. AcroTEX: Acrobat and TEX team up. *TUGboat*, 20(3):196–201, Sep. 1999.

10. Donald P. Story. Techniques of introducing document-level JavaScript into a PDF file from LATEX source. *TUGboat*, 22(3):161–167, September 2001.

11. Hán Thé Thánh. Micro-typographic extensions to the TEX typesetting system. *TUGboat*, 21(4):317–434, December 2000.

12. W3C. *Scalable Vector Graphics (SVG) 1.1 Specification*, January 2003.

13. Andrew H. Watt. *Designing SVG Web Graphics*. New Riders Publishing, September 2001.

iTeXMac:
An Integrated TeX Environment for Mac OS X

Jérôme Laurens

Université de Bourgogne
jerome.laurens@u-bourgogne.fr

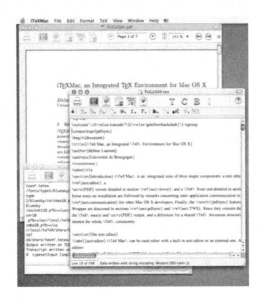

1 Introduction

iTeXMac is an integrated suite of three major components: a text editor detailed in section 2, a PDF viewer detailed in section 3, and a TeX front end detailed in section 4. Some notes on installation are followed by remarks concerning inter-application communication in section 6 for other Mac OS X developers. Finally, the pdfsync feature and the TeX Wrapper are discussed in sections 7 and 8. Since they concern the synchronization between the TeX source and PDF output, and a definition for a shared TeX document structure, both will certainly interest the whole TeX community.

2 The Text Editor

iTeXMac can be used either with a built-in text editor or an external one. All standard text editors like TextEdit, BBEdit, AlphaX, vi, and emacs are supported and configuring iTeXMac for other editors is very easy, even when coming from the X11 world.

A. Syropoulos et al. (Eds.): TUG 2004, LNCS 3130, pp. 192–202, 2004.

The built-in text editor comes with flavours similar to emacs and AlphaX modes. It relies on a plug-in architecture that allows very different kinds of user interfaces according to the type of the file being edited. Whereas AlphaX uses Tcl and emacs uses Lisp, iTEXMac utilizes the benefits of Objective-C bundles, giving plug-ins great potential power together with the application.

Among the standard features shared by advanced text editors (like key binding management, advanced regular expressions, command completion), an interesting feature of iTEXMac's text editor is the syntax parsing policy. The syntax highlighting deeply depends on the kind of text edited, whether it is Plain, LATEX or METAPOST (support for HTML is planned). The text properties used for highlighting include not only the color of the text, but also the font, the background color and some formatting properties.

Moreover, the command shortcuts that refer to mathematical and text symbols are replaced by the glyph they represent, thus replacing \alpha with α and so on. Conversely the built-in editor can show a character palette with 42 menus gathering text and mathematical symbols, as they would appear in the output. The editor thus serves as a graphical front-end to the standard LATEX packages, `amsfonts.sty`, `amssymb.sty`, `mathbb.sty`, `mathrsfs.sty`, `marvosym.sty` and `wasysym.sty`, which makes thousands of symbols available with just one click. The result is a text editor that contains much more WYSIWYG than others, with no source file format requirement.

There is also advanced management of string encoding, and iTEXMac supports more than 80 of them with an efficient user interface. The text files are scanned for hints about the text encoding:

LATEX	`\usepackage`[*encoding*]`{inputenc}`
ConTEXt	`\enableregime`[*encoding*]
emacs	`%-*-coding:` *character encoding*`;-*-`
	`%!iTeXMac(charset):`
	character encoding
	Mac OS X hidden internals

But this is not user friendly practice and will be enhanced by the forthcoming discussion of TEX wrappers in section 8.

Spell checking for TEX input is available with Rick Zaccone's LATEX-aware Excalibur[1] and Anton Leuski's TEX-aware cocoAspell[2], a port of the Free and Open Source spell checker aspell. The latter also knows about HTML code and is integrated to Mac OS X allowing iTEXMac to check spelling as you type, with misspelled words being underlined in red. While this service is provided to all applications for free, iTEXMac is the only one that truly enables TEX support by managing the language and the list of known words on a file by file basis using TEX Wrappers.

---

[1] `http://www.eg.bucknell.edu/~excalibr/`
[2] `http://cocoAspell.leuski.net/`

3   The PDF Viewer

iTeXMac can be used either with a built-in PDF viewer or an external one. The built-in viewer lacks many advanced features of Acrobat or Preview, but it updates the display automatically when a PDF file has been changed externally. Moreover, it allows you to make selections and export them to other applications, like Word, TextEdit or Keynote for example. Finally, it has support for the useful PDF synchronization discussed below and is very well integrated in the suite.

iTeXMac can open PS, EPS and DVI files with a double click, by first converting them to PDF. It thus plays the role of a PostScript or a DVI viewer. This feature is now partially obsolete since Mac OS X version 10.3 provides its own PS to PDF translator used by the Preview application shipped with the system.

4   The TeX Front End

This component of the software serves two different purposes. On one hand it is a bridge between the user and the utilities of a standard TeX distribution: a graphical user interface for the commands `tex`, `latex`, `pdftex`, and so on. On the other hand, it has to properly manage the different kinds of documents one wants to typeset.

Actually, the iTeXMac interface with its underlying TeX distribution is fairly simple. Five basic actions are connected to menu items, toolbar buttons or command shortcuts to

- typeset (e.g., running `latex` once, or twice in advanced mode)
- make the bibliography (e.g. running `bibtex`)
- make the index (e.g., running `makeindex`)
- render graphics (e.g., running `dvipdf`)

All these actions are connected to shell scripts stored on a per document basis. If necessary, the user can customize them or even change the whole process by inserting an in-line instruction at the very beginning of a source file. For example, the following directive, if present, will run `pdflatex` in escape mode.

```
%!iTeXMac(typeset): pdflatex
--shell-escape $iTMInput
```

The `makeindex` and `bibtex` command options can be set from panels, and other commands are supported. Moreover, the various log files are parsed, warnings and errors are highlighted with different colors and HTML links point to lines where an error occurred. Some navigation facilities from log file to output are also provided, a string like [a number...], pointing to the output page.

As for documents, iTeXMac manages a list of default settings that fit a wide range of situations, including for example

- LATEX documents with DVI, PS or PDF engines
- books
- METAPOST documents
- ConTEXt documents
- HTML documents
- B. Gaulle's French Pro documents.

Users can extend this list with a built-in editor, adding support for MusicTEX, maybe `gcc`, and so on.

5 Installing TEX and iTEXMac

The starting point for a detailed documentation is the MacOS X TEX/LATEX Web Site[3] where one will find an overview of the TEX related tools available on Mac OS X. As a graphical front-end, iTEXMac needs a TEX distribution to be fully functional. Gerben Wierda maintains on his site[4] the TEX Live[5] distribution and a set of useful packages. Other teTEX 2.0.2 ports are available from fink[6] (and through one of its graphical user interfaces, such as finkcommander[7]) and from Darwin Ports[8], through a CVS interface.

The official web site of iTEXMac is hosted by the Open Source software development SourceForge website at: `http://itexmac.sourceforge.net/`. One can find in the download section the disk images for the following products:

- iTEXMac, both stable and developer release
- an external editor for iTEXMac key binding
- the Hypertext Help With LATEX wrapped as a searchable Mac OS X help file
- the TEX Catalog On line wrapped as a searchable Mac OS X help file
- the French LATEX FAQ wrapped as a searchable Mac OS X help file.

An updater allows you to check easily for new versions. To install iTEXMac, just download the latest disk image archive, double click and follow the instructions in the read-me file.

Due to its Unix core, Mac OS X is no longer focused on only one user. To support multiple users, iTEXMac configuration files can be placed in different locations to change defaults for all, or just certain users. The search path is:

- the built-in domain as shipped with the application (with default, read-only settings)
- the network domain (`/Network/Library/ApplicationSupport/iTeXMac`), where an administrator can put material to override or augment the default behaviour of all the machines on a network

---

[3] `http://www.esm.psu.edu/mac-tex/`
[4] `http://www.rna.nl/tex.html`
[5] `http://www.tug.org/texlive/`
[6] `http://fink.sourceforge.net/pdb/package.php/tetex`
[7] `http://finkcommander.sourceforge.net/`
[8] `http://darwinports.opendarwin.org/ports/?by=cat&substr=print`

- the local domain (`/Library/Application\-Sup\-port/iTeXMac`), where an administrator can put material to override or augment the network or default behaviour
- the user domain (`~/Library/Application\-Sup\-port/iTeXMac`), where the user can put material to override or augment the local or default behaviour

This is a way to apply modifications to iTeXMac as a whole.

6   Inter-application Communication

This section describes how iTeXMac communicates with other components, in the hope that this syntax will also be used by other applications when relevant, to avoid the current situation where there are as many AppleScript syntaxes as there are available applications for TeX on the Macintosh. It also shows why iTeXMac integrates so well with other editors or viewers.

6.1   Shell Commands

iTeXMac acts as a server, such that other applications can send it messages. Each time it starts, iTeXMac installs an alias to its own binary code in `~/Library/TeX/bin/iTeXMac`. With the following syntax[9], either from the command line, an AppleScript or shell script, one can edit a text file at the location corresponding to the given line and column numbers

```
~/Library/TeX/bin/iTeXMac edit -file   "filename"
     -line lineNumber -column colNumber
```

The following syntax is used to display a PDF file at the location corresponding to the given line column and source file name

```
~/Library/TeX/bin/iTeXMac display -file   "filename.pdf"
   -source "sourcename.tex" -line lineNumber -column colNumber
```

6.2   AppleScript

The same feature is implemented using this scripting language. It would be great for the user if other TeX front ends on Mac OS X would implement the same syntax.

```
tell application "iTeXMac" to edit   "filename.tex"
     at line lineNumber column colNumber

tell application "iTeXMac" to display   "filename.pdf"
     at line lineNumber column colNumber
     in source "Posix source name.tex"
```

---

[9] These commands should be entered all on one line. They are broken here due to the relatively narrow columns.

iTEXMac support for AppleScript likewise covers the compile, bibliography and index actions. They are not given here since there is no Apple Events Suite dedicated to TEX. However, configuration files and instructions are given to let third-party applications like Alpha X, BBEdit or emacs control iTEXMac using those scripts.

6.3 HTML

iTEXMac implements support for a URL scheme named `file-special` for editing, updating or displaying files, for example

```
file-special://localhost/"filename.tex";
    action=edit;line=lineNumber; column=columnNumber
```

```
file-special://localhost/"filename.pdf"; action=display;
line=lineNum;      column=columnNum; source="Posix source name.tex"
```

will ask iTEXMac to edit a TEX source file or display the given file (assumed to be PDF) and when synchronization information is available, scroll to the location corresponding to the given line and column in source (assumed to be TEX). This allows adding dynamic links in HTML pages, in a TEX tutorial for example.

7 The pdfsync Feature

7.1 About Synchronization

As the TEX typesetting system heavily relies on a page description language, there is no straightforward correspondence between a part of the output and the original description code in the input. A workaround was introduced a long time ago by commercial TEX frontends Visual TEX[10] and TEXtures[11] with a very efficient implementation. Then LaTEX users could access the same features – though in a less-efficient implementation – through the use of `srcltx.sty`, which added source specials in the DVI files. The command line option `-src-specials` now gives this task to the TEX typesetting engine.

When used with an external DVI viewer or an external text editor, through an X11 server or not, iTEXMac fully supports this kind of synchronization feature.

For the PDF file format, Piero d'Ancona and the author elaborated a strategy that works rather well for Plain TEX, ConTEXt and LaTEX users. While typesetting a `foo.tex` file with LaTEX for example, the `pdfsync` package writes extra geometry information in an auxiliary file named `foo.pdfsync`, subsequently used by the front ends to link line numbers in source documents with locations in pages of output PDF documents. iTEXMac and TEXShop[12] both support `pdfsync`.

---

[10] http://www.micropress-inc.com/

[11] http://www.bluesky.com/

[12] http://www.uoregon.edu/~koch/texshop

The official **pdfsync** web site is:

http://itexmac.sourceforge.net/pdfsync.html

It was more convenient to use an auxiliary file than to embed the geometric information in the PDF output using **pdftex** primitives. The output file is not polluted with extraneous information and the front ends need not parse the PDF output to retrieve such metrics.

7.2 The pdfsync Mechanism

A macro is defined to put **pdfsync** anchors at specific locations (for hbox's, paragraphs and maths). There are essentially three problems we must solve: the position of an object in the PDF page is not known until the whole page is composed, the objects don't appear linearly in the output[13] and finally, an input file can be entirely parsed long before its contents are shipped out. To solve these, at each **pdfsync** anchor the known information (line number and source file name) is immediately written to the **pdfsync** auxiliary file and the unknown information (location and page number) will be written only at the next ship out.

7.3 The .pdfsync File Specifications

This is an ASCII text file organized into lines. There is no required end of line marker format from among the standard ones used by operating systems.

Only the two first lines described in table 1 are required, the other ones are optional. The remaining lines are described according to their starting characters, they consist of 2 interlaced streams. A synchronous one detailed in table 2 is obtained with \immediate\writes and concerns the input information. An asynchronous one detailed in table 3 is obtained with delayed \writes and concerns the output information.

Table 1. **pdfsync** required lines format.

Line	Format	Description	Comment
1st	*jobName*	*jobName*: case sensitive TeX file name	In general, the extensionless name of the file as the result of an \immediate\write\file{\jobname}
2nd	version *V*	*V*: a 0 based nonnegative integer	The current version is 0

The correspondence between the two kinds of information is made through a record counter, which establishes a many-to-many mapping from line numbers in TeX sources to positions in PDF output.

---

[13] The footnote objects provide a good example.

Table 2. pdfsync line specifications of the synchronous stream.

Line	Format	Description	Comment
"b"	b *name*	*name*: TEX file name	TEX is about to begin parsing *name*, all subsequent line and column numbers will refer to *name*. The path is relative to the directory containing the .pdfsync file. Path separators are the Unix "/". The file extension is not required, "tex" is the default if necessary. Case sensitive.
"e"	e		The end of the input file has been reached. Subsequent line and column numbers now refer to the calling file. Optional, but must match a corresponding "b" line.
"l"	l *R L* l *R L C*	*R*: record number, *L*: line number, *C*: optional column number.	

Table 3. pdfsync line specification of the asynchronous stream.

Line	Format	Description	Comment
"s"	s *S*	*S*: physical page number	TEX is going to ship out a new page.
"p" "p*"	p *R x y* p* *R x y*	*R*: record number, *x*: horizontal coordinate, *y*: vertical coordinate.	Both coordinates are respectively given by \the\pdflastxpos and \the\pdflastypos

7.4 Known Problems

Unfortunately, the various pdfsync files for Plain, LATEX or ConTEXt are not completely safe. Some compatibility problems with existing macro packages may occur. Moreover, sometimes pdfsync actually influences the final layout; in a case like that, it should only be used in the document preparation stage.

Another mechanism widely used by ConTEXt makes pdfsync sometimes inefficient, where the macro expansion only occurs long after it has been parsed, such that the \inputlineno is no longer relevant and the significant line number is no longer accessible. This makes a second argument for the implementation of the pdfsync feature at a very low level, most certainly inside the pdftex engine itself.

8 TWS: A TEX Wrapper Structure

In general, working with TEX seems difficult due to the numerous auxiliary files created. Moreover, sharing TEX documents is often delicate as soon as we do not use very standard LATEX. The purpose of this section is to lay the foundation for the TEX Wrapper Structure, which aims to help the user solve these problems.

Table 4. Contents of the TEX Project directory *document.* `texp`.

Name	Contents
`Info.plist`	XML property list for any general purpose information wrapped in an `info` dictionary described in Table 5. Optional.
spellingKey.`spelling`	XML property list for lists of known words wrapped in a `spelling` dictionary defined in table 9 and uniquely identified by *spellingKey*. This format is stronger than a simple comma separated list of words. Optional.
`frontends`	directory dedicated to front-ends only.
`frontends/`*name*	private directory dedicated to the front-end identified by *name*. The further contents definition is left under the front-end responsibility.
`users`	directory dedicated to users. Should not contain any front-end specific data.
`users/`*name*	directory dedicated to the user identified by *name* (not its login name). Not yet defined, but private and preferably encrypted.

First, it is very natural to gather all the files related to one TEX document in one folder we call a TEX Wrapper. The file extension for this directory is `texd`, in reference to the `rtf` and `rtfd` file extensions already existing on Mac OS X. The contents of a TEX wrapper named *document.*`texd` is divided according to different criteria:

- required data (source, graphics, bibliography database)
- helpful data and hints (tex, bibtex, makeindex options, known words)
- user-specific data
- front-end-specific data
- cached data
- temporary data

It seems convenient to gather all the non-required information in one folder named *document.*`texd/`*document.*`texp` such that silently removing this directory would cause no harm. As a consequence, no required data should stay inside *document.*`texp`, and this is the only rule concerning the required data. The `texp` file extension stands for "TEX Project".

In Tables 4 to 9 we show the core file structure of the *document.*`texp` directory. This is a minimal definition involving only string encoding and spelling information because there is no consensus yet among users and all the developers of TEX solutions, on Mac OS X at least. We make use of the XML property list data format storage as defined by

`http://www.apple.com/DTDs/PropertyList-1.0.dtd`

Table 5. `info` dictionary description.

Key	Class	Contents
`isa`	String	Required with value: `info`
`version`	Number	Not yet used but reserved
`files`	Dictionary	The paths of the files involved in the project wrapped in a `files` dictionary. Optional.
`properties`	Dictionary	Attributes of the above files wrapped in a `properties` dictionary. Optional.
`main`	String	The *fileKey* of the main file, if relevant, where *fileKey* is one of the keys of the `files` dictionary. Optional.

Table 6. `files` dictionary description.

Key	Class	Contents
fileKey	String	The path of the file identified by the string *fileKey*, relative to the directory containing the TEX project. No two different keys should correspond to the same path.

Table 7. `properties` dictionary description.

Key	Class	Contents
fileKey	Dictionary	Language, encoding, spelling information and other attributes wrapped in an `attributes` dictionary described in table 8. *fileKey* is one of the keys of the `files` dictionary.

Table 8. `attributes` dictionary description.

Key	Class	Contents
`isa`	String	Required with value: `attributes`
`version`	Number	Not yet used but reserved
`language`	String	According to latest ISO 639. Optional.
`codeset`	String	According to ISO 3166 and the IANA A ssigned Character Set Names. If absent the standard C++ locale library module is used to retrieve the `codeset` from the `language`. Optional.
`eol`	String	When non void and consistent, the string used as end of line marker. Optional.
`spelling`	String	One of the *spellingKeys* of table 4, meaning that *spellingKeys*.`spelling` contains the list of known words of the present file. Optional.

Table 9. `spelling` dictionary description.

Key	Class	Contents
`isa`	String	Required with value: `spelling`
`version`	Number	Not yet used but reserved
`words`	Array	The array of known words

However, this mechanism doesn't actually provide the concrete information needed to typeset properly (engine, format, output format). For that we can use `Makefiles` or shell scripts either embedded in the TEX Wrapper itself or shipped as a standard tool in a TEX distribution. This latter choice is less powerful but much more secure. Anyway, a set of default actions to be performed on a TEX Wrapper should be outlined (compose, view, clean, archive...).

Technically, iTEXMac uses a set of private, built-in shell scripts to typeset documents. If this is not suitable, customized ones are used instead, but no warning is given then. No security problem has been reported yet, most certainly because such documents are not shared.

Notice that iTEXMac declares `texd` as a document wrapper extension to Mac OS X, which means that *document*.`texd` folders are seen by other applications just like other single file documents, their contents is hidden at first glance. Using another file extension will prevent this Mac OS X feature without losing the benefit of the TEX Wrapper Structure.

A final remark concerns the version control system in standard use among TEX users. In the current definition, only one directory level should be supported in a *document*.`texp` folder. The contents of the `frontend` and `users` should not be monitored.

9   Nota Bene

Some features discussed here are still in the development stage and are still being tested and validated (for example, advanced syntax highlighting and full TWS support).

MlBibTeX: Beyond LaTeX

Jean-Michel Hufflen

LIFC (FRE CNRS 2661)
University of Franche-Comté
16, route de Gray
25030 Besançon Cedex
France
hufflen@lifc.univ-fcomte.fr
http://lifc.univ-fcomte.fr/~hufflen

Abstract. This article sums up our experience with MlBibTeX, our multilingual implementation of BibTeX, and points out some possible improvements for better co-operation between LaTeX and MlBibTeX. Also, MlBibTeX may be used to generate bibliographies written according to other formalisms, especially formalisms related to XML, and we give some ways to ease that.

Keywords: Bibliographies, multilingual features, BibTeX, MlBibTeX, bst, nbst, XML, XSLT, XSL-FO, DocBook.

1   Introduction

MlBibTeX (for 'MultiLingual BibTeX') is a reimplementation of BibTeX [21], the bibliography processor associated with LaTeX [19]. The project began in October 2000, and has resulted in two experimental versions [9, 11] and the present version (1.3), that will be available publicly by the time this article appears. As we explained in [15], a prototype using the Scheme programming language is working whilst we are developing a more robust program written in C. The prototype has allowed us to get some experience with real-sized bibliographies: this is the purpose of the first part of this article, after a short review of the *modus operandi* of MlBibTeX.

MlBibTeX's present version no longer uses the bst language of BibTeX for bibliography styles [20]. Such .bst files were used in MlBibTeX's first version, but since this old-fashioned language, based on simple stack manipulations, is not modular, we quickly realised that this choice would have led us to styles that were too complicated [12]. Thus, Version 1.3 uses the nbst (for 'New Bibliography STyles') language, described in [13] and similar to XSLT[1], the language of transformations designed for XML texts [32]. More precisely, MlBibTeX 1.3 uses XML[2] as a central formalism in the sense that parsing files containing *bibliographical*

---

[1] EXtensible Stylesheet Language Transformations.

[2] EXtensible Markup Language. A good introduction to this formalism issued by the w3c (**W**orld **W**ide **W**eb **C**onsortium) is [24].

A. Syropoulos et al. (Eds.): TUG 2004, LNCS 3130, pp. 203–215, 2004.

```
@BOOK{silke1988,
        AUTHOR = {James~R. Silke},
        TITLE = {Prisoner of the Horned Helmet},
        PUBLISHER = {Grafton Books},
        YEAR = 1988,
        NUMBER = 1,
        SERIES = {Frank Frazetta's Death Dealer},
        NOTE = {[Pas de traduction fran\c{c}aise
                connue] ! french
                [Keine deutsche Übersetzung]
                ! german},
        LANGUAGE = english}
```

Fig. 1. Example of a bibliographical entry in MlBibTeX.

entries (.bib files) results in a DOM[3] tree. Bibliography styles written using nbst are XML texts, too.

Of course, nbst can be used to generate bibliographies for documents other than those processed with LaTeX[4]. In particular, nbst eases the generation of bibliographies for documents written using XML-like syntax. Nevertheless, dealing with .bib files raises some problems: we go into them thoroughly in Section 4.

Reading this article requires only a basic knowledge of LaTeX, BibTeX and XML. Some examples given in the next section will use the commands provided by the multilingual babel package of LaTeX 2_ε [2]. Other examples given in Section 4 will use the Scheme programming language, but if need be, referring to an introductory book such as [28] is sufficient to understand them.

2   Architecture of MlBibTeX

2.1   How MlBibTeX Works

As a simple example of using MlBibTeX with LaTeX, let us consider the silke1988 bibliographical entry given in Figure 1. As we explain in [15], the sequence '[...] ! ⟨*idf*⟩' is one of the multilingual features provided by MlBibTeX, defining a string to be included when the language of a corresponding reference, appearing within a bibliography, is *idf*. So if this entry is cited throughout a document written in French and the 'References' section is also written in French, it will appear as:

[1] James R. SILKE: *Prisoner of the Horned Helmet*. N° 1 *in Frank Frazetta's Death Dealer*. Grafton Books, 1988. Pas de traduction française connue.

---

[3] Document **O**bject **M**odel. This is a W3C recommendation for a standard tree-based programming approach [24, p. 306–308], very often used to implement XML trees.

[4] This is also the case with the bst language of BibTeX, but in practice, it seems that this feature has not been used, except for documents written in SCRIBE [25], a predecessor of LaTeX.

Here and in the bibliography of this article, we use a 'plain' style, that is, references are labelled with numbers. More precisely, the source processed by LATEX, included into the .bbl file generated by MlBiBTEX, is:

```
\begin{thebibliography}{...}
...
\bibitem{silke1988}
\begin{otherlanguage*}{english}
James~R. \textsc{Silke}: \emph{Prisoner of the
Horned Helmet}.
\foreignlanguage{french}{\bblno~1 \bblof}
\emph{Frank Frazetta's Death Dealer}. Grafton
Books, 1988. \foreignlanguage{french}{Pas de
traduction fran\c{c}aise connue}.
\end{otherlanguage*}
...
\end{thebibliography}
```

Let us examine this source text. We can notice the use of additional LATEX commands to put some keywords ('\bblin' for '*in*', '\bblno' for 'N°', that is, 'number' in French). In [14], we explain how to put them into action within LATEX and how MlBiBTEX uses them. This source also shows how English words, originating from an entry in English (see the value of the LANGUAGE field in Figure 1), are processed. If the document uses the babel package, and if the french option of this package is selected, we use the \foreignlanguage command of this package [2], as shown above. Users do not have to select its english option; if it is not active, the source text generated by MlBiBTEX looks like:

```
\bibitem{silke1988}James~R. \textsc{Silke}:
\emph{Prisoner of the Horned Helmet}. \bblno~1
\bblof\ \emph{Frank Frazetta's Death Dealer}.
Grafton Books, 1988. Pas de traduction
fran\c{c}aise connue.
```

but the English words belonging to this reference will be taken as French by LATEX and thus may be processed or hyphenated incorrectly.

2.2   The Modules of MlBiBTEX

As mentioned in the introduction, parsing a .bib file results in a DOM tree. In fact, .bib files are processed as if they were XML trees, but without whitespace nodes[5]. Following this approach, the entry silke1988 given in Figure 1 is viewed

---

[5] These are text nodes whose contents are only whitespace characters, originating from what has been typed between two tags [27, p. 25–26]. For example, if the XML text of Figure 2 is parsed, there is a whitespace node, containing a newline and four space characters between the opening tags <author> and <name>. XML parsers are bound by the 'all text counts' constraint included in the XML specification [33, § 2.10], and cannot ignore such whitespace characters.

```
<book id="silke1988" language="english">
  <author>
    <name>
      <personname>
        <first>James R.</first>
        <last>Silke</last>
      </personname>
    </name>
  </author>
  <title>Prisoner of the Horned Helmet</title>
  <publisher>Grafton Books</publisher>
  <year>1988</year>
  <number>1</number>
  <series>
    Frank Frazetta's Death Dealer
  </series>
  <note>
    <group language="french">
      Pas de traduction française connue
    </group>
    <group language="german">
      Keine deutsche Übersetzung
    </group>
  </note>
</book>
```

Fig. 2. The XML tree corresponding to the entry of Figure 1.

as the tree of Figure 2, except that the whitespace nodes that an XML parser would produce are excluded.

We can see that some LaTeX commands and special characters are converted according to the conventions of XML.

– The commands used for accents and special letters are replaced by the letter itself. This poses no problem since DOM trees are encoded in Unicode [29]. As an example, the '\c{c}' sequence in the value of the NOTE field in Figure 1 is replaced by 'ç' in Figure 2. (By the way, let us remark that MlBIBTEX can handle the 8-bit latin1 encoding[6]: notice the 'Ü' character inside this value.)
– Likewise, the commands:
  - '\␣' for a simple space character,
  - '\\' for an end-of-line character,
  and the sequences of characters:
  - '~', for an unbreakable space character,
  - '--', and '---' for dash characters,
  are replaced by the corresponding Unicode values for these characters[7]:

---

[6] See [7, Table C.4] for more details.

[7] That was not the case in earlier versions; for instance, [12, Figure 3] improperly includes a tilde character in a text node. This bug was fixed at the end of 2003.

```
<nbst:template match="group">
  <nbst:if test="@language=$language">
    <!-- The $language variable is set to the current language.  -->
    <nbst:value-of select="call(language_open_change,@language)"/>
    <!-- If the babel package is used and a known option has been selected,
         this external function writes the \foreignlanguage command...
      -->
    <nbst:apply-templates use-language="@language"/>
    <nbst:value-of select="call(language_close_change,@language)"/>
    <!-- ... and this external function puts a closing brace.  -->
  <nbst:if>
</nbst:template>
```

Fig. 3. Example of calling an external function.

     – —

An example is given by the value of the AUTHOR field, see Figures 1 & 2.

– Some characters escaped in LATEX (for example, '$', '%', '&') lose the escape character:

$$\text{\textbackslash\%} \implies \%$$

The escape is restored if MlBibTEX generates a .bbl file to be processed by LATEX. Other characters are replaced by a reference to a character entity[8]:

$$\text{\textbackslash\&} \implies \text{\&} \qquad < \implies \text{\<} \qquad > \implies \text{\>}$$

– Balanced delimiters for quotations (" ' " and " ' " or ' ' ' and ' ' ') are replaced by an emph element[9]:

```
'Tooth and Claw' =>
  <emph emf='no' quotedf='yes'>
    Tooth and Claw
  </emph>
```

If ' ' ' or ' " ' characters are unbalanced, they are replaced by references to character entities used in XML documents:

$$' \implies \text{\'} \qquad " \implies \text{\"}$$

Such an XML tree, resulting from our parser, may be validated using a DTD[10]; more precisely, by a revised version of the DTD sketched in [10].

Some examples of using nbst for bibliography styles are given in [12–14]. We give another example in Figure 3. We can see that this language is close to XSLT

---

[8] See [24, p. 48] for more details.

[9] 'emph' is of course for 'emphasise': all the attributes (for example, 'quotedf' for 'quoted-flag', used for specifying a quotation) default to no, except emf, which defaults to yes. The complete specification is given in [10].

[10] Document Type Definition. A DTD defines a document markup model [24, Ch.5].

and it uses *path expressions* as in the XPath language [31]. Also, the example shows how multilingual features (for example, the sequence '[...] ! ...') are processed: we use some external functions in order to determine which LaTeX command can be used to switch to another language. These external functions are written using the language of MlBibTeX's implementation: Scheme for the prototype, C for the final program.

3   MlBibTeX with LaTeX

When BibTeX generates a .bbl file, it does not use the source file processed by LaTeX, but only the auxiliary (.aux) file, in which the definition of all the labels provided by the commands \label and \bibitem is stored. This file also contains the name of the bibliography style to be used and the paths of bibliography data bases to be searched, so BibTeX need not look at any other file.

This is not true for MlBibTeX. It still uses the .aux file as far as possible, but it also has to determine which multilingual packages are used: first of all babel, but also some packages devoted to particular languages: french [6], german [23], ... So we have to do a *partial parsing* of the .tex file for that. For better co-operation between LaTeX and MlBibTeX, this could be improved, in that information about multilingual packages used, and languages available, could be put in the .aux file. In fact, the external functions of our new bibliography styles are only used to manage information extracted from a .tex file. Expressing such operations using nbst would be tedious.

Another improvement regarding the natural languages known by LaTeX would be a connection between:

a) the language codes used in XML, specified by means of a two-letter language abbreviation, optionally followed by a two-letter country code [1] (for example, 'de' for '*d*eutsch' ('German'), 'en-UK', 'en-US, etc.)'; and

b) the *resources* usable to write texts in these languages.

For example, a default framework could be the use of the babel package, and 'de' would get access to the german option of this package, although it could be redefined to use the *ad hoc* package name german. In the future, such a framework would allow us to homogenise all the notations for natural languages to those of XML. In addition, let us notice that ConTeXt[11] [8], already uses these two-letter codes in its \selectlanguage command.

And last but not least, auxiliary files should include information about the encoding used in the source text. As can be seen in the examples of Section 2.1, accented letters are replaced by the commands used to produce them in LaTeX, even though LaTeX can of course handle 8-bit encodings (provided that the inputenc package is loaded with the right option). This is to avoid encoding

---

[11] TeX, defined by Donald E. Knuth [18], provides a general framework to format texts. To be fit for use, the definitions of this framework need to be organised in a *format*. Two such formats are plain TeX and LaTeX, and another is ConTeXt, created by Hans Hagen.

```
<nbst:bst version="1.3" id="plain" xmlns:nbst=
 "http://lifc.univ-fcomte.fr/~hufflen/mlbibtex"
 >

  <nbst:output method="LaTeX"/>
  ...
</nbst:bst>
```

Fig. 4. Root element for a bibliography style written using nbst.

problems. In addition, such information would ease the processing of languages written using non-Latin alphabets.

4   Towards the XML World

Since a .bib file can be processed as an XML tree by a bibliography style written in nbst, MlBɪʙTᴇX opens a window on XML's world. A converter from .bib files to a file written using HTML[12], the language of Web pages, becomes easy to write. So does a tool to write a bibliography as an XSL-FO[13] document [34]. More precisely, we give in Figure 4 an example of using the root element of nbst. Possible values for the `method` of the `nbst:output` element are:

LaTeX   xml   html   text

Nevertheless, this approach has an important limitation in practice. Since BɪʙTᴇX has traditionally been used to generate files suitable for LᴬTᴇX, users often put LᴬTᴇX commands inside values of BɪʙTᴇX fields[14]. For example:

ORGANIZATION = {\textsc{tug}}

In such a case, we would have to write a mini-LᴬTᴇX program (or perhaps a new output mode for LᴬTᴇX) that would transform such a value into a string suitable for an XML parser.

The problem is more complicated when commands are defined by end-users. For instance:

ORGANIZATION = {\logo{tug}}

works with BɪʙTᴇX – or MlBɪʙTᴇX when we use it for generating LᴬTᴇX output – even though \logo has an arbitrary definition; for example,

```
\newcommand{\logo}[1]{\textsc{#1}}
```

---

[12] **H**yper**T**ext **M**arkup **L**anguage.

[13] **EX**tensible **S**tylesheet **L**anguage – **F**ormatting **O**bjects: this language aims to describe high-quality print outputs. Such documents can be processed by the shell command `xmltex` (resp. the shell command `pdfxmltex`) from PassiveTᴇX [22, p. 180] to get .dvi files (resp. .pdf files).

[14] The author personally confesses to using many \foreignlanguage commands within the values of BɪʙTᴇX fields, before deciding to develop MlBɪʙTᴇX.

```
<bibliography>

  <title>References</title>

  <biblioentry>
    <abbrev>silke1989</abbrev>
    <authorgroup>
      <author>
        <firstname>James R.</firstname>
        <surname>Silke</surname>
      </author>
    </authorgroup>
    <copyright><year>1989</year></copyright>
    <isbn>0-586-07018-4</isbn>
    <publisher>
      <publishername>
        Grafton Books
      </publishername>
    </publisher>
    <title>Lords of Destruction</title>
    <seriesinfo>
      <title>
        <othercredit>
          <firstname>Frank</firstname>
          <surname>Frazetta</surname>
        </othercredit>'s Death Dealer
      </title>
      <volumenum>2</volumenum>
    </seriesinfo>
  </biblioentry>

</bibliography>
```

Fig. 5. The bibliographical reference from Figure 1 expressed in DocBook. Note the *ad hoc* tag `<othercredit>`.

according to LATEX's conventions, or:

```
\def\logo#1{\textsc{#1}}
```

if a style close to plain TEX is used. Likewise, such commands can be known when an output file from MlBIBTEX is processed by ConTEXt.

Moreover, let us consider the bibliographical reference given in Figure 5, according to the conventions of DocBook, a system for writing structured documents [36] (we use the conventions of the XML version of DocBook, described in [26]). We can see that some information is more precise than that provided in Figure 1. But there are still complexities: the person name given in the value of the SERIES field is surrounded by an *ad hoc* element in the DocBook version.

If we want to take advantage of the expressive power of DocBook, we can:

- directly process an XML file for bibliographical entries. In this case, our DTD should be extended; that is possible, but we still need a solution to process the huge number of existing .bib files;
- introduce some new syntax inside .bib files, that might be complicated and thus perhaps unused in practice,
- introduce new LATEX commands, to process like the \logo example mentioned above.

We have experimentally gone quite far in the third direction, which also allows to us to deal with the LATEX commands already in .bib files. In Figure 6, we give some examples of such processing, as implemented in the prototype[15].

As can be seen, we have defined a new function in Scheme, named **define-pattern**, with two formal arguments. The first is a string viewed as a *pattern*, following the conventions of TEX for defining commands, that is, the arguments of a command are denoted by '#1', '#2', ... (cf. [18, Ch. 20]). The second argument may also be a string, in which case it specifies a replacement. The arguments of the corresponding command are processed recursively. In case of conflict among patterns, the longest is chosen. So, the pattern "\\logo{#1}"[16] takes precedence over the pattern "{#1}".

If the second argument of the **define-pattern** function is not a string, it must be a zero-argument function that results in a string. In this case, all the operations must be specified explicitly, using the following functions we wrote:

pattern-matches? returns a *true* value if its first argument matches the second, a *false* value otherwise;

pattern-process recursively processes its only argument, after replacing sub-patterns by corresponding values[17];

pattern-replace replaces the sub-patterns of its argument by corresponding values; these value are not processed, just replaced *verbatim*.

Whether given directly as the second argument to **define-pattern** or resulting from applying a zero-argument function, the string must be well-formed w.r.t. XML's conventions, that is, tags must be balanced, attributes must be well-formed, etc. In other words, such a string must be acceptable to an XML parser: in our case, the parser is SSAX[18] [17].

The examples given in Figure 6 allow us to see that we can deal with simple commands, like:

$$\text{\textbackslash logo\{...\}} \implies \text{<emph ...>...</emph>}$$

as well as more complicated cases, like a cascade of \iflanguage commands [2]:

---

[15] This feature has not yet been implemented in the final version.

[16] Let us recall that in Scheme, the backslash character ('\') is used to escape special characters in string constants. To include it within a string, it must itself be escaped.

[17] In fact, using a string *s* as a second argument of **define-pattern** yields the evaluation of the expression (lambda () (pattern-process *s*)).

[18] Scheme implementation of SAX. 'SAX' is for 'Simple API (**A**pplication **P**rogramming **I**nterface) for XML': this name denotes a kind of parser, see [24, p. 290–292].

```
(define-pattern "{#1}"
  ;; The asitis element is used for words that should never be uncapitalised, that is, proper names. In BIBTEX,
  ;; we specify such behaviour by surrounding words by additional braces.
  "<asitis>#1</asitis>")

(define-pattern "\\logo{#1}" "<emph emf='no' scf='yes'>#1</emph>")

(define-pattern "\\foreignlanguage{#1}{#2}"
  "<foreigngroup language='#1'>#2</foreigngroup>")

(define-pattern "\\iflanguage{#1}{#2}{#3}"
  (lambda ()   ; Zero-argument function.
    (string-append ; Concatenation of strings.
      "<nonemptyinformation>"
      "<group language='" (pattern-replace "#1") "'>" (pattern-process "#2")
      "</group>"
      (let loop ((pattern (pattern-replace "#3")))
        ;; This form—named let (cf. [28, Exercise 14.8])—defines an internal function loop and
        ;; launches its first call:
        (if (pattern-matches? "\\iflanguage{#4}{#5}{#6}" pattern)
            (string-append "<group language='" (pattern-replace "#4") "'>"
              (pattern-process "#5")
              "</group>"
              ;; The internal function loop is recursively called with a new value:
              (loop (pattern-replace "#6")))
            (string-append "<group>" (pattern-process pattern) "</group>")))
      "</nonemptyinformation>")))
```

Fig. 6. Patterns for some LaTeX commands in Scheme.

```
\iflanguage{...}{...}{%
 \iflanguage{...}{...}{ ...  }}
```

which becomes:

```
<nonemptyinformation>
  <group language='...'>...</group>
  <group language='...'>...</group>
  ...
</nonemptyinformation>
```

The `nonemptyinformation` element is used for information that must be output, possibly in a default language if no translation into the current language is available.

What we do by means of our `define-pattern` function is like the additional procedures in Perl[19] that the converter `LaTeX2HTML` [4] can use to translate additional commands.

5   Conclusion

Managing several formalisms can be tedious. This fact was one of main elements in XML's design: giving a central formalism, able to be used for representing trees, and allowing many tools using different formalisms to communicate.

BIBTEX deals with three formalisms: .aux files, .bib files and .bst files. As Jonathan Fine notes in [5], the applications devoted to a particular formalism cannot be shared with other applications. MlBIBTEX attempts to use XML as far as possible, although there is still much to do. For example, defining a syntax for the entries for which we are looking, when using MlBIBTEX to generate XSL-FO or DocBook documents. (For our tests, this list of entry names is simply given on the command line).

The next step will probably be a more intensive use of XML, that is, the direct writing of bibliographical entries using XML conventions. For this, we need something more powerful than DTDs, with a richer type structure, namely, *schemas*[20]. In addition, we should be able to easily add new fields to bibliographical entries: the example given using DocBook shows that additional information must be able to be supplied to take advantage of the expressive power of this system. But such additions are difficult to model with DTDs[21]. We are presently

---

[19] Practical **E**xtraction and **R**eport **L**anguage.

[20] Schemas have more expressive power than DTDs, because they allow users to define types precisely, which in turn makes for a better validation of an XML text. In addition, this approach is more homogeneous since schemas are XML texts, whereas DTDs are not.

There are currently four ways to specify schemas: Relax NG [3], Schematron [16], Examplotron [30], XML Schema [35]. At present, it seems to us that XML Schema is the most suitable for describing bibliographical entries.

[21] Whereas that is easy with 'old' BIBTEX, provided that you use a bibliography style able to deal with additional fields.

going thoroughly into replacing our DTD by a schema; when this work reaches maturity, bibliographical entries using XML syntax could be directly validated using schemas.

Acknowledgements

Many thanks to Karl Berry for his patience while waiting for this article. In addition he proofread a first version and gave me many constructive criticisms. Thanks also to Barbara Beeton.

References

1. Harald Tveit ALVESTRAND: *Request for Comments: 1766. Tags for the Identification of Languages.* UNINETT, Network Working Group. March 1995.
   http://www.cis.ohio-state.edu/cgi-bin/rfc/rfc1766.html
2. Joannes BRAAMS: *Babel, a Multilingual Package for Use with LaTeX's Standard Document Classes.* Version 3.7. May 2002.
   CTAN:macros/latex/required/babel/babel.dvi
3. James CLARK *et al.: Relax NG.*
   http://www.oasis-open.org/committees/relax-ng/. 2002.
4. Nicos DRAKOS: *The LaTeX2HTML Translator.* March 1999. Computer Based Learning Unit, University of Leeds.
5. Jonathan FINE: "TeX as a Callable Function." In: *EuroTeX 2002,* (26–30). Bachotek, Poland. April 2002.
6. Bernard GAULLE: *Notice d'utilisation du style french multilingue pour LaTeX.* Version pro V5.01. January 2001.
   CTAN:loria/language/french/pro/french/ALIRE.pdf
7. Michel GOOSSENS, Sebastian RAHTZ and Frank MITTELBACH: *The LaTeX Graphics Companion. Illustrating Documents with TeX and PostScript.* Addison-Wesley Publishing Company, Reading, Massachusetts. 1997.
8. Hans HAGEN: *ConTeXt, the Manual.* November 2001.
   http://www.pragma-ade.com
9. Jean-Michel HUFFLEN: "MlBibTeX: A New Implementation of BibTeX." In: *EuroTeX 2001,* (74–94). Kerkrade, The Netherlands. September 2001.
10. Jean-Michel HUFFLEN: "Multilingual Features for Bibliography Programs: From XML to MlBibTeX." In: *EuroTeX 2002,* (46–59). Bachotek, Poland. April 2002.
11. Jean-Michel HUFFLEN: *Towards MlBibTeX's Versions 1.2 & 1.3.* MaTeX Conference. Budapest, Hungary. November 2002.
12. Jean-Michel HUFFLEN: "European Bibliography Styles and MlBibTeX". EuroTeX 2003, Brest, France. June 2003. (To appear in TUGBoat.)
13. Jean-Michel HUFFLEN: *MlBibTeX's Version 1.3.* TUG 2003, Outrigger Waikoloa Beach Resort, Hawaii. July 2003.
14. Jean-Michel HUFFLEN: "Making MlBibTeX Fit for a Particular Language. Example of the Polish Language." *Biuletyn* GUST. Forthcoming. Presented at the BachoTeX 2003 conference. 2004.
15. Jean-Michel HUFFLEN: "A Tour around MlBibTeX and Its Implementation(s)." *Biuletyn* GUST, 20(21–28). In *Proc. BachoTeX Conference.* April 2004.

16. ISO/IEC 19757: *The Schematron. An* XML *Structure Validation Language Using Patterns in Trees.*
    `http://www.ascc.net/xml/resource/schematron/schematron.html`. June 2003.

17. Oleg KISELYOV: "A Better XML Parser through Functional Programming." In: *4th International Symposium on Practical Aspects of Declarative Languages*, Vol. 2257 of *Lecture Notes in Computer Science*. Springer-Verlag. 2002.

18. Donald Ervin KNUTH: *Computers & Typesetting. Vol. A: The TEXbook.* Addison-Wesley Publishing Company, Reading, Massachusetts. 1984.

19. Leslie LAMPORT: *LATEX. A Document Preparation System. User's Guide and Reference Manual.* Addison-Wesley Publishing Company, Reading, Massachusetts. 1994.

20. Oren PATASHNIK: *Designing BIBTEX styles.* February 1988. Part of the BIBTEX distribution.

21. Oren PATASHNIK: *BIBTEXing.* February 1988. Part of the BIBTEX distribution.

22. Dave PAWSON: XSL-FO. O'Reilly & Associates, Inc. 2002.

23. Bernd RAICHLE: *Die Makropakete "'german"' und "'ngerman"' für LATEX 2ε, LATEX 2.09, Plain-TEX and andere darauf Basierende Formate.* Version 2.5. July 1998. Im Software LATEX.

24. Erik T. RAY: *Learning* XML. O'Reilly & Associates, Inc. 2001.

25. Brian Keith REID: SCRIBE *Document Production System User Manual.* Technical Report, Unilogic, Ltd. 1984.

26. Thomas SCHRAITLE: *DocBook-*XML *– Medienneutrales und plattformunabhändiges Publizieren.* SuSE Press. 2004.

27. John E. SIMPSON: *XPath and XPointer.* O'Reilly & Associates, Inc. 2002.

28. George SPRINGER and Daniel P. FRIEDMAN: *Scheme and the Art of Programming.* The MIT Press, McGraw-Hill Book Company. 1989.

29. *The Unicode Standard Version 3.0.* Addison-Wesley. February 2000.

30. Eric VAN DER VLIST: *Examplotron.* `http://examplotron.org`. February 2003.

31. W3C: XML *Path Language (XPath). Version 1.0.* W3C Recommendation. Edited by James Clark and Steve DeRose. November 1999.
    `http://www.w3.org/TR/1999/REC-xpath-19991116`

32. W3C: XSL *Transformations (*XSLT*). Version 1.0.* W3C Recommendation. Written by Sharon Adler, Anders Berglund, Jeff Caruso, Stephen Deach, Tony Graham, Paul Grosso, Eduardo Gutentag, Alex Milowski, Scott Parnell, Jeremy Richman and Steve Zilles. November 1999.
    `http://www.w3.org/TR/1999/REC-xslt-19991116`

33. W3C: *Extensible Markup Language (*XML*) 1.0 (Second Edition).* W3C Recommendation. Edited by Tim Bray, Jean Paoli, C. M. Sperberg-McQueen and Eve Maler. October 2000. `http://www.w3.org/TR/2000/REC-xml-20001006`

34. W3C: *Extensible Stylesheet Language (*XSL*). Version 1.0.* W3C Recommendation. Edited by James Clark. October 2001.
    `http://www.w3.org/TR/2001/REC-xsl-20011015/`

35. W3C: XML *Schema.* November 2003. `http://www.w3.org/XML/Schema`

36. Norman WALSH and Leonard MUELLNER: *DocBook: The Definitive Guide.* O'Reilly & Associates, Inc. 1999.

Managing TeX Resources with XML Topic Maps

Tomasz Przechlewski

Uniwersytet Gdański, Wydział Zarzadzania
81-824 Sopot
ul. Armii Krajowej 119/121
Poland
tomasz@gnu.univ.gda.pl

Abstract. For many years the Polish TeX Users Group newsletter has been published online on the GUST web site. The repository now contains valuable information on TeX, METAFONT, electronic document, computer graphics and related subjects. However, access to the content is very poor: it is available as PS/PDF files with only a simple HTML page facilitating navigation. There is no integration with information resources from other sections of the site, nor with the resources from other LUG or CTAN sites.

Topic maps were initially developed for efficient preparation of indices, glossaries and thesauruses for electronic documents repositories, and are now codified as both the ISO standard (ISO/IEC 13250) and the XTM 1.0 standard. Their applications extend to the domain of electronic publishing. Topic maps and the similar RDF standard are considered to be the backbone of corporate knowledge management systems and/or the Semantic Web [3].

The paper contains an introduction to the Topic Maps standard and discusses selected problems of Topic Map construction. Finally the application of Topic Maps as an interface to the repository of TeX related resources is presented, as well as the successes and challenges encountered in the implementation.

1   Introduction

All the papers published for the last 10 years in the bulletin of the Polish TeX Users' Group (GUST, http://www.gust.org.pl/) are now available on-line from the GUST Web site. The repository contains valuable information on TeX, METAFONT, electronic documents, computer graphics, typography and related subjects. However, access to the content itself is very poor: the papers are available as PS/PDF files with only a simple HTML interface facilitating navigation. There is no integration with other resources from that site. As CTAN and other LUGs' sites provide more resources it would obviously be valuable to integrate them too.

At first glance, the Topic Maps framework appears to be an attractive way to integrate vast amounts of dispersed TeX related resources. A primary goal of the proposed interface should be to support learning. If the project succeeds,

A. Syropoulos et al. (Eds.): TUG 2004, LNCS 3130, pp. 216–228, 2004.

we hope it will change slightly the opinion of TEX as a very difficult subject to become acquainted with.

The paper is organized as follows. The standard is introduced and selected problems of topic maps construction are discussed in the subsequent three sections. Then a short comparison of Topic Maps and RDF is presented. The application of Topic Maps as an interface to the GUST resource repository is described in the last two sections.

2   What Is a Topic Map?

Topic Maps are an SGML/HYTIME based standard defined in [1] (ISO/IEC 13250, often referred to as HYTM). The standard was recently rewritten by an independent consortium, TopicMaps.org [19] and renamed to XML Topic Maps (XTM). XTM was developed in order to simplify the ISO specification and enable its usage for the Web through XML syntax. Also, the original linking scheme was replaced by XLINK/XPOINTER syntax. XTM was recently incorporated as an Annex to [1].

The standard enumerates the following possible applications of TMs [1][1]:

- To qualify the content and/or data contained in information objects as topics, to enable navigational tools such as indexes, cross-references, citation systems, or glossaries.
- To link topics together in such a way as to enable navigation between them.
- To filter an information set to create views adapted to specific users or purposes. For example, such filtering can aid in the management of multilingual documents, management of access modes depending on security criteria, delivery of partial views depending on user profiles and/or knowledge domains, etc.
- To add structure to unstructured information objects, or to facilitate the creation of topic-oriented user interfaces that provide the effect of merging unstructured information bases with structured ones.

In short, a *topic map* is a model of knowledge representation based on three key notions: *topics* which represent subjects, *occurrences* of topics which are links to related resources, and *associations* (relations) among topics.

A topic represents, within an application context, any clearly identified and unambigous subject or concept from the real world: a person, an idea, an object etc.

A topic is a instance of a topic type. Topic types can be structured as hierarchies organized by superclass-subclass relationships. The standard does not provide any predefined semantics to the classes. Finally, topic and topic type form a class-instance relationship.

Topic have three kinds of characteristics: *names* (none, one, or more), *occurrences*, and *roles* in associations. The links between topics and their related

---

[1] Examples of application of Topic Maps to real world problems can be found in [9, 21, 5, 18, 11, 12].

information (web page, picture, etc.) are defined by *occurrences*. The linked resources are usually located outside the map. XTM uses a simple link mechanism as defined in XLINK, similar to HTML hyperlinks.

As with topics, occurrences can be typed; occurrence types are often referred as *occurrence roles*. Occurrence types are also defined as topics. Using XML syntax, the definition of topic is quite simple:

```
<topic id="t-przechlewska-wanda">
  <instanceOf> <topicRef xlink:href="#person"/> </instanceOf>
    <baseName>
      <baseNameString>Plata-Przechlewska, Wanda</baseNameString>
    </baseName>
</topic>
```

Topic associations define relationships between topics. As associations are independent of the resources (i.e., the data layer) they represent added-value information. This independency means that a concrete topic map can describe more than one information pool, and vice versa. Each association can have an *association type* which is also a topic. There are no constraints on how many topics can be related by one association. Topics can play specific roles in associations, described with *association role types* – which are also topics.

The concepts described above are shown in Fig. 1. Topics are represented as small ovals or circles in the upper half of the picture while the large oval at the bottom indicates data layer. Small objects of different shapes contained in the data layer represent resources of different types. The lines between the data layer and topics represent occurrences, while thick dashed ones between topics depict associations.

Besides the above three fundamental concepts, the standard provides a notion of *scope*. All characteristics of topics are valid within certain bounds, called a *scope*, and determined in terms of other topics. Typically, scopes are used to model multilingual documents, access rights, different views, and so on.

Scopes can also be used to avoid name conflicts when a single name denotes more than one concept. An example of scope for the topic *latex* might be *computer application* or *rubber industry* depending on the subject of the topic. Only the topic characteristics can be scoped, not the topic itself.

3   Subject Identity and Map Merging

From the above short tour of TM concepts it should be clear that there is an exact one-to-one correspondence between subjects and topics. Thus, the identification of subjects is crucial to individual topic map applications and to interoperability between different topic maps.

The simplest and most popular way of identifying subjects is by identifyng them via some system of unique labels (usually URIs). A subject identifier is simply a URI unambiguously identifying the subject. If the subject identifier points to a resource (not required) the resource is called a subject indicator. The

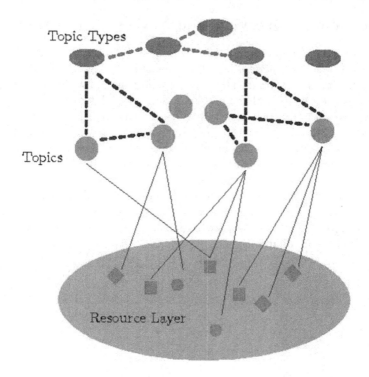

Fig. 1. Topic map and resource layer.

subject indicator should contain human-readable documentation describing the non-addressable subject [22].

As there are no restrictions to prevent every map author from defining their own subject identifiers and resource indicators, there is a possibility that semantic or syntactic overlap will occur. To overcome this, *published subject indicators* (PSIs) are proposed [17]. PSIs are stable and reliable indicators published by an institution or organization that desires to promote a specific standard. Anyone can publish PSIs and there is no registration authority. The adoption of PSIs can therefore be an open and spontaneous process [17, 6][2].

Subject identity is of primary importance for topic map merging when there is a need to recognize which topics describe the same subject.

Two topics and their characteristics can be *merged* (aggregated) if the topics share the same name in the same scope (*name-based merging*), or if they refer to the same subject indicator (*subject-based merging*). Merging results in a single topic that has the union of all characteristics of merged topics. Merged topics play the roles in all the associations that the individual topics played before [22, 15].

---

[2] For example, the XTM 1.0 specification contains a set of PSIs for core concepts, such as class, instance, etc., as well as for the identification of countries and languages [19].

4   Constraining, Querying, and Navigating the Map

The notion of a topic map template is used frequently in literature. As the name suggests, a *topic map template* is a sort of schema imposing constraints on topic map objects with TM syntax. The standard does not provide any means by which the designer of the TM template can put constraints onto the topic map itself. Standardisation of such constraints are currently in progress [14].

Displaying lists of indexes which the user can navigate easily is the standard way of TM visualization. As this approach does not scale well for larger maps, augmenting navigation with some sort of searching facility is recommended. Other visualization techniques such as hyperbolic trees [15], cone trees, and hypergraph views (Fig. 2) can be used for visualization and navigation of topic maps. They display TMs as a graph, with the topics and occurrences as nodes and the associations as arcs. The drawback of such 'advanced' techniques is that users are usually unfamilar with them.

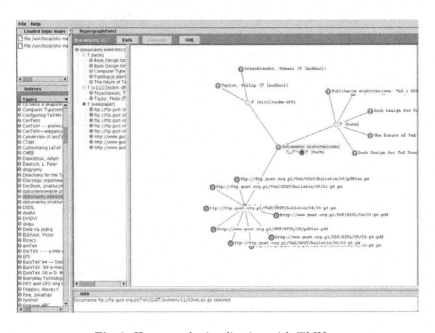

Fig. 2. Hypergraph visualization with TMNav.

There are several proposed query languages for topic maps. None of them are part of the standard and there are inconsistencies in different TM engines. Two of the most prominent proposals are:

- TMQL (*Topic Maps Query Language*, [9]), with SQL-like syntax, provides both for querying and modifying topic maps (select, insert, delete, update).
- Tolog, inspired by the logic programming language Prolog, supports requirements for TMQL with clearer and simpler syntax.

The introduction to the TM standard presented in this paper does not cover all the details of the technology. Interested readers can find an exhaustive description in [15], which contains a detailed introduction with numerous examples, and [16].

5   Topic Maps and RDF

The W3C promotes the Resource Description Framework (RDF) [10] as another framework for expressing metadata. RDF is a W3C standard envisioned to be a foundational layer of the Semantic Web.

The fundamental notion in the RDF data model is a *statement*, which is a triple composed of a *resource*, *property*, and *value*. The RDF Schema (RDFS) [4] is a W3C working draft aimed at defining a description language for vocabularies in RDF. More expressive RDFS models have been proposed recently [23].

One key difference between RDF and topic maps is that topic maps are modelled on a concept-centric view of the world. For example, in RDF there are no 'predefined' properties, so to assign a name to a resource one has to use another standard (such as Dublin Core), something that is not necessary with topic maps. The notion of scope is also absent from RDF too.

The RDF and Topic Maps standards are similar in many respects [7]. Both offer simple yet powerful means of expressing concepts and relationships.

6   Building Topic Maps
for the GUST Bibliographic Database

Similar to writing a good index for a book, creating a good topic map is carried out by combining manual labour with the help of some software applications. It is usually a two-stage task, beginning with the modelling phase of building the 'upper-part' of the map, i.e., the hierarchy of topic and association types (the *schema* of the map) and then populating the map with instances of topic types, their associations and occurrences.

Approaches for developing a topic map out of a pool of information resources include [2]:

- using standard vocabularies and taxonomies (i.e., www.dmoz.org) to be the initial source of topics types.
- generating TMs from the structured databases or documents with topic types and association types derived from the scheme of the database/ document.
- extraction of topics and topic associations from pools of unstructured or loosely structured documents using NLP (Natural Language Processing) software combined with manual labour.

The first approach is concerned with the modelling phase of topic map creation, while the third one deals with populating the map.

Following the above guidelines, the structure of the BibTEX records was an obvious candidate to start with in modelling our map of GUST articles. It provides a basic initial set of topics including: *author, paper, keyword*, and the following association types: *author-paper, paper-keyword* and *author-keyword*. Abstracts (if present in BibTEX databases) can be considered as occurrences of the topic *paper*. The publication date and language can be used as scopes for easy navigation, using them as constraints.

Other TAOs (topics, associations, and occurrences [16]) to consider are: author home pages (occurrence type), applications described in the paper (association type), papers referenced (association type). This information is absent from BibTEX files but, at least theoretically, can be automatically extracted from the source files of papers.

We started by analyzing the data at our disposal, i.e., TEX and BibTEX source files. Unfortunately, in the case of the GUST bulletin the BibTEX database was not maintained. This apparent oversight was rectified with simple Perl scripts and a few days of manual labour. The bibliographic database was created and saved in a XML-compatible file[3].

TEX documents are typically visually tagged and lack information oriented markup. The only elements marked up consistently and unambiguously in the case of the GUST bulletin are the paper titles and authors' names. Authors' home pages were rarely present, while email addresses were available but not particularly useful for our purposes. Neither abstracts nor keyword lists had been required and as a consequence were absent from the majority of the papers. Similarly, any consistent scheme of marking bibliographies (or attaching .bib files) was lacking, so there was no easy way to define the *related to* association between papers.

The benefit derived from keywords is much greater if they are applied consistently according to some fixed classification; otherwise, the set of keywords usually consists of many random terms which are nearly useless. Since we didn't want to define yet another 'standard' in this area, we would have liked to adopt an existing one. The following sources were considered: the TEX entry at `dmoz.org`, Graham Williams' catalogue[4], collections of BibTEX files and .tpm files [20]

The accuracy of the TEX taxonomy subtree at `dmoz.org` was somewhat questionable, and we quickly rejected the idea of using it. Williams' catalogue of TEX resources does not include any information except the location of the resource in the structure of CTAN. As for BibTEX files, it appeared only MAPS and TUGBoat were complete and up-to date[5] but only the latter contains keywords. Unfortunately, they do not comply with any consistent scheme. Due to the lack of any existing standard, the keywords were added manually on a

---

[3] We reused the XML schema developed for the MAPS bulletin (`http://www.ntg.org.ln/maps/`).

[4] `http://www.ctan.org/tex-archive/help/Catalogue`

[5] Cahiers GUTenberg was not found, but the impressive portal of Association GUTenberg indicates appropriate metadata are maintained, but not published.

commonsense basis, with the intention of being 'in sync' with the most frequent terms used in MAPS[6].

Finally the following TAOs were defined (the language of the publication was considered to be the only scope):

- topic types: *author*, *paper*, and *keyword*;
- association types: *author-paper*, *paper-keyword*, and *author-keyword*;
- occurrence types: *papers* and *abstracts*.

The schema of the map was prepared manually and then the rest of the map was generated from intermediate XML file with an XSLT stylesheet [8, 13]. The resulting map consists of 454 topics, 1029 associations, and 999 occurrences. A fragment of the map rendered in a web browser with Ontopia Omnigator (a no-cost but closed-source application, http://www.ontopia.net/download/) is shown in Fig. 3.

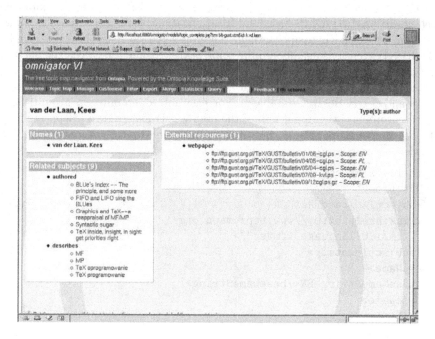

Fig. 3. A fragment of GUST topic map rendered with Omnigator.

Omnigator shows the map as a list of links arranged in panels. Initially only a list of subjects (index of topic types) is displayed. When a link for a topic is clicked on, the topic is displayed with all the information about its characteristics

---

[6] There are 814 bibliographic entries in MAPS base and 895 different keywords. The most popular keywords in MAPS BibTEX file are: LaTEX–51, NTG–42, plain TEX–37, PostScript–28, ConTEXt, TEX-NL, METAFONT, SGML, and so forth. There are small number of inconsistent cases (special commands vs. specials, or configuration vs. configuring) and fine-grained keywords (Portland, Poland, Bachotek, USSR!).

(names, associations, occurrences). In Fig. 3, an example page for author *Kees van der Laan* is shown. The right panel contains all the relevant resources while the lower left has all the related topics, i.e., papers written by Kees and other subjects covered. The user can easily browse both papers authored by him and switch to pages on some other interesting subject. The panel with resources contains information on the resource type allowing fast access to the required data.

Similar functionality can be obtained with the freely available TM4Nav or even by using a simple XSLT stylesheet [13].

7   Integrating Other TeX Resources

So far there is nothing in TMs that cannot be obtained using other technologies. The same or better functionality can be achieved with any database management system (DMS). But integrating TeX resources on a global scale needs flexibility, which traditional RDBMS-based DMS applications lack. For example, topic maps can be extended easily through merging separate maps into one, while DMS-based extensions usually require some prior agreement between the parties (e.g., LUGs), schema redefinitions, and more.

To verify this flexibility in practice, we extended the GUST map with the MAPS and TUB BibTeX databases. For easy interoperability in a multi-language environment, the upper half of the map was transferred to a separate file. With the use of scope, the design of multi-language topic types was easy, for example:

```
<topic id="english">
 <subjectIdentity>
   <subjectIndicatorRef
   xlink:href="http://www.topicmaps.org/\
      xtm/1.0/language.xtm#en"/>
   </subjectIdentity>
   <baseName>
    <baseNameString>EN</baseNameString>
   </baseName>
</topic>
  ...
<topic id="author">
 <baseName><scope>
   <topicRef xlink:href="#english"/></scope>
   <baseNameString>author</baseNameString>
 </baseName>
 <baseName><scope>
    <topicRef xlink:href="#polish"/> </scope>
   <baseNameString>autor</baseNameString>
  </baseName>
</topic>
```

Other topic types were designed similarly. Scopes for other languages can easily be added.

The 'lower part' of the map was generated from (cleaned) BIBTeX records with `bibtex2xml.py` (`http://bibtexml.sf.net`) and than transformed to MAPS XML with an XSLT stylesheet. Keywords were added to TUB entries using a very crude procedure[7].

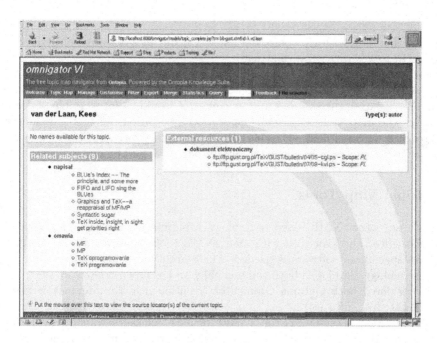

Fig. 4. Topic map fragment from Fig. 3 scoped to Polish language.

Simple name-based merging of all three maps results in over 25,000 TAOs (≈ 1000 authors, more than 2000 papers). Some of the subjects were represented with multiple topics. As an example the Grand Wizard was represented as the following four distinct topics: 'Knuth, Don', 'Knuth, Donald', 'Knuth, Donald E.', 'Knuth., Donald E.'[8].

As identity-based merging is regarded as more robust, some identifiers have to be devised first. Establishing a PSI for every TeX author seemed overly ambitious. Instead, a dummy subject identifier was chosen, such as: `http://tug.org/authors#initials-surname`. This can still produce multiple topics for the same subject, but now we can eliminate unwanted duplicates by defining an additional map consisting solely of topics like the following [18]:

---

[7] Acronyms, such as LaTeX, METAFONT, or XML, present in the title were used as keywords.

[8] First name variants, abbreviations and middle names cause problems in many more cases.

```
<topic id="de-knuth">
 <subjectIdentity>
  <subjectIndicatorRef
    xlink="http://tug.org/authors#d-knuth"/>
  <subjectIndicatorRef
    xlink="http://tug.org/authors#d-e-knuth"/>
 </subjectIdentity>
</topic>
```

Merging this map with the 'base' map(s) will result in a map free of unwanted duplicated topics with all variant names preserved.

For further extensions, we plan to incorporate CTAN resources. For that purpose, Williams' catalogue and/or the TPM files from TEX Live project can be used. As the catalogue contains author names, it would be for example possible to enrich the map with the *author-application* association. Further enrichment will result if we can link applications with documents describing them. However, some robust classification scheme of TEX resources should be devised first.

8   Topic Map Tools

As with any other XML-based technology, topic maps can be developed with any text editor and processed with many XML tools. However, for larger-scale projects specialized software is needed. There are a few tools supporting topic map technology, developed both commercially and as Open Source projects. We have considered both Ontopia Omnigator (mentioned in the previous section) and TM4J (free software).

TM4J (http://tm4j.org) is a suite of Java packages which provide interfaces and default implementations for the import, manipulation and export of XML Topic Maps. Features of the TM4J engine include an object model which supports XTM specification with the ability to store topic map in an object-oriented or relational database, and an implementation of the tolog query language.

Based on TM4J a few projects are in progress: TMNav for intuitive navigation and editing of topic maps, and TMBrowse for publishing maps as set of HTML pages (similarly to Omnigator).

These projects are in early stages and our experience with TMBrowse indicates that current version frequently crashes with bigger maps and is significantly slower than Omnigator. There were problems with tolog queries as well.

As all these projects are actively maintained progress may be expected in the near future.

9   Summary

Topic maps are an interesting new technology which can be used to describe the relation between TEX resources. The main problem is topic map visualization.

Available tools are in many cases unstable and non-scalable, but we can expect improvement.

The system presented here can certainly be improved. It is planned to extend it with the content of Williams' catalogue. The maps developed in the project are available from `http://gnu.univ.gda.pl/~tomasz/tm/`. At the same address, the interested reader can find links to many resources on topic maps.

References

1. ISO/IEC. Topic Maps, ISO/IEC 13250, 2002. `http://www.y12.doe.gov/sgml/`
2. Kal Ahmed, Danny Ayers, Mark Birbeck, and Jay Cousins. *Professional* XML *Meta Data.* Wrox Press, 2001.
3. Tim Berners-Lee, James Hendler, and Ora Lassila. The Semantic Web. *Scientific American*, 284(5):35–43, 2001.
   `http://www.sciam.com/2001/0501issue/0501berners-lee.html`
4. Dan Brickley and R. V. Guha. RDF vocabulary description language 1.0: RDF schema, 2002. `http://www.w3.org/TR/rdf-schema/`
5. Anna Carlstedt and Mats Nordborg. An evaluation of topic maps. Master's thesis, Göteborg University, 2002. `http://www.cling.gu.se/~cl8matsn/exjobb.html`
6. Paolo Ciancarini, Marco Pirruccio, and Fabio Vitali. Metadata on the Web. On the integration of RDF and topic maps. In *Extreme Markup Languages*, 2003. `http://www.mulberrytech.com/Extreme/Proceedings/xslfo-pdf/2003/Presutti01/EML2003Presutti01.pdf`
7. Lars M. Garshol. Living with Topic Maps and RDF.
   `http://www.ontopia.net/topicmaps/materials/tmrdf.html`, 2002.
8. Michael Kay. XSLT *Programmer's Reference 2nd Edition.* Wrox Press, 2001.
9. Rafał Księżyk. Trying not to get lost with a topic map. In XML *Europe Conference*, 1999. `http://www.infoloom.com/gcaconfs/WEB/granada99/ksi.HTM`
10. Ora Lassila and Ralph R. Swick. Resource description framework (RDF). Model and syntax specification, 1999. `http://www.w3.org/TR/REC-rdf-syntax/`
11. Xia Lin and Jian Qin. Building a topic map repository, 2000. `http://www.knowledgetechnologies.net/proceedings/presentations/lin/xialin.pdf`
12. Ashish Mahabal, S. George Djorgovski, Robert Brunner, and Roy Williams. Topic maps as a virtual observatory tool, 2002. `http://arxiv.org/abs/astro-ph/0110184`
13. Sal Mangano. XSLT *Cookbook.* O'Reilly, 2002.
14. Mary Nishikawa and Graham Moore. Topic map constraint language requirements, 2002. `http://www.isotopicmaps.org/tmcl/`
15. Jack Park and Sam Hunting, editors. XML *Topic Maps. Creating and using Topic Maps for the Web.* Addison-Wesley, 2002.
16. Steve Pepper. The TAO of topic maps, 2000.
   `http://www.ontopia.net/topicmaps/materials/tao.html`
17. Steve Pepper. Published subject: Introduction and basic requirements, 2003.
   `http://www.oasis-open.org/committees/`.
18. Steve Pepper and Marius L. Garshol. Lessons on applying topic maps.
   `http://www.ontopia.net/topicmaps/materials/xmlconf.html`, 2002.
19. Steve Pepper and Graham Moore. XML topic maps (XTM) 1.0, 2000.
   `http://www.topicmaps.org/xtm/1.0/`.

20. Fabrice Popineau. Directions for the TeXlive systems. In *EuroTEX 2001, The Good, the Bad and the Ugly, Kerkrade*, pages 152–161. NTG, 2001.
`http://www.ntg.nl/maps/pdf/26_20.pdf`.

21. Tomasz Przechlewski. Wykorzystanie map pojęć w zarzadzaniu repozytoriami dokumentów elektronicznych. In *Materiały Konferencji: MSK 2003*, 2003.

22. Hans Holger Rath. Semantic resource exploitation with topic maps. In *Proceedings of the GLDV-Spring Meeting 2001*, 2001.
`http://www.uni-giessen.de/fb09/ascl/gldv2001/`.

23. Michael K. Smith, Chris Welty, and Deborah L. McGuinness. OWL Web ontology language guide, 2003. `http://www.w3.org/TR/owl-guide/`.

ŞäferTEX: Source Code Esthetics for Automated Typesetting

Frank-Rene Schaefer

Franzstr. 21
50931 Cologne
Germany
fschaef@users.sourceforge.net
http://safertex.sourceforge.net

Abstract. While TEX [4] provides high quality typesetting features, its usability suffers due to its macro-based command language. Many tools have been developed over the years simplifying and extending the TEX interface, such as LATEX [5], LATEX3 [6], pdfTEX [2], and NTS [8]. Front-ends such as TEXmacs [10] follow the visual/graphical approach to facilitate the coding of documents. The system introduced in this paper, however, is radical in its targetting of optimized *code appearance*.

The primary goal of ŞäferTEX is to make the typesetting source code as close as possible to human-readable text, to which we have been accustomed over the last few centuries. Using indentation, empty lines and a few triggers allows one to express interruption, scope, listed items, etc. A minimized frame of 'paradigms' spans a space of possible typesetting commands. Characters such as '_' and '$' do not have to be backslashed. Transitions from one type of text to another are automatically detected, with the effect that environments do not have to be bracketed explicitly. The following paper introduces the programming language ŞäferTEX as a user interface to the TEX typesetting engine. It is shown how the development of a language with reduced redundancy increases the beauty of code appearance.

1 Introduction

The original role of an author in the document production process is to act as an *information source*. To optimize the flow of information, the user has to be freed from tasks such as text layout and document design. The user should be able to delegate the implementation of visual document features and styles to another entity. With this aim in mind, the traditional relationship between an author and his typesetter before the electronic age can be considered the optimal case. Modern technology has increased the speed and reduced the cost of document processing. However, the border between *information specification* and *document design* has blurred or even vanished.

In typesetting engines with a graphical user interface, an editor often takes full control over page breaks, font sizes, paragraph indentation, references and so

A. Syropoulos et al. (Eds.): TUG 2004, LNCS 3130, pp. 229–239, 2004.

on. Script-oriented engines such as TEX take care of most typesetting tasks and provide high quality document design. However, quite often the task to produce a document requires detailed insight into the underlying philosophy.

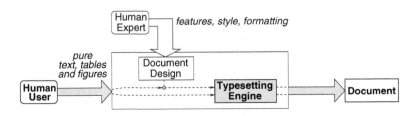

Fig. 1. Neo-traditional typesetting.

ŞäferTEX tries to get back to the basics, as depicted in Figure 1. Like the traditional writer, a user shall specify information as *redundancy-free* as possible with a minimum of commands that are alien to him. Layout, features, and styles shall be implemented according to predefined standards with a minimum of specification by the user.

To the user, the engine provides a simple interface, only requiring plain text, tables and figures. A second interface allows a human expert to adapt the engine to local requirements of style and output. Ideally, the added features in the second interface do not appear to the user, but are activated from the context. Then, the user can concentrate on the core information he wants to produce, and not be distracted by secondary problems of formatting.

The abovementioned ideal configuration of engine, user, and expert can hardly be achieved with present automated text formatting systems. While relying on TEX as a typesetting engine, ŞäferTEX tries to progress towards a minimal-redundancy programming language that is at the same time intuitive to the human writer.

2   The ŞäferTEX Engine

As shown in Figure 2, the ŞäferTEX engine is based on a three-phase compilation, namely: lexical analysis, parsing and code generation. Along with the usual advantages of such modularization, this structure allows us to describe the engine in a very formal manner. In this early phase of the project, it further facilitates adding new features to the language. Using interfacing tools such as SWIG [1] and .NET [9], it should be possible in the future to pass the generated parse tree to different programming languages. Such an approach would open a whole new world to typesetters and document designers. Plug-ins for ŞäferTEX could then be designed in the person's favorite programming language (C++, Java, Python, C#, anything). Currently, automated document production mainly happens by preprocessing LATEX code. Using a parse tree, however, gives access to document

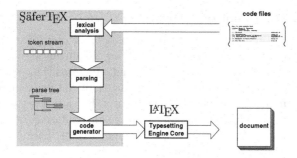

Fig. 2. The ŞäferTEX compilation process.

contents in a structured manner, i.e., through dedicated data structures such as objects of type `section`, `item group`, and so on.

GNU flex [7] (a free software package), is used to create the lexical analyzer. It was, though, necessary to deviate from the traditional idea of a lexical analyzer as a pure finite state automaton. A wrapper around flex implements inheritance between modes (start conditions). Additionally, the lexical analyzer produces implicit tokens and deals with indentation as a scope delimiter.

The parser is developed using the Lemon parser generator [3] (also free software). Using such a program, the ŞäferTEX language can be described with a context-free grammar. The result of the parser is a parse tree, which is currently processed in C++. The final product is a LATEX file that is currently fed into the LATEX engine. A detailed discussion of the engine is not the intention of this paper, though. The present text focuses on the language itself.

3   Means for Beauty

ŞäferTEX tries to optimize code appearance. The author identifies three basic means by which this can be achieved:

1. The first means is intuitive treatment of characters. For example, '$' and '_' are used as normal characters and do not function as commands, as they do in LATEX.
2. The second is to use indentation as the scope delimiter. This is reminiscent of the Python programming language. It allows the user to reduce brackets and enforces proper placement of scopes. For table environments, this principle is extended so that the column positions can be used as cell delimiters.
3. The third principle is automatic environment detection. If an item appears, then the 'itemize' environment is automatically assumed. This reduces redundancy, and makes the source file much more readable.

Applying these principles leads to the eight rules of ŞäferTEX as they are explained at the end (section 5). We now discuss them in more detail.

3.1 Intuitive Treatment of Characters

In the design of a typesetting language, the user has to be given the ability to enter both normal text and commands specifying document structure and non-text content. This can be achieved by defining functions, i.e., using character sequences as triggers for a specific functionality. This happens when we define, say, `sin(x)` as a function computing the sine of `x`. For a typesetter this is not a viable option, since the character chain can be easily confused with normal text. As a result, one would have to 'bracket' normal text or 'backslash' functions. Another solution is to use extra characters. This was the method Donald Knuth chose when he designed TEX [4]. The first solution is still intuitive to most users. The second, however, is rather confusing, implying that '%', '$' and '_' have a meaning different from what one sees in the file.

Historically, at the time TEX was designed, keyboards had a very restricted number of characters. Moreover, ASCII being the standard text encoding in Knuth's cultural context, the high cost of data storage, and the lack of advanced programming languages also all may have contributed to the design choices made. Although the documents produced still equal and even outclass most commercial systems of our days, the input language, it must be admitted, is rather cryptic.

The first step towards readability of code is to declare a maximum number of characters as 'normal'. In ŞäferTEX, the only character that is not considered normal is the backslash. All other characters, such as '%', '$' and '_', appear in the text as they are. Special characters only act abnormal if they appear twice without whitespace in between. These tokens fall into the category of *alien things*, meaning that they look strange and thus are expected to not appear verbatim in the output.

Table 1 compares LATEX code to ŞäferTEX code, showing the improvement with respect to code appearance. The advantages may seem minor. Consider, however, the task of learning the difference between the characters that can be typed normally and others that have to be backslashed or bracketed. The abovementioned simplification already removes the chance of subtle errors appearing when LATEX code is compiled. The subsequent sections show how the code appearance and the ease of text input can be further improved.

3.2 Scope by Indentation

We have discussed how commands are best defined in a typesetting engine. One way to organize information is to create specific regions, called scopes or environments. Most programming languages use explicit delimiters for scopes without giving any special meaning to white space of any kind. This implies that the delimiters must be visible. C++, for example, uses curly braces, while LATEX uses \begin{...} ... \end{...} constructs to determine scope. This approach allows one to place the scopes very flexibly. However, it pollutes the text with symbols not directly related to the information being described. The more scopes that are used, and the deeper they are nested, the more the source text loses readability.

Table 1. Comparison of treatment of special characters in LaTeX and ŞäferTEX.

LaTeX:	```According to Balmun \& Refish $<$www.b-and-r.org$>$ a conversion of module \#5, namely 'propulsion_control,' into a metric system increases code safety up to 98.7\% at cost of \~ \ \$17,500.```
ŞäferTEX:	```According to Balmun & Refish <www.b-and-r.org> a conversion of module #5, namely 'propulsion_control,' into a metric system increases code safety up to 98.7% at cost of ~ $17,500.```

Another approach is *scoping by indentation*. A scope of a certain indentation envelopes all subsequent lines and scopes as long as they have more indentation. Figure 3 shows an example of scope by indentation. LaTeX's redundancy-rich delimiters add nothing but visual noise to the reader of the file. ŞäferTEX, however, uses a single backslashed command \quote in order to open a quote domain. The scope of the quote is then simply closed by the lesser indentation of the subsequent sentence.

```
Einstein clearly stated his disbelief in the
boundedness of the human spirit as becomes
clear through his sayings:

\quote The difference between genius and
        stupidity is that genius has its limits.

        Only two things are infinite, the
        universe and human stupidity, and I'm
        not sure about the former.

Similar reports have been heard from Frank
Zappa and others.
```

Fig. 3. Scope by indentation.

This simple example was chosen to display the principle. It is easy to imagine that for more deeply nested scopes (e.g., picture in minipage in center in figure), LaTeX code converges to unreadability, while ŞäferTEX code still allows one to get a quick overview about the document structure. Scope by indentation has proven to be a very convenient and elegant tool.

An extension of this concept is using *columns as cell delimiters* in a table scope. The implementation of tables in ŞäferTEX allows the source to omit many 'parboxes' and explicit '&'-cell delimiters. To begin with, a row is delimited by an empty line. This means that line contents are glued together as long as only one line break separates them. The cell content, though, is collected using the position of the cell markers '&&' and '||'. Additionally, the symbol '~~' glues two cells together. This makes cumbersome declarations with \multicolumn and \parbox unnecessary. Figure 4 shows an example of a ŞäferTEX table definition.

```
\table Food suppliers, prices and amounts.
       ---------------------------------------------------------------
Product     || Price/kg && Supplier           && kg || Total Price
       ===============================================================
Sugar       ||   $0.25 && Jackie O'Neil       && 34 ||   $8.50
       ---------------------------------------------------------------
Yellow Swiss ||  $12.2 && United Independent && 100 || $1220.00
Cheese                      Farmers of
                            Switzerland
       ---------------------------------------------------------------
Green Pepper ||  $25.0 && Anonymous           &&  2 ||  $50.00
Genuine                     Indians Tribes
Mexican
       ===============================================================
Sum          ~~          ~~                    ~~    && $1278.50
       ---------------------------------------------------------------
```

Fig. 4. Example of writing a table: identifying cell borders by column.

4   Implicit Environment Detection

A basic means of improving convenience of programming is reducing redundancy. In LATEX, for example, the environment declarations are sometimes unnecessary. To declare a list of items, one has to specify something like

```
\begin{itemize}
   \item This is the first item and
   \item this one is the second.
\end{itemize}
```

Considering the information content, the occurrence of the \item should be enough to know that an itemize environment has started. Using our second paradigm, 'scope by indentation', the closing of the environment could be detected by the first text block that has less indentation than the item itself. The \begin and \end statements are therefore redundant. In ŞäferTEX, the token '--' (two dashes) is used to mark an item. Thus, in ŞäferTEX, the item list above simply looks like:

```
   -- This is the first item and
   -- this one is the second.
```

As implied previously, this paradigm's power really unfolds in combination with scope by indentation. Subsequent paragraphs simply need to be indented more than the text block to which they belong. Nested item groups are specified by higher levels of indentation, as seen in figure 5.

```
Items provide a good means to

    -- structure information
    -- emphasize important points. There are
       three basic ways to do this:

       [[Numbers]]: Enumerations are good when
                    there is a sequential order
                    in the information being
                    presented.

       [[Descriptions]]: Descriptions are
                         suitable if keywords
                         or key phrases are
                         placeholders for more
                         specific information.

       [[Bullets]]: Normal items indicate that
                    the presented set of
                    information does not
                    define any priorization.

    -- classify basic categories

There may be other things to consider of
which the author is currently unaware.
```

Fig. 5. Example code showing 'scope by indentation'.

Some important points from the example:

- The appearance of a '--' at the beginning of a line tells ŞäferTEX that there is an item and that an implicit token 'list begin' has to be created before the token 'item start' is sent. The next '--' signals the start of the next item.
- The '[['-symbol appears at the beginning of the line. It indicates a descriptor item. Since it has a higher indentation than the '--' items, it is identified as a nested list. Therefore, an implicit token 'list begin' has to be created again.
- The final sentence having less indentation than anything before closes all lists, i.e., it produces implicit 'list end' tokens for all lists that are to be closed. Thus, the parser and code generator are able to produce environment commands corresponding to the given scopes.

Now that the fundamental ideas to improve programming convenience for a typesetting system have been discussed, we turn to defining a best set of rules for expressions that implement these rules.

5 The Eight Rules of ŞäferTᴇX

Rules for command design shall be consistent with the paradigms of intuitive treatment of characters, scope by indentation, and automatic environment detection. The following set of rules was designed to meet these goals for ŞäferTᴇX while striving for a intuitive code appearance:

[1] Every character and every symbol in the code appears in the final output as in the source document, except for Alien things.

[2] Alien things look alien.

In plain TᴇX, characters such as '$', '%' and '_' do not appear in the document as typed. The fact that they look natural but trigger some TᴇX specific behavior is prone to confuse the layman. In ŞäferTᴇX, they appear as typed on the screen. Alien things can be identified by their look. The next four rules define the 'alien look:'

[3] Any word starting with a single backslash \. Examples are \figure and \table.

[4] Any non-letter character that appears twice or more, such as '##' (this triggers the start of an enumeration item at the beginning of the line).

[5] Parentheses (at the beginning of a line) that only contain asterisks '*' or whitespace. Sequences such as '(*)', '( )', '(***)' indicate sections and subsections.

[6] The very first paragraph of the file. It is interpreted as the title of the document.

Except for the first case, alien things do not interfere with readability. In fact, the double minus '--' for items and the '(*)' for sections are used naturally in many ASCII files. Internally, alien things are translated into commands for the typesetting engine, but the user does not need to know.

The last two issues are separation of the text stream and identification of scope of an environment:

[7] Termination of paragraphs, interruptions of the text flow, etc., are indicated by an EMPTY LINE.

[8] The scope of an environment, table cells, etc. is determined by its INDENTATION. A line with less indentation closes all scopes of higher indentation.

These are the eight rules of ŞäferTᴇX that enable one to operate the typesetter. They are defined as 'rules' but, in fact, they do not go much beyond common organization of text files.

```
                      Details about
                 The Elves and The Shoemaker


   \Author Original:
             Brothers Jakob & Wilhelm Grimm
             Somewhere in Germany

 ( ) Abstract ................................... abstract.st

 (*) Nocturne shoe productions ..................... strange.st
     (**) Living in confusion ....................... confusion.st
     (**) Women make trouble ........................ trouble.st

 (*) Midnight observations ..........:............... midnight.st
     (**) Elves in the cold ......................... freezing-elves.st

 (*) New era for elves: luxury ..................... luxury.st

 (*) Elves leave their job undone .................. spoiled-elves.st
```

Fig. 6. Example input 'main.st'.

6   Commands

This section gives a brief overview of the commands that are currently implemented. In this early stage of development, the system's structure and language design has been in the foreground, in order to build the framework for a more powerful typesetting engine. In the current version of ŞäferTEX, the following commands are implemented:

--, ++   starts a bullet item. The two can be used interchangeably to distinguish different levels of nested item groups.

starts an enumeration item.

[[ ]] bracket the beginning of a description item.

\table opens a table environment. It is followed by a caption and the table body as described in section 3.2.

\figure opens a figure environment. The text following this command is interpreted as the caption. Then file names of images are to be listed. Images that are to be shown side by side are separated by '&&'. Vertically adjacent images are separated by empty lines.

\quote opens a quote environment.

(*) starts a section. The number of asterisks indicates the level of the section.

( ) starts a section without a section number. The number of blanks indicates the section level.

.... includes a file (more than four dots is equivalent to four). The next non-whitespace character sequence is taken as the filename to be included.

\author specifies information about the author of the document.

```
\figure ::fig:plots:: Performance a) productivity of shoemaker. b) gain.

ferry-tales/prod.eps   &&   ferry-tales/capital.eps
```

Reviewing the plots of shoes produced (figure --<fig:plots>), the shoemaker realized an instantaneous increase during the night period. He only could think of two possible reasons:

He was sleepworking. Since he even used to work few when awake this assumption was quickly refuted.

Elves must have come over night and did some charity work.

He further based his theory on the influence of the tanning material used. In fact, there were differences in the number of shoes produced depending on acid number and pH value (see table --<tab:tan-mat>).

```
\table ::tab:tan-mat::Influence of tanning materials on shoe production.


   Tanning Mat. && pH value   && acid number && shoes prod.

 ----------------------------------------------------------------
   European  && 3.4 - 3.7 && 30 - 40  && 32          @@
   Indian        2.0 - 2.1    31 - 45     35          @@
   African       4.5 - 4.6    33 - 37     36          @@
   Australian    3.0 - 7.0    27 - 45     15          @@


 ----------------------------------------------------------------
```

Resourcing several leathers from indian & african suppliers allowed him to increase profit ranges tremendously. Moreover, these shoes were sold at an even higher price around $0.50. Pretty soon, the shoemaker was able to save a good sum of $201.24.

Fig. 7. Example input 'confusion.st'.

Commands have been designed for footnotes, labels, and more. However, due to the early stage of development, no definite decision about their format has been made. In the appendix, two example files are listed in order to provide an example of ŞäferTEX code in practical applications.

7   Conclusion and Outlook

Using simple paradigms for improving code appearance and reducing redundancy, a language has been developed that allows more user-friendly input than is currently possible with TEX and LATEX. These paradigms are: the intuitive processing of special characters, the usage of indentation for scope and the implicit identification of environments. As an implementation of these paradigms, the eight rules of ŞäferTEX were formed, which describe the fundamental structure of the language.

While developing ŞäferTEX, the author quickly realized that the ability to provide the parse tree to layout designers extends the usage beyond the domain of TEX. Currently, much effort remains to provide appropriate commands for document production. Functionality of popular tools such as psfrag, fancyheaders, bibtex, makeindex, etc., are to be implemented as part of the language. In the long run, however, it may be interesting to extend its usage towards a general markup language.

Acknowledgments

The author would like to thank the TEX Stammtisch of Cologne in Germany for their valuable comments. Special thanks to Holger Jakobs who helped translate this text from Genglish to English.

References

1. D. M. Beazley. Automated scientific software scripting with SWIG. In *Tools for program development and analysis*, volume 19, pages 599–609. Elsevier Science Publishers B. V., Amsterdam, The Netherlands, 2003.
2. T. T. Hàn, S. Rahtz, and H. Hagen. The pdftex manual. http://www.ntg.nl/doc/han/pdftex-a.pdf, 1999.
3. R. D. Hipp. The Lemon Parser Generator. http://www.hwaci.com/sw/lemon, 1998.
4. D. E. Knuth. *The TEXbook*. Addison Wesley, 1983.
5. H. Kopka and P. Daly. *A Guide to LATEX*. Addison Wesley, 1992.
6. Frank Mittelbach and Chris Rowley. The LATEX3 Project. *TUGboat*, 18(3):195–198, 1997.
7. J. Poskanzer and V. Paxson. Flex, a fast lexical analyzer generator. http://sourceforge.net/projects/lex, 1995.
8. P. Taylor, J. Zlatuška, and K. Skoupy. *The NTS project: from conception to implementation*. Cahiers GUTenberg, May 2000.
9. A. Troelsen. *C# and the .NET Platform*. APress, 2001.
10. Joris van der Hoeven. GNU TEXmacs. http://www.texmacs.org/tmweb/home/welcome.en.html, 2003.

Creating Type 1 Fonts from METAFONT Sources
Comparison of Tools, Techniques and Results

Karel Píška

Institute of Physics, Academy of Sciences
182 21 Prague
Czech Republic
piska@fzu.cz
http://www-hep.fzu.cz/~piska/

Abstract. This paper summarizes experiences in converting METAFONT fonts to PostScript fonts with TEXtrace and mftrace, based on programs of autotracing bitmaps (AutoTrace and potrace), and with systems using analytic conversion (MetaFog and MetaType1, using METAPOST output or METAPOST itself). A development process is demonstrated with public Indic fonts (Devanagari, Malayalam). Examples from the Computer Modern fonts have been also included to illustrate common problems of conversion. Features, advantages and disadvantages of various techniques are discussed. Postprocessing – corrections, optimization and (auto)hinting – or even preprocessing may be necessary, before even a primary contour approximation is achieved. To do fully automatic conversion of a perfect METAFONT glyph definition into perfect Type 1 outline curves is very difficult at best, perhaps impossible.

Keywords: font conversion, bitmap fonts, METAFONT, METAPOST, outline fonts, PostScript, Type 1 fonts, approximation, Bézier curves.

1 Introduction

In recent years, several free programs for creating PostScript outline fonts from METAFONT sources have been developed. The aim of this paper is to give a short comparison of these programs, with references to original sources and documentation, and to provide a brief description of their use. We will discuss advantages and drawbacks, and demonstrate numerous examples to compare important features and to illustrate significant problems. We omit technical details described in the original documentation and concentrate our attention on the quality of the output, including hinting issues.

The programs TEXtrace and mftrace read original METAFONT sources, generate high-resolution pk bitmaps, call autotracing programs (AutoTrace or potrace) and finally generate the files in the Type 1 format (pfb or pfa).

MetaType1 creates Type 1 output from METAPOST sources. Therefore it requires rewriting font definitions from METAFONT into METAPOST.

Similarly, MetaFog converts the PostScript files generated by METAPOST to other PostScript files containing only outlines, that can be subsequently

A. Syropoulos et al. (Eds.): TUG 2004, LNCS 3130, pp. 240–256, 2004.

assembled into Type 1 fonts. MetaFog is not a new product, but its excellent results remain, in our comparisons, unsurpassed.

Additionally, we may need adequate encoding files. If none are available, a TEX encoding (e.g., the standard TEX T1 encoding) is usually used as the default.

2   Autotracing Bitmaps

2.1   TEXtrace with AutoTrace

Péter Szabó developed TEXtrace [18]. It is a collection of Unix scripts. It reads the original METAFONT sources, rendering the font bitmaps into PostScript (via dvips). For converting the resulting bitmaps to outlines, it calls (in the version of 2001) the AutoTrace program [21] created by Martin Weber, and, finally, composes the final files in the Type 1 format. TEXtrace works fully automatically and can be invoked by a command like this:

bash traceall.sh *mfname psname psnumber*

where *mfname*.mf is the name of the METAFONT font, *psname*.pfb is the name of the Type 1 font file, and *psnumber* denotes a Type 1 UniqueID [1].

The *Adobe Type 1 Font Format* documentation [1, pp. 29–33] recommends observing certain *Type 1 conventions:* 1) points at extremes; 2) tangent continuity; 3) conciseness; and 4) consistency.

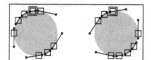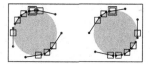

Fig. 1. TEXtrace: """" in cmr10.

The outline results from TEXtrace (that is, from AutoTrace) are relatively faithful to the original bitmaps. Some artifacts exist, but they are invisible in usual font sizes and magnifications and for practical purposes may be negligible. Nonetheless, they spoil our attempts to automatically produce perfect, hinted, outline fonts.

The underlying reason is that the information about the control points in the original METAFONT is lost, and the Type 1 conventions are not satisfied, as exemplified in Figure 1. The endpoints (double squares) are not placed at extremes (rule 1), most of the horizontal and vertical points of extrema are missing. On the other hand, the outline definition is not concise (rule 3) – due to the large numbers of control points in the glyph definitions, the font files generated by TEXtrace are huge. Furthermore, the two identical periods in the dieresis glyph """" are approximated by different point sets (rule 4).

The following examples show the results of conversion of Indic fonts submitted to TUG India 2002 [16], devanagari (dvng10) and Malayalam (mm10).

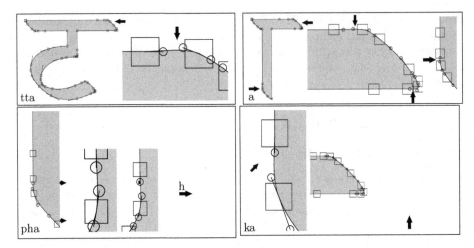

Fig. 2. Results of TEXtrace (AutoTrace): bumps and a hole (h).

Typical irregularities produced by conversion with TEXtrace are *bumps* and *holes*. Figure 2 demonstrates bumps caused by the envelope being stroked along a path with a rapid change of curvature, and by cases of transition from a straight line to a particularly small arc. The second clipped part of the letter "pha" shows a hole.

I tried to remove those bumps and holes, and (partially) other irregularities at the Type 1 level with a set of special programs manually marking places to be changed in a "raw" text, translated by `t1disasm` and by `t1asm` back after modifications (both programs are from the `t1utils` package [13]), which achieves a better outline approximation, as shown in Figure 3. The postprocessing consisted

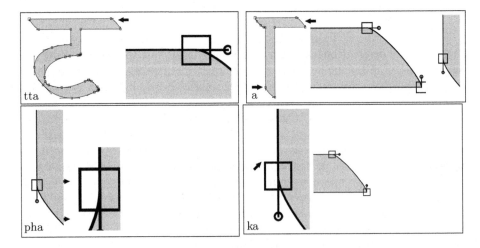

Fig. 3. Improved results achieved with postprocessing.

of: inserting missing extrema points, changing the first nodes of contour paths (if desirable), and the optimization of merging pairs (or sequences) of Bézier segments together, and joining nodes in horizontal or vertical straight parts to eliminate redundant nodes.

However, when this process was applied to the Malayalam fonts, we meet another problem: undetected corners in Figure 4. Instead of attempting to correct them, I stopped my postprocessing attempts, and switched to experiments with analytic methods of conversion.

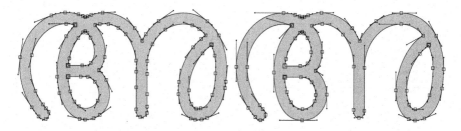

Fig. 4. TEXtrace (AutoTrace) first without and then with postprocessing for the Malayalam "a", showing undetected corners.

Examples of CM-super. Type 1 fonts [20] generated by Vladimir Volovich (first announced in 2001) inherit typical bugs produced by tracing bitmaps by AutoTrace (as invoked by TEXtrace) such as bumps and holes, improper selection of starting points of contour paths, and problems in distinguishing sharp corners and small arcs. We illustrate them in several following figures, in order to demonstrate that fixing such irregularities automatically is difficult.

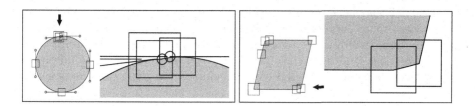

Fig. 5. CM-super: period in `sfrm1000` and `sfsi1000`, with redundant node.

In the period "." from the `sfrm1000` font (its source is the original `cmr10`), an optimization cannot exclude the redundant node (Figure 5) (it is still the starting point of the path).

The minus "−" derived from `cmr10` contains a bump, and minus from `cmtt10` two bumps (Figure 6). Moreover, these bumps have been hinted and have their own hints (probably as results of autohinting).

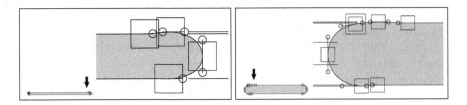

Fig. 6. CM-super: minus in `sfrm1000` and `sftt1000`, with bumps.

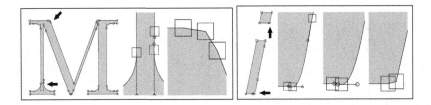

Fig. 7. CM-super: "M" in `sfrm1000` and "i" in `sfsi1000`.

In the letter "M" from `cmtt10`, we observe missing dishes, a hole and a bad approximation of an arc (Figure 7). On the contrary, in "i" the corners are not detected properly, we also have a hinted bump.

2.2   TEXtrace with potrace

The 2003 version of TEXtrace supports alternative bitmap tracing with `potrace` [17], developed by Peter Selinger. In this version, the real corners are detected or at least detected better than with AutoTrace (Figure 8). Thus, bumps and holes have been suppressed, but smooth connections have often been changed to sharp corners (not present originally). While the bumps demonstrated violation of consistency and may produce invalid hinting zone coordinates (Figure 6), the unwanted sharp corners mean loss of tangent continuity (the middle clip in Figure 8). Unfortunately, the approximation does not preserve horizontal and vertical directions (the right clip), the stem edges are oblique – the difference between the two arrows on the left edge is 2 units in the glyph coordinate space.

2.3   mftrace

Han-Wen Nienhuys created mftrace [15, 3], a Python script that calls AutoTrace or potrace (as with TEXtrace) to convert glyph bitmap images to outlines. The results of tracing are thus expected to be very similar to those of TEXtrace. In fact, for the analyzed Indic fonts, they are identical, as we can see in the first image in Figure 9 (compare with TEXtrace results in Figure 4). With the `--simplify` option, mftrace calls FontForge [22] (previously named PfaEdit) to execute postprocessing simplification; this helps to exclude redundant nodes from outline contours, as in the second image in Figure 9.

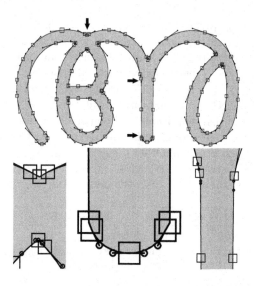

Fig. 8. TEXtrace (using potrace), with different corners.

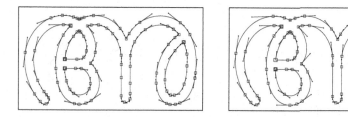

Fig. 9. mftrace without and with --simplify.

3 Analytic Conversions

3.1 MetaType1

MetaType1 [8, 9] is a programmable system for auditing, enhancing and generating Type 1 fonts from METAPOST sources. MetaType1 was designed by Bogusław Jackowski, Janusz M. Nowacki and Piotr Strzelczyk. The MetaType1 package is available from ftp://bop.eps.gda.pl/pub/metatype1 [10].

This "auditing and enhancing" is a process of converting the Type 1 font into MetaType1 (text) files, generating proof sheets, analysis, making corrections and regenerating modified Type 1 fonts. It is an important tool for checking, verifying and improving existing Type 1 fonts.

MetaType1 works with the METAPOST language. Therefore the METAFONT font sources must be converted/rewritten into METAPOST. Macro package extensions of METAPOST and other miscellaneous programs provide generation of proper structure of the Type 1 format, evaluate hints (not only the basic outline curves), and create **pfb** and also **afm** and **pfm** files.

During the rewriting process, users define several parameters of the Type 1 font, including the PostScript font encoding – PostScript glyph names and their codes – because METAFONT sources do not contain this data in a form directly usable for Type 1 encoding vectors. METAFONT output commands have to be changed to their METAPOST alternatives. Similarly, it is necessary to substitute METAFONT commands not available in METAPOST, to define METAPOST variants of pen definitions and pen stroking, etc.

Alternative METAPOST commands are defined in the MetaType1 files fontbase.mp, plain_ex.mp, et al. Other (new) commands may be defined by the user. Correspondence between METAFONT and METAPOST is approximately as shown in the following table (of course, the details may vary from font to font):

METAFONT	METAPOST
fill *path;*	Fill *path;*
draw *path;*	pen_stroke() (*path*) (*glyph*) ;
	Fill *glyph;*
penlabels(1,2);	justlabels(1,2);
beginchar(…	beginglyph(…
endchar;	endglyph;

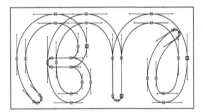 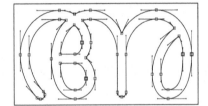

Fig. 10. MetaType1 – primary outlines and overlap removal.

Many METAFONT commands have no counterpart in METAPOST [6]. For example, operations with bitmap pictures: in METAPOST, font data is represented as PostScript curves, not bitmaps. As a result, writing METAPOST code that would produce equivalent results as original METAFONT code using these or other such features would be very difficult.

After the basic conversion, the next step is removing overlaps (if any are present) using the MetaType1 command find_outlines. Figure 10 shows the results before and after overlap removal for the Malayalam vowel a (font mm10 using pen stroking with a circular pen). This operation is not necessary in META-FONT, since it generates bitmaps. In the METAPOST environment of PostScript outlines, however, we need to reduce overlapping curves to single or pairs of paths.

MetaType1 also allows insertion of commands for automatic computation of horizontal and vertical hints (FixHStems, FixVStems). The Type 1 font can be visualized in a proof sheet form containing the control point labels (numbers) and hinting zones (Figure 11).

So far, so good. But there are two crucial problems. First, the METAFONT Malayalam fonts designed by Jeroen Hellingman [5], use the command

```
currenttransform := currenttransform
                    shifted (.5rm, 0);
```

So all the glyphs should be shifted to the right. METAFONT saves the transformation command and does this operation automatically. By contrast, in METAPOST we need to insert the **shift** commands explicitly in all glyph programs. Also the labels must be shifted! In my experiments, I did this shift operation later, before final assembly of the Type 1 fonts.

The second problem is that in MetaType1 (I used MetaType1 version 0.40 of 2003) a regular pen stroking algorithm is not available, only a simplified method of connecting the points 'parallel' to the nodes on the path. Therefore the approximation of the envelope is not correct. For example, in Figure 12 it should be asymmetric, but it is symmetric. Inserting additional nodes cannot help, because the bisection results will again be asymmetric. The Figure shows the outline curves do not correspond to the real pen in two midpoint locations. The envelope there looks narrow and it is in fact narrower than it should be. I hope that this problem could be solved in a future release, at least for pen stroking with a circular pen.

Even more serious is a situation with the rotated elliptic pen used in the Devanagari fonts designed by Frans Velthuis [19] (and also other Indic fonts derived from **dvng**). Absence of a regular pen stroking in MetaType1 makes it impractical for such complicated fonts. MetaType1 approximates the pen statically in path nodes, tries to connect their static end points, and ignores complicated dynamic correlations between the path, the pen and the envelope. Unfortunately, in this case the results of the envelope approximation are not correct and cannot be used (Figure 13).

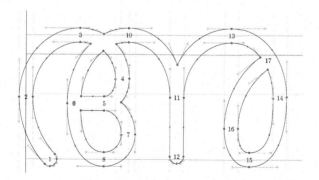

Fig. 11. MetaType1 – proof sheet.

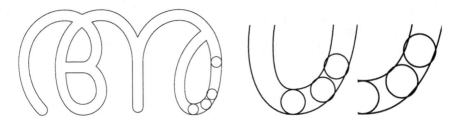

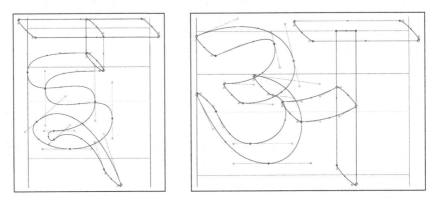

Fig. 12. MetaType1 – bad pen stroking.

Fig. 13. MetaType1 – Devanagari "i", "a".

3.2 MetaFog

Two programs using analytic conversion were presented in 1995. Basil K. Malyshev created his BaKoMa collection [14] and Richard J. Kinch developed MetaFog [11]. BaKoMa is a PostScript and TrueType version of the Computer Modern fonts. Malyshev's paper discusses some problems of conversion, especially regarding hinting, but his programs and detailed information about the conversion algorithm are not available.

R. Kinch created MetaFog along with weeder, which supports interactive processing of outlines, and a package for making final fonts from outlines generated by MetaFog in TrueType, Type 1 and other formats. MetaFog itself (I used an evaluation version graciously donated by Richard) reads the METAPOST output from the command:

<pre>mpost '&mfplain options;' input fontname.mf</pre>

Thus, the conversion (from METAFONT sources) is limited to fonts that can be processed by METAPOST, that is, do not contain METAFONT-specific definitions and commands. MetaFog generates another PostScript file consisting only of the outline structures. A conversion process is described also in the paper written by Taco Hoekwater [7].

MetaFog evaluates outline contours and precisely computes envelopes of an elliptical pen stroking along a Bézier curve. We must notice that the envelopes

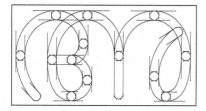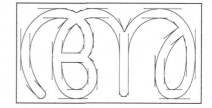

Fig. 14. MetaFog – initial input contour and final result.

in general are not cubic Bézier curves and their representation in a Type 1 font must be an approximation. The results for a circular pen, on the other hand, can be considered perfect. Figures 14 and 15 show an example of the Malayalam letter "a" (font `mm10`): the initial and final contours and the final Type 1 font with control points (stroked version) and its visual comparison with METAPOST output embedded in a Type 3 font, respectively.

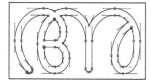

Fig. 15. MetaFog – final Type 1 font.

Problems with Complex Pen-Stroking. A more complicated situation is the conversion of fonts using pen stroking with a rotated elliptical pen, such as the Devanagari font. Figure 16 illustrates this case. The initial input contour and final result contour (tta1) look good – in the first image we can see the projections of the pen in nodes corresponding to METAFONT source. But exact comparison with the original METAPOST output embedded in a Type 3 font (tta2) and primary MetaFog conversion displayed together with the METAPOST source (tta3) shows that this approximation is not correct. Because these elements are very common in shapes of all but the simplest Devanagari glyphs, corrections are necessary.

I therefore applied a simple pen-dependent preprocessing step before the MetaFog conversion, thus adapting the METAPOST output as a modified form of bisection, as discussed in a paper by R. Kinch [11]. The preprocessing scans curves, searching for points where the path direction and the direction of main axis of the pen coincide (namely 135°) and inserts these points as additional path nodes. In our case, the transformation matrix is $\cos\theta * [1, 1, -1, 1]$, so we solve only a quadratic equation and can find 0, 1 or 2 (at most) of these points. This technique corrects the MetaFog approximation of all such occurrences in

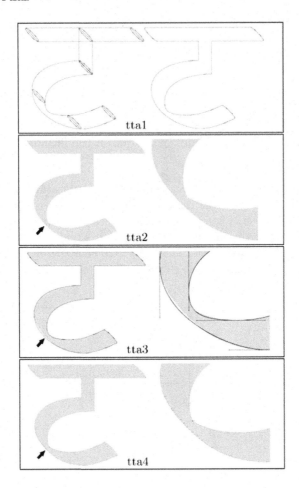

Fig. 16. MetaFog contours, METAPOST output, primary and secondary conversion on the METAPOST background.

the **dvng** font. The result of this secondary MetaFog conversion with METAPOST source is shown in the last panel of Figure 16 (tta4).

Similar improvements for the Devanagari letters "a" and "pha" are shown in figure 17. For "pha", the first 135° node was already present in the path defined by the METAFONT source (first panel, pha1); on the contrary, the second occurrence of a 135° point was absent, and therefore it was inserted in the METAPOST output (last panel, pha2).

Of course, this improvement is not universal, it only solves a special problem with a special pen for a special font.

Figure 18 illustrates movement of a rotated elliptical pen stepping along a "nice" path (panel 1). However, correlations with the pen are not trivial: changes of curvature of the outer wingtip curve do not have simple monotonic behavior, and the inner wingtip curve (panel 2) is even more complicated. This

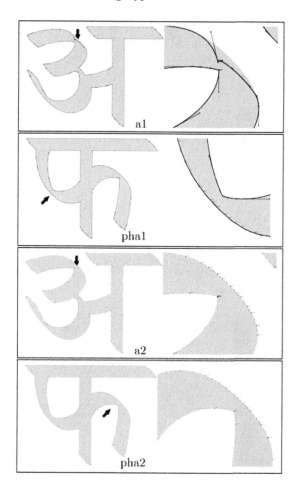

Fig. 17. MetaFog output before and after modification of METAPOST source.

means that the pen-stroked wingtip curves along a single Bézier curve cannot be approximated by single Bézier curves (compare with the starting Figure 16, panel tta1), i.e., an envelope edge of a pen along a *simple* path is *not simple*.

Automatic Conversion Problems. A "dark side" of improving the curve approximation is a fragmentation of an envelope curve into many segments (often more than 10, and up to 16 in Devanagari!). We achieve a faithful approximation (limited only by numerical accuracy) at the expense of conciseness. To make up for this, postprocessing is needed. The original MetaFog output and a result of my (preliminary) optimization assembled into Type 1 fonts are shown in Figure 19.

Unfortunately, even a small computational inaccuracy can make automatic conversion and optimization impossible, and even make it very difficult to design

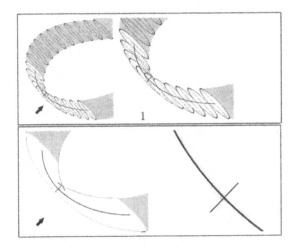

Fig. 18. Wingtip curves in METAPOST source.

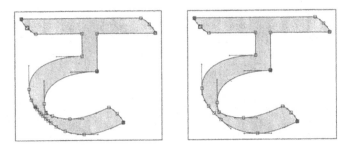

Fig. 19. MetaFog converted to Type 1 – before and after postprocessing.

postprocessing algorithms. In Figure 20, we demonstrate problems with the primary approximation of an envelope stroked by a rotated elliptical pen, and also difficulties with automatic optimization of the Devanagari ligature "d+g+r".

In the first panel of Figure 20, we observe an artifact produced by MetaFog due to a complicated correlation of the pen and the path. Fortunately, those cases are very rare (less than 1 % of glyphs in Devanagari).

In the second panel, the path and subsequently the corresponding envelope edges are not absolutely horizontal, thus (probably) MetaFog cannot properly find intersection points and join reconstructed outline components. Those defects are present in more than 12 % of the Devanagari glyphs. In all cases, they have been successfully solved manually by the interactive weeder program.

In the last two details in Figure 20 (the lower ending part of the left stem) we can see that both nodes of the left segment are outside the filled area boundary defined by the METAPOST curve. The outer wingtip edge is split there into many segments, some being straight lines – and they should not be, e.g., the first and

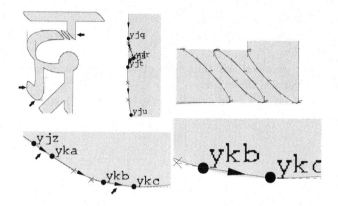

Fig. 20. MetaFog – problems with automatic conversion.

the third segment marked by 2 arrows in the clip – their curvatures are for us undefined. Additionally, we cannot detect the last segment (magnified in the figure) as horizontal because its angle is "greater than some ε".

Thus, neither node coordinates, nor segment directions, nor curvatures are reliable. It gives a *visual* comparison of the METAPOST output with its outline approximation. Therefore, my (first and "simple") idea cannot succeed. This was to classify the behavior of directions and curvatures of *all* the segments *automatically*, and then to divide segments into groups according to directions and curvatures, then *automatically* merging the groups to single Bézier segments. As demonstrated, this optimization may fail or produce incorrect results and, unfortunately, human assistance is needed.

4   Summary

Here we summarize the most important features of the conversion programs found in our experiments.

4.1   Approximate Conversions: TEXtrace, mftrace

Advantages:

- approximation covers original METAFONT fonts and correspondence to **pk** bitmaps is (reasonably) close
- simple invocation, robust solution
- fully automatic processing can generate complete, final Type 1 fonts

Disadvantages:

- approximate conversions give only approximate outlines
- lost information about nodes and other control points

- final fonts do not satisfy the *Type 1 conventions*
- AutoTrace: problems with recognizing corners, generation of unwanted bumps and holes
- potrace: sharp connections, thus loss of tangent continuity, violation of horizontal or vertical directions
- automatic and correct (auto)hinting may yield poor results due to these irregularities

4.2   MetaType1

Advantages:

- complete support for Type 1 font generation
- manual insertion of hinting information possible via simple hinting commands
- font file compression via subroutines

Disadvantages:

- conversion of METAFONT to METAPOST often requires manual rewriting, possibly non-trivial and time-consuming
- bad pen stroking algorithm; in particular, results for complicated fonts using rotated elliptical pens are unusable
- difficulties with removing overlaps in tangential cases

4.3   MetaFog

Advantages:

- fully automatic conversion of METAPOST output to outlines
- "typical" fonts usually achieve perfect results
- even for very complex fonts (again, with rotated elliptical pens), adaptations of METAPOST output and manual editing with weeder make it plausible to obtain perfect outlines
- results fulfill the *Type 1 conventions* in most cases (except for those very complex fonts)

Disadvantages:

- MetaFog reads METAPOST output, thus cannot process METAFONT-specific definitions
- complex fonts may still need manual reduction with weeder or subsequent optimization of outlines to reach conciseness
- processing is slow

4.4 Final Font Processing and Common Problems

The conversion systems discussed here, with the exception of MetaType1, do not include internal hinting subsystems. To insert hints, we can use font editors, for example FontForge [22]. For successful automatic hinting, however, the font outlines must fulfill certain conditions. Irregularities – absence of nodes at extrema or presence of bumps and holes – are not compatible with autohinting, because extrema points correspond to hinting zones while bumps or holes do not fit them, thus causing outliers. The resulting difference of ± 1 unit in the integer glyph coordinate system, after rounding to integers, is not acceptable for high-quality fonts. Problems may also be caused by other "rounding to integer" effects, and by the presence of close doublets or triplets.

In my view, these experiments show that the quality of primary outline approximation is crucial to achieve perfect final Type 1 fonts. It is virtually impossible to recreate discarded METAFONT information, or to find exact conditions for a secondary fit that corrects primary contours that were created with irregularities or artifacts. Starting with high-resolution bitmaps is problematic, as too much information has been lost, making subsequent processes of improvement, optimization and hinting difficult at best, not possible to automate and usually not successful.

Acknowledgements

I would like to thank all the authors of the free conversion programs, Richard Kinch for donating his MetaFog and weeder, the authors of the public META-FONT fonts for Indic languages and other sources used in the contribution, and Karl Berry for help with editing of this article.

References

1. Adobe Systems Inc. *Adobe Type 1 Font Format.* Addison-Wesley, 1990.
2. Alfred V. Aho, Brian W. Kernighan, and Peter J. Weinberger, *The AWK Programming Language*, Addison-Wesley, 1988.
3. Karl Berry. "Making outline fonts from bitmap images." *TUGboat*, **22**(4), pp. 281–285, 2001.
4. Free Software Foundation. GNU awk, http://www.gnu.org/software/gawk.
5. Jeroen Hellingman. Malayalam fonts, CTAN:language/malayalam.
6. John D. Hobby. A User's Manual for METAPOST. AT&T Bell Laboratories, Computing Science Technical Report 162, 1994.
7. Taco Hoekwater. "Generating Type 1 Fonts from METAFONT Sources", *TUGboat*, **19**(3), pp. 256–266, 1998.
8. Bogusław Jackowski, Janusz M. Nowacki, Piotr Strzelczyk. "MetaType1: A META-POST-based Engine for Generating Type 1 Fonts", *Proceedings of the XII EuroTeX 2001 conference*, pp. 111–119, Kerkrade, the Netherlands, 23–27 September 2001.
9. Bogusław Jackowski, Janusz M. Nowacki, Piotr Strzelczyk. "Programming Post-Script Type 1 Fonts Using MetaType1: Auditing, Enhancing, Creating. *Preprints of the XIV EuroTeX 2003 conference*, pp. 151–157, Brest, France, 24–27 June 2003 (to appear in TUGBoat).

10. MetaType1distribution: `ftp://bop.eps.gda.pl/pub/metatype1`.
11. Richard J. Kinch. "MetaFog: Converting METAFONT Shapes to Contours", *TUGboat*, **16**(3), pp. 233–243, 1995.
12. Donald E. Knuth. *The METAFONTbook*. Addison-Wesley, 1986. Volume C of *Computers and Typesetting*.
13. Eddie Kohler. t1utils (Type 1 tools), `http://freshmeat.net/projects/t1utils`.
14. Basil K. Malyshev, "Problems of the conversion of METAFONT fonts to PostScript Type 1", *TUGboat*, **16**(1), pp. 60–68, 1995.
15. Han-Wen Nienhuys. mftrace, `http://www.cs.uu.nl/~hanwen/mftrace`.
16. Karel Píška. "A conversion of public Indic fonts from METAFONT into Type 1 format with TEXtrace." *TUGboat*, **23**(1), pp. 70–73, 2002.
17. Peter Selinger. potrace, `http://potrace.sourceforge.net`.
18. Péter Szabó. "Conversion of TEX fonts into Type 1 format", *Proceedings of the XII EuroTEX 2001 conference*, pp. 192–206, Kerkrade, the Netherlands, 23–27 September 2001.
    `http://www.inf.bme.hu/~pts/textrace`; `http://textrace.sourceforge.net`.
19. Frans J. Velthuis. Devanagari fonts, `CTAN:language/devanagari`.
20. Vladimir Volovich: CM-super fonts: `CTAN:fonts/ps-type1/cm-super`.
21. Martin Weber. AutoTrace, `http://autotrace.sourceforge.net`.
22. George Williams. FontForge: A PostScript Font Editor, `http://fontforge.sourceforge.net`.

Beyond Glyphs,
Advanced Typographic Features of Fonts

George Williams

FontForge
444 Alan Rd.
Santa Barbara, CA 93109, USA
gww@silcom.com
http://bibliofile.duhs.duke.edu/gww/

Abstract. Two hundred years ago a font was a collection of small pieces of metal. Using that font required the services of a skilled typesetter to handle the niceties of kerning and ligatures. Modern fonts are expected to encapsulate both the letter shapes found on the pieces of metal, and the intelligence of the typesetter by providing information on how to position and replace glyphs as appropriate. As our view of typography extends beyond the familiar Latin, Greek and Cyrillic scripts into the more complex Arabic and Indic we need greater expressive power in the font itself. As of this writing there are two fairly common methods to include these metainformation within a font, that used by Apple (GX technology) and that used by MicroSoft and Adobe (OpenType). I shall compare these two formats and describe how FontForge , a modern open source font editor, may be used to implement either or both.

1 Introduction

Modern fonts are more that just collections of glyph shapes, they must also contain information on how those glyphs are put together. In West-European typography the two most obvious examples of this are kerning and ligatures.

In Arabic most character should have at least four variants depending on what other characters surround it, a vast number of ligatures and marks.

Indic scripts require glyph rearrangement, and a complex system of glyph replacements.

Apple has developed one way to describe these metainformation as part of its GX font technology, and MicroSoft and Adobe have developed another mechanism as part of OpenType. Although both of these systems have the same ultimate goals the philosophy behind them, the mechanisms used, and the expressive powers of the formats are markedly different.

2 Comparing GX and OpenType

On one level the difference between these two technologies is similar to the different approaches toward hinting used by PostScript and TrueType fonts. In

A. Syropoulos et al. (Eds.): TUG 2004, LNCS 3130, pp. 257–263, 2004.

the approach used by PostScript and OpenType the font contains information describing what needs to be accomplished, while TrueType and GX provide provide little programs that actually accomplish it.

GX puts a greater burden on the font designer. Writing a state machine that converts the glyph sequence "f" "i" to the "fi" glyph is harder than just stating that 'f" "i" should become "fi."

Looking at a GX state machine and attempting to figure out what glyphs are converted into what ligatures in what situations is, in general, impossible (equivalent to the halting problem). While in an OpenType font this ligature composition is exactly the information provided in the font.

Both technologies allow a font to attach a high level description (called a feature or feature setting) to a set of glyph transformations. Some features will be turned on automatically if appropriate conditions are met, others are designed to be invoked by the user when s/he deems it appropriate.

3   Comparing GX and OpenType Transformations

The expressive powers of the two formats for non-contextual transformations (simple kerning, substitutions, ligatures) are very similar, so similar that Font-Forge can use the same interface for both.

In the area of contextual transformations the two formats differ wildly. Open-Type provides a series of fixed length patterns. At every glyph position in the glyph stream each pattern is tried in sequence. If one matches at that position then any transformations specified are applied and the process moves on to the next glyph position.

GX provides a state machine. The state machine processes the entire glyph stream. There may be several places within the stream where a match is found, and at those places a maximum of two transformations may be applied.

Neither format is a sub-set of the other. Both can express things the other cannot.

A GX state machine can easily match the regular expression "ab*c" and then replace "a" with "d". In OpenType this would require an infinite number of patterns. GX provides a mechanism for determining if a glyph is at the start or end of a text line (so swash substitutions could be made dependent on this) while OpenType does not.

On the other hand replacing the string "abc" with "def" can be done easily in OpenType but not at all in GX (three substitutions need to be applied after the match is found, and GX only supports two). OpenType allows different types of substitutions to be applied within a pattern (for example a ligature at one point and a simple substitution at another) while GX does not. OpenType matches a pattern against every glyph position in the stream, and each pattern may have multiple substitutions. This means it is possible for several substitutions to be applied to one position. This cannot be expressed with GX.

FontForge uses the same User Interface (or UI for short) UI for specifying non-contextual substitutions but must use different UIs for contextual ones.

4   Non-contextual Transformations in FontForge

Many transformations affect one glyph at a time. In the `Element -> Char Info` dialog FontForge shows all the transformations that may affect the current glyph.

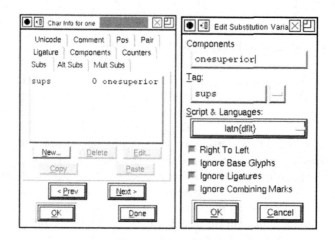

Fig. 1. Simple substitutions of "one"

In this case the glyph named "one" can be replaced by the glyph "onesuperior" under the control of the 'sups' feature (presumably the 'sups' feature would transform "two" to "twosuperior," but that will be shown in the dialog for "two," not here).

Double-clicking on an entry in the list (or pressing the [New] button) will invoke another dialog showing information about the current substitution.

Every transformation must have a tag, script, and flag set associated with it. The tag is either a four letter OpenType feature tag, or a two number GX feature/setting either format may be used to identify the transformation. Some OpenType features correspond directly to a GX feature setting (OpenType 'sups' matches GX 10,1), in this case FontForge will use the OpenType feature tag to describe the transformation (as the more mnemonic of the two) and will translate it into the appropriate GX tag when an Apple font is generated.

The script and language information is only meaningful in OpenType fonts. It specifies the conditions under which the current transformation is to be applied. Generally, the script is obvious from the current glyph, and the language information is irrelevant – the transformation should always be applied in that script and the language is set to "default." FontForge can generally guess the appropriate script by looking at the current glyph. But some glyphs, like the digits, are used in multiple scripts (e.g., Latin-based scripts, the Greek script, and Cyrillic script among others share those glyphs), and in this case the user may need to adjust the script pulldown.

When outputting a GX table FontForge will ignore any transformations which do not have a "default" language in their script/language list.

The right to left flag is meaningful in both GX and OpenType. The others are only meaningful in OpenType. FontForge is usually able to determine the proper setting of right to left by looking at the glyph itself, but you can always correct it if necessary.

5   Contextual Transformations for OpenType

Contextual transformations have two different aspects. One is a set of simpler transformations that actually do the work, and the other provides the context in which they are active. Let us suppose the user has a script font where most letter combinations join at the baseline, but after a few ("b", "o", "v" and "w") the join is at the x-height. After these letters we need a different variant of the following letter. So in OpenType the user must specify two different transformations, the first substitutes the normal form of a letter for the variant that looks right after a "b", and the second specifies the context in which the first is active.

The transformations which do all the work are created glyph by glyph much like any other simple substitution described above. The only difference is that instead of specifying a script/language combination you should use the special entry in the script menu called "- Nested -". This tells FontForge that the substitution will only be used under the control of a contextual transformation.

Contextual transformations features are complex to specify. These apply to more than one glyph at a time and are reachable through `Element -> Font Info`. There are essentially two different formats for these—contextual and chaining contextual. Chaining contextual is a superset of contextual and allows you to use characters previously processed (earlier in the glyph stream) as part of your context.

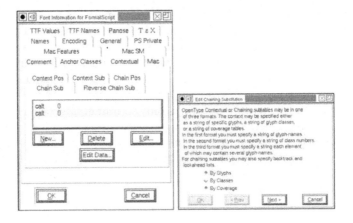

Fig. 2. OpenType Contextual formats

Such a feature requires a tag, script, and set of flags specified in a dialog very similar to that used for simple features.

The context in these transformations may be specified as patterns of glyphs, patterns of classes of glyphs, or patterns of a choice of glyphs.

The glyph stream is divided into three parts, glyphs before the current glyph which may not be changed but which are matched for context, a few glyphs starting at the current glyph which may be changed and are matched, and glyphs ahead of the current glyph which are only matched for context.

Fig. 3. OpenType Contextual by classes

The glyphs provided by the font are divided into different classes. There may be a different set of glyph classes for each region of the glyph stream. In the following example, there are three classes defined for the region around the current glyph. By convention class 0 contains all glyphs which are not explicitly allocated to another class. Class 1 contains the glyphs "b o v w b.high..." Class 2 contains the glyphs "a c d e...". The buttons underneath the class display allow the user to modify these classes.

At the top of the screen are the patterns which will be matched. Here there is a single pattern, which says: "The character before the current glyph must be in class 1, and the current glyph must be in class 2. If this pattern is matched then the glyph which is at position 0 (the current glyph) should be altered by applying the simple substitution defined by feature tag 'high'."

6   Contextual Transformations for GX

As with OpenType there are two aspects to a GX contextual transformation. There is a set of simple non-contextual transformations which do the work, and a state machine which controls when a simple transformation is activated.

The glyphs of the font are divided into a set of classes (each state machine defines its own class sets), GX provides four predefined classes some of these classes do not represent actual glyphs but concepts like "end of line". The state machine looks like a two dimensional array of transitions. On one axis we have the glyph classes, and on the other we have the states. GX provides two predefined states, start of text and start of line. Usually these two states are identical but the distinction is present if the user wishes to take advantage of it.

The transitions are slightly different depending on the type of state machine. Here I shall only discuss contextual substitution transitions. If the state machine is in a given state, and the current glyph is in a given class, then the transition specified for that class in the given state will be applied to figure out what to do next. A transition specifies the next state (which may be the same as the current state), two flags, and two substitutions. One flag controls whether to read another glyph from the glyph stream, or continue with the same current glyph. The other flag allows you to mark the current glyph for future reference. Two transformations may be specified one applies to the current glyph, and the other applies to any previously marked glyph. Either substitution may be empty.

Fig. 4. GX state machine types

Again these state machines apply to more than one glyph at a time and are specified by `Element -> Font Info`.

In a few cases, FontForge will be able to convert an OpenType contextual substitution to a GX state machine. The `[Convert From OpenType]` button at the bottom of the dialog will show a list of OpenType features FontForge thinks it can convert. You can also create your own (or edit an old) state machine from here.

Every state machine must be associated with a GX feature/setting, and the context in which it executes may be controlled with the vertical and right to left check boxes.

This state machine executes the same script example discussed earlier. Again the glyph set is divided into two interesting classes: those glyphs that are followed by a high join, and those glyphs that are not. The state machine has two real states: in one the current glyph needs to be converted to a high variant, in the other the current glyph remains the low variant. State 2 maps the current glyph to its high variant, while both states 0 & 1 retain the current glyph unchanged

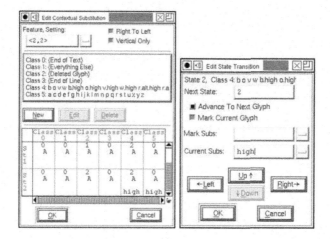

Fig. 5. GX state machine

(this example makes no distinction between the first two states, but the format requires that both be present).

If we are in state 0 and we get a normal glyph (class 5) then we read the next glyph, stay in state 0 and nothing much happens. If we get a glyph that needs a high connection after it then we read the next glyph, change to state 2 and nothing else happens.

If we are in state 2 and we get any letter glyph then we apply the 'high' substitution to convert that glyph to its high variant. If it is a normal glyph we drop back to state 0, but if it needs a high connection after it we stay in state 2.

If the user wishes to change a transition s/he may click on it and a new dialog pops up giving control over the transition. The arrow buttons on the bottom of the dialog allow the user to change which transition s/he is editing.

7   Summary

Both OpenType and GX attempt to provide similar effects. For simple concepts (non-contextual substitutions like "superscript") FontForge uses the same format internally to express both. This means the user only needs to specify these data once rather than do so for both OpenType and GX. But the expressive powers of the more complicated concepts (contextual substitutions for example) are so different that FontForge requires users to specify this information in both formats.

Author Index

Lecture Notes in Computer Science

For information about Vols. 1–3053

please contact your bookseller or Springer-Verlag